THE PRACTICE OF MANAGEMENT

Other books by Peter F. Drucker:

MANAGING FOR RESULTS

MANAGEMENT: TASKS, RESPONSIBILITIES, PRACTICES

PEOPLE AND PERFORMANCE

THE PRACTICE OF MANAGEMENT

By PETER F. DRUCKER

ALLIED PUBLISHERS PVT. LIMITED
NEW DELHI MUMBAI KOLKATA CHENNAI NAGPUR
AHMEDABAD BANGALORE HYDERABAD LUCKNOW

ALLIED PULIBLISERS PRIVATE LIMITED

1/13-14 Asaf Ali Road, **New Delhi**–110002
Ph.: 011-23239001 • E-mail: delhi.books@alliedpublishers.com

47/9 Prag Narain Road, Near Kalyan Bhawan, **Lucknow**–226001
Ph.: 0522-2209942 • E-mail: lko.books@alliedpublishers.com

17 Chittaranjan Avenue, **Kolkata**–700072
Ph.: 033-22129618 • E-mail: cal.books@alliedpublishers.com

15 J.N. Heredia Marg, Ballard Estate, **Mumbai**–400001
Ph.: 022-42126969 • E-mail: mumbai.books@alliedpublishers.com

60 Shiv Sunder Apartments (Ground Floor), Central Bazar Road, Bajaj Nagar, **Nagpur**–440010
Ph.: 0712-2234210 • E-mail: ngp.books@alliedpublishers.com

F-1 Sun House (First Floor), C.G. Road, Navrangpura, Ellisbridge P.O., **Ahmedabad**–380006
Ph.: 079-26465916 • E-mail: ahmbd.books@alliedpublishers.com

751 Anna Salai, **Chennai**–600002
Ph.: 044-28523938 • E-mail: chennai.books@alliedpublishers.com

5th Main Road, Gandhinagar, **Bangalore**–560009
Ph.: 080-22262081 • E-mail: bngl.books@alliedpublishers.com

3-2-844/6 & 7 Kachiguda Station Road, **Hyderabad**–500027
Ph.: 040-24619079 • E-mail: hyd.books@alliedpublishers.com

Website: www.alliedpublishers.com

First Indian Edition, 1970
First Allied Paperback, 1975
Edition, 2016

ISBN 81-7764-186-7

Published by Sunil Sachdev and printed by Ravi Sachdev at Allied Publishers Pvt. Ltd., Printing Division, A-104 Mayapuri Phase II, New Delhi -110064

CONTENTS

PART THREE. THE STRUCTURE OF MANAGEMENT

PART FOUR. THE MANAGEMENT OF WORKER AND WORK

PART FIVE. WHAT IT MEANS TO BE A MANAGER

CONCLUSION: THE RESPONSIBILITIES OF MANAGEMENT

PREFACE

We have available today the knowledge and experience needed for the successful practice of management. But there is probably no field of human endeavor where the always tremendous gap between the knowledge and performance of the leaders and the knowledge and performance of the average is wider or more intractable. This book does not exclude from its aims the advancement of the frontier of knowledge; it hopes, indeed, to make some contribution to it. But its first aim is to narrow the gap between what can be done and what is being done, between the leaders in management and the average.

Though not concerned with techniques this is a practical book. It is written out of many years of experience in working with managements—managements of small companies as well as managements of large and very large companies. And it aims at being a guide for men in major management positions, enabling them to examine their own work and performance, to diagnose their weaknesses and to improve their own effectiveness as well as the results of the enterprise they are responsible for. For younger men in management—and for men who plan to make management their career—this book should provide both a vision of what management is and concrete guidance in the knowledge, performance and discipline that are needed to qualify for a major management position.

But this book is written fully as much for the citizen without direct management experience. He, perhaps more than anyone else, needs to know what management is, what it does and what he can rightfully expect from it. For the ignorance of the function of management, of its work, of its standards and of its responsibilities is one of the most serious weaknesses of an industrial society—and it is almost universal.

Footnotes, acknowledgments and other references have been avoided throughout this book except where necessary to identify a direct quotation, or where likely to be helpful to the reader by guiding him to books that give full treatment to important subjects only touched upon in this text. Readers familiar with the work of Joseph A. Schumpeter will recognize without special reference how much the author owes to this most fruitful of modern economists; to others a footnote acknowledging the debt would be neither helpful nor meaningful. Readers interested in organization theory need no "X" to mark the spot where the author falls off the tightrope of organization orthodoxy. All my readers, I am sure, will assume that this book, like any other, has a long and mixed intellectual ancestry. And all, I trust, are more concerned with what is right than with who is right, and, accordingly, are neither assuaged by appeal to authority nor alarmed by its absence.

But I want to acknowledge the special debt I owe to some friends in American management: to Charles R. Hook, Jr., now Deputy-Postmaster General of the United States (formerly with the Chesapeake and Ohio Railroad); James C. Worthy, now Assistant Secretary of Commerce (formerly with Sears, Roebuck and Company); Frank C. Householder, Jr., John E. Kusik and Vernon C. Mickelson of the Chesapeake and Ohio Railway Company; Fred J. Borch, L. Byron Cherry, Russell Colley, M. L. Hurni, T. M. Linville, P. E. Mills and Moorhead Wright of General Electric; Donaldson Brown, Chester E. Evans, Walter G. Morris, L. N. Laseau, Alfred P. Sloan, Jr., and the late Henry G. Weaver of General Motors Corporation; Kendrick Porter of Lester B. Knight and Associates; Ewing W. Reilley, Bernard Muller-Thym and Robert K. Stolz of McKinsey & Company; Leo Cherne, David Emery, Aaron Levenstein, Jack Livingston and Auren Uris of The Research Institute of America; Clarence B. Caldwell of Sears, Roebuck and Company. To a greater extent than any number of footnotes could express, this book rests on their thought and on their work on management problems in which they allowed me to share. And I am in debt to Hermine Popper, Roxanne Wright Smith, John Fischer, Eldridge Haynes and Daniel Maue for generous help in the writing and editing of this book.

Above all I wish here to acknowledge the debt this book and I owe to Harold F. Smiddy of the General Electric Company. Despite misgivings and dissents he gave to this book of his counsel, advice and help, freely and far beyond the call of friendship. He is truly the book's Godfather; and I can only hope that the Godchild will prove itself worthy of the care he bestowed on it.

Montclair, New Jersey
March 1, 1954

PETER F. DRUCKER

INTRODUCTION

THE NATURE OF MANAGEMENT

CHAPTER 1

THE ROLE OF MANAGEMENT

The dynamic element in every business—A distinct and a leading group—The emergence of management—The free world's stake in management.

THE manager is the dynamic, life-giving element in every business. Without his leadership the "resources of production" remain resources and never become production. In a competitive economy, above all, the quality and performance of the managers determine the success of a business, indeed they determine its survival. For the quality and performance of its managers is the only effective advantage an enterprise in a competitive economy can have.

Management is also a distinct and a leading group in industrial society. We no longer talk of "capital" and "labor"; we talk of "management" and "labor." The "responsibilities of capital" have disappeared from our vocabulary together with the "rights of capital"; instead, we hear of the "responsibilities of management," and (a singularly hapless phrase) of the "prerogatives of management." We are building up a comprehensive and distinct system of "education for management." And when the Eisenhower Administration was formed in 1952, it was formed consciously as a "Management Administration."

The emergence of management as an essential, a distinct and a leading institution is a pivotal event in social history. Rarely, if ever, has a new basic institution, a new leading group, emerged as fast as has management since the turn of this century. Rarely in human history has a new institution proven indispensable so quickly;

and even less often has a new institution arrived with so little opposition, so little disturbance, so little controversy.

Management will remain a basic and dominant institution perhaps as long as Western civilization itself survives. For management is not only grounded in the nature of the modern industrial system and in the needs of the modern business enterprise to which an industrial system must entrust its productive resources—both human and material. Management also expresses basic beliefs of modern Western society. It expresses the belief in the possibility of controlling man's livelihood through systematic organization of economic resources. It expresses the belief that economic change can be made into the most powerful engine for human betterment and social justice—that, as Jonathan Swift first overstated it two hundred and fifty years ago, whoever makes two blades of grass grow where only one grew before deserves better of mankind than any speculative philosopher or metaphysical system builder.

This belief that the material can and should be used to advance the human spirit is not just the age-old human heresy "materialism." In fact, it is incompatible with materialism as the term has always been understood. It is something new, distinctly modern, distinctly Western. Prior to, and outside of, the modern West, resources have always been considered a limit to man's activities, a restriction on his control over his environment—rather than an opportunity and a tool of his control over nature. They have always been considered God-given and unchangeable. Indeed all societies, except the modern West, have looked upon economic change as a danger to society and individual alike, and have considered it the first responsibility of government to keep the economy unchangeable.

Management, which is the organ of society specifically charged with making resources productive, that is, with the responsibility for organized economic advance, therefore reflects the basic spirit of the modern age. It is in fact indispensable—and this explains why, once begotten, it grew so fast and with so little opposition.

The Importance of Management

Management, its competence, its integrity and its performance will be decisive both to the United States and to the free world in the decades ahead. At the same time the demands on management will be rising steadily and steeply.

A "Cold War" of indefinite duration not only puts heavy economic burdens on the economy, which only continuous economic advance can make bearable; it demands ability to satisfy the country's military needs while building up, at the same time, an expanding peacetime economy. It demands, indeed, an unprecedented ability of the entire economy to shift back and forth between peacetime and defense production, practically at an instant's notice. This demand, on the satisfaction of which our survival may well depend, is above all a demand on the competence of the managements, especially of our big enterprises.

That the United States is the leader today, economically and socially, will make management performance decisive—and adequate management performance much harder. From the peak there is only one easy way to go: downwards. It always requires twice as much effort and skill to stay up as it did to climb up. In other words, there is real danger that in retrospect the United States of 1950 will come to look like the Great Britain of 1880—doomed to decline for lack of vision and lack of effort. There are evidences of a tendency in this country to defend what we have rather than advance further; capital equipment is getting old in many industries; productivity is improving fast only in the very new industries, and may be stagnant if not declining in many others. Only superior management competence and continuously improved management performance can keep us progressing, can prevent our becoming smug, self-satisfied and lazy.

Outside the United States management has an even more decisive function and an even tougher job. Whether Europe regains her economic prosperity depends, above all, on the performance of her managements. And whether the formerly colonial and raw-material producing countries will succeed in developing their economies as free nations or will go Communist, depends to a large extent on their ability to produce competent and responsible managers in a hurry. Truly, the entire free world has an immense stake in the competence, skill and responsibility of management.

CHAPTER 2

THE JOBS OF MANAGEMENT

Management the least known of our basic institutions—The organ of the enterprise—The first function: economic performance—The first job: managing a business—Managing as creative action—Management by objectives—Managing managers—The enterprise as a genuine whole—Managers must manage—"It's the abilities, not the disabilities, that count"—Managing worker and work—The two time dimensions of management—The integrated nature of management.

DESPITE its crucial importance, its high visibility and its spectacular rise, management is the least known and the least understood of our basic institutions. Even the people in a business often do not know what their management does and what it is supposed to be doing, how it acts and why, whether it does a good job or not. Indeed, the typical picture of what goes on in the "front office" or on "the fourteenth floor" in the minds of otherwise sane, well-informed and intelligent employees (including, often, people themselves in responsible managerial and specialist positions) bears striking resemblance to the medieval geographer's picture of Africa as the stamping ground of the one-eyed ogre, the two-headed pygmy, the immortal phoenix and the elusive unicorn. What then is management: What does it do?

There are two popular answers. One is that management is the people at the top—the term "management" being little more than euphemism for "the boss." The other one defines a manager as someone who directs the work of others and who, as a slogan puts it "does his work by getting other people to do theirs."

But these are at best merely efforts to tell us who belongs in management (as we shall see, they don't even tell us that). They do not attempt to tell us what management is and what it does. These questions can only be answered by analyzing management's function. For management is an organ; and organs can be described and defined only through their function.

Management is the specific organ of the business enterprise. Whenever we talk of a business enterprise, say, the United States Steel Company or the British Coal Board, as deciding to build a new plant, laying off workers or treating its customers fairly, we actually talk of a management decision, a management action, a management behavior. The enterprise can decide, act and behave only as its managers do—by itself the enterprise has no effective existence. And conversely any business enterprise, no matter what its legal structure, must have a management to be alive and functioning. (In this respect there is no difference between private enterprise, the nationalized industries of Great Britain, such old-established government monopolies as a Post Office, and the "ministries" and "trusts" of Communist Russia.)

That management is the specific organ of the business enterprise is so obvious that it tends to be taken for granted. But it sets management apart from all other governing organs of all other institutions. The Government, the Army or the Church—in fact, any major institution—has to have an organ which, in some of its function, is not unlike the management of the business enterprise. But management as such is the management of a *business* enterprise. And the reason for the existence of a business enterprise is that it supplies economic goods and services. To be sure, the business enterprise must discharge its economic responsibility so as to strengthen society, and in accordance with society's political and ethical beliefs. But these are (to use the logician's term) accidental conditions limiting, modifying, encouraging or retarding the economic activities of the business enterprise. The essence of business enterprise, the vital principle that determines its nature, is economic performance.

The First Function: Economic Performance

Management must always, in every decision and action, put economic performance first. It can only justify its existence and its authority by the economic results it produces. There may be great non-economic results: the happiness of the members of the enterprise, the contribution to the welfare or culture of the community, etc. Yet management has failed if it fails to produce economic results. It has failed if it does not supply goods and services desired by the consumer at a price the consumer is willing to pay. It has failed if it does not improve or at least maintain the wealth-producing capacity of the economic resources entrusted to it.

In this management is unique. A General Staff will ask itself quite legitimately whether its basic military decisions are compatible with the economic structure and welfare of the country. But it would be greatly remiss in its duty were it to start its military deliberations with the needs of the economy. The economic consequences of military decisions are a secondary, a limiting factor in these decisions, not their starting point or their rationale. A General Staff, being the specific organ of a military organization, must, by necessity, put military security first. To act differently would be a betrayal of its responsibility and dangerous malpractice. Similarly, management, while always taking into consideration the impact of its decisions on society, both within and without the enterprise, must always put economic performance first.

The first definition of management is therefore that it is an economic organ, indeed the specifically economic organ of an industrial society. Every act, every decision, every deliberation of management has as its first dimension an economic dimension.

Management's first job is managing a business

This apparently obvious statement leads to conclusions that are far from being obvious or generally accepted. It implies both severe limitations on the scope of management and manager, and a major responsibility for creative action.

It means in the first place that the skills, the competence, the experience of management cannot, as such, be transferred and applied to the organization and running of other institutions. In particular a man's success in management carries by itself no promise—let alone a guarantee—of his being successful in government. A career in management is, by itself, not a preparation for major political office—or for leadership in the Armed Forces, the Church or a university. The skills, the competence and the experience that are common and therefore transferable are analytical and administrative—extremely important, but secondary to the attainment of the primary objectives of the various non-business institutions. Whether Franklin D. Roosevelt was a great President or a national disaster has been argued hotly in this country for twenty years. But the patent fact that he was an extremely poor administrator seldom enters the discussion; even his staunchest enemies would consider it irrelevant. What is at issue are his basic political decisions. And no one would claim that these should be determined by the supply of goods and services desired by the consumer at the price the consumer is willing to pay, or by the maintenance or improvement of wealth-producing resources. What to the manager must be the main focus is to the politician, of necessity, only one factor among many.

A second negative conclusion is that management can never be an exact science. True, the work of a manager can be systematically analyzed and classified; there are, in other words, distinct professional features and a scientific aspect to management. Nor is managing a business just a matter of hunch or native ability; its elements and requirements can be analyzed, can be organized systematically, can be learned by anyone with normal human endowment. Altogether, this entire book is based on the proposition that the days of the "intuitive" managers are numbered. This book assumes that the manager can improve his performance in all areas of management, including the managing of a business, through the systematic study of principles, the acquisition of organized knowledge and the systematic analysis of his own performance in all areas of his work and job and on all levels of management. Indeed, nothing else can contribute so much to his skill, his effectiveness and his performance. And underlying this theme is the conviction that the impact of the manager on modern society and its citizens is so great as to require of him the self-discipline and the high standards of public service of a true professional.

And yet the ultimate test of management is business performance. Achievement rather than knowledge remains, of necessity, both proof and aim. Management, in other words, is a practice, rather than a science or a profession, though containing elements of both. No greater damage could be done to our economy or to our society than to attempt to "professionalize" management by "licensing" managers, for instance, or by limiting access to management to people with a special academic degree.

On the contrary, it is the test of good management that it enables the successful business performer to do his work—whether he be otherwise a good manager or a poor one. And any serious attempt to make management "scientific" or a "profession" is bound to lead to the attempt to eliminate those "disturbing nuisances," the unpredictabilities of business life—its risks, its ups and downs, its "wasteful competition," the "irrational choices" of the consumer—and, in the process, the economy's freedom and its ability to grow. It is not entirely accident that some of the early pioneers of "Scientific Management" ended up by demanding complete cartelization of the economy (Henry Gantt was the prime example); that the one direct outgrowth of American "Scientific Management" abroad, the German "Rationalization" movement of the twenties, attempted to make the world safe for professional management by cartelizing it; and that in our own country men who were steeped in "scientific management" played a big part in "Technocracy" and in the attempted nation-wide super-cartel of the National Recovery Act in the first year of Roosevelt's New Deal.

The scope and extent of management's authority and responsibility are severely limited. It is true that in order to discharge its business responsibility management must excercise substantial social and governing authority within the enterprise—authority over citizens in their capacity as members of the enterprise. It is also a fact that because of the importance of the business enterprise, management inevitably becomes one of the leading groups in industrial society. Since management's responsibility is always founded in economic performance, however, it has no authority except as is necessary to discharge its economic responsibility. To assert authority for management over the citizen and his affairs beyond that growing out of management's responsibility for business performance is usurpation of authority. Furthermore management can only be one leading group among several; in its own self-interest it can never and must never be *the* leading group. It has partial rather than comprehensive social responsibility—hence partial rather than comprehensive social authority. Should management claim to be *the* leading group—or even to be the most powerful of leading groups—it will either be rebuffed and, in the process, be shorn of most of the authority it can claim legitimately, or it will help into power a dictatorship that will deprive management as well as all other groups in a free society of their authority and standing.

But while the fact that management is an organ of the business enterprise limits its scope and potential, it also embodies a major responsibility for creative action. For management has to *manage.* And managing is not just passive, adaptive behavior; it means taking action to make the desired results come to pass.

The early economist conceived of the businessman and his behavior as purely passive: success in business meant rapid and intelligent adaptation to events occurring outside, in an economy shaped by impersonal, objective forces that were neither controlled by the businessman nor influenced by his reaction to them. We may call this the concept of the "trader." Even if he was not considered a parasite, his contributions were seen as purely mechanical: the shifting of resources to more productive use. Today's economist sees the businessman as choosing rationally between alternatives of action. This is no longer a mechanical concept; obviously what choice the businessman makes has a real impact on the economy. But still, the economist's "businessman"—the picture that underlies the prevailing economic "theory of the firm" and the theorem of the "maximization of profits"—reacts to economic developments. He is still passive, still adaptive—though with a choice between various ways to adapt. Basically this is a concept of the "investor" or the "financier" rather than of the manager.

Of course, it is always important to adapt to economic changes rapidly, intelligently and rationally. But managing goes way beyond passive reaction and adaptation. It implies responsibility for attempting to shape the economic environment, for planning, initiating and carrying through changes in that economic environment, for constantly pushing back the limitations of economic circumstances on the enterprise's freedom of action. What is possible—the economist's "economic conditions"—is therefore only one pole in managing a business. What is desirable in the interest of the enterprise is the other. And while man can never really "master" his environment, while he is always held within a tight vise of possibilities, it is management's specific job to make what is desirable first possible and then actual. Management is not just a creature of the economy; it is a creator as well. And only to the extent to which it masters the economic circumstances, and alters them by conscious, directed action, does it really manage. To manage a business means, therefore, to *manage by objectives*. Throughout this book this will be a keynote.

Managing Managers

To obtain economic performance there must be an enterprise. Management's second function is therefore to make a productive enterprise out of human and material resources. Concretely this is the function of managing managers.

The enterprise, by definition, must be capable of producing more or better than all the resources that comprise it. It must be a genuine whole: greater than—or at least different from—the sum of its parts, with its output larger than the sum of all inputs.

The enterprise cannot therefore be a mechanical assemblage of resources. To make an enterprise out of resources it is not enough to put them together in logical order and then to throw the switch of capital as the nineteenth-century economists firmly believed (and as many of their successors among academic economists still believe). What is needed is a transmutation of the resources. And this cannot come from an inanimate resource such as capital. It requires management.

But it is also clear that the "resources" capable of enlargement can only be human resources. All other resources stand under the laws of mechanics. They can be better utilized or worse utilized, but they can never have an output greater than the sum of the inputs. On the contrary, the problem in putting non-human resources together is always to keep to a minimum the inevitable output-shrinkage through friction, etc. Man, alone of all the resources available to man, can grow and develop. Only what a great medieval political writer (Sir John Fortescue) called the "intencio populi," the directed, focused, united effort of free human beings, can produce a real whole. Indeed, to make the whole that is greater than the sum of its parts has since Plato's days been the definition of the "Good Society."

When we speak of growth and development we imply that the human being himself determines what he contributes. Yet, we habitually define the rank-and-file worker—as distinguished from the manager—as a man who does as he is directed, without responsibility or share in the decisions concerning his work or that of others. This indicates that we consider the rank-and-file worker in the same light as other material resources, and as far as his contribution to the enterprise is concerned as standing under the laws of mechanics. This is a serious misunderstanding. The misunderstanding, however, is not in the definition of rank-and-file *work*, but rather in the failure to see that many rank-and-file *jobs* are in effect managerial, or would be more productive if made so. It does not, in other words, affect the argument that it is managing managers that makes an enterprise.

That this is true is shown in the terms we use to describe the various activities needed to build a functioning and productive enterprise. We speak of "organization"—the formal structure of the enterprise. But what we mean is the organization of managers and of their functions; neither brick and mortar nor rank-and-file workers have any place in the organization structure. We speak of "leadership" and of the "spirit" of a company. But leadership is given by managers and effective primarily within management; and the spirit is made by the spirit within the management group. We talk of "objectives" for the company, and of its performance. But the objectives are goals for management people; the performance is management performance. And if an enterprise fails to perform, we rightly hire not different workers but a new president.

Managers are also the costliest resource of the enterprise. In the big companies one hears again and again that a good engineer or accountant with ten or twelve years of working experience represents a direct investment of $50,000 over and above the contribution he has made so far to the company's success. The figure is, of course, pure guess—though the margin of error may well be no greater than that in the accountant's meticulous and detailed calculation of the investment in, and profitability of, a piece of machinery or a plant. But even if the actual figure were only a fraction, it would be high enough to make certain that the investment in managers, though, of course, never shown on the books, outweighs the investment in every other resource in practically all businesses. To utilize this investment as fully as possible is therefore a major requirement of managing a business.

To manage managers is therefore to make resources productive by making an enterprise out of them. And management is so complex and multi-faceted a thing, even in a very small business, that managing managers is inevitably not only a vital but a complex job.

Managing Worker and Work

The final function of management is to manage workers and work. Work has to be performed; and the resource to perform it with is workers—ranging from totally unskilled to artists, from wheelbarrow pushers to executive vice-presidents. This implies organization of the work so as to make it most suitable for human beings, and organization of people so as to make them work most productively and effectively. It implies consideration of the human being as a resource —that is, as something having peculiar physiological properties, abilities and limitations that require the same amount of engineering attention as the properties of any other resource, e. g., copper. It implies also consideration of the human resource as human beings having, unlike any other resource, personality, citizenship, control over whether they work, how much and how well, and thus requiring motivation, participation, satisfactions, incentives and rewards, leadership, status and function. And it is management, and management alone, that can satisfy these requirements. For they must be satisfied through work and job and within the enterprise; and management is the activating organ of the enterprise.

There is one more major factor in every management problem, every decision, every action—not, properly speaking, a fourth function of management, but an additional dimension: time. Management always has to consider both the present and the long-range future. A management problem is not solved if immediate profits are purchased by endangering the long-range profitability, perhaps even the survival, of the company. A management decision is irresponsible if it risks disaster this year for the sake of a grandiose future. The all too common case of the management that produces great economic results as long as it runs the company but leaves behind nothing but a burned-out and rapidly sinking hulk is an example of irresponsible managerial action through failure to balance present and future. The immediate "economic results" are actually fictitious and are achieved by paying out capital. In every case where present and future are not both satisfied, where their requirements are not harmonized or at least balanced, capital, that is, wealth-producing resources, is endangered, damaged or destroyed.

The time dimension is inherent in management because management is concerned with decisions for action. And action is always aimed at results in the future. Anybody whose responsibility it is to act—rather than just to know—operates into the future. But there are two reasons why the time dimension is of particular importance in management's job, and of particular difficulty. In the first place, it is the essence of economic and technological progress that the time-span for the fruition and proving out of a decision is steadily lengthening. Edison, fifty years ago, needed two years or so between the start of laboratory work on an idea and the start of pilot-plant operations. Today it may well take Edison's successors fifteen years. A half century ago a new plant was expected to pay for itself in two or three years; today, with capital investment per worker ten times that of 1900, the pay-off period in the same industry is ten or twelve years. The human organization, such as a sales force or a management group, may take even longer to build and to pay for itself.

The second peculiar characteristic of the time dimension is that management—almost alone—has to live always in both present and future. A military leader, too, knows both times. But rarely does he have to live in both at the same time. During peace he knows no "present"; all the present is is a preparation for the future of war. During war he knows only the most short-lived "future"; he is concerned with winning the war at hand to the practical exclusion of everything else. But management must keep the enterprise successful and profitable in the present—or else there will be no enterprise left to enjoy the future. It must simultaneously make the enterprise capable of growing and prospering, or at least of surviving in the future—otherwise it has fallen down on its responsibility of keeping resources productive and unimpaired, has destroyed capital. (The only parallel to this time-squeeze is the dilemma of the politician between the responsibility for the common good and the need to be re-elected as a prerequisite to making his contribution to the common good. But the cynical politician can argue that promises to the voters and performance once in office need not resemble each other too closely. The manager's action on present results, however, directly determines future results, his action on future results—research expenditures, for instance, or plant investment—profoundly influences visible present results.)

The Integrated Nature of Management

The three jobs of management: managing a business, managing managers and managing worker and work, can be analyzed separately, studied separately, appraised separately. In each a present and a future dimension can be distinguished. But in its daily work management cannot separate them. Nor can it separate decisions on present from decisions on future. Any management decision always affects all three jobs and must take all three into account. And the most vital decisions on the future are often made as decisions on the present—on present research budgets or on the handling of a grievance, on promoting this man and letting that one go, on maintenance standards or on customer service.

It cannot even be said that one job predominates or requires the greater skill or competence. True, business performance comes first—it is the aim of the enterprise and the reason for its existence. But if there is no functioning enterprise, there will be no business performance, no matter how good management may be in managing the business. The same holds true if worker and work are mismanaged. Economic performance that is being achieved by mismanaging managers is illusory and actually destructive of capital. Economic performance that is being achieved by mismanaging work and worker is equally an illusion. It will not only raise costs to the point where the enterprise ceases to be competitive; it will, by creating class hatred and class warfare, end by making it impossible for the enterprise to operate at all.

Managing a business has primacy because the enterprise is an economic institution; but managing managers and managing workers and work have primacy precisely because society is not an economic institution and is therefore vitally interested in these two areas of management in which basic social beliefs and aims are being realized.

In this book we shall always bring together both present and future. But we shall discuss separately each of the three major jobs of management: managing a business, managing managers, managing work and worker. We must, however, never allow ourselves to forget that in actual practice managers always discharge these three jobs in every one action. We must not allow ourselves to forget that it is actually the specific situation of the manager to have not one but three jobs at the same time, discharged by and through the same people, exercised in and through the same decision. Indeed we can only answer our question: "What is management and what does it do?" by saying that it is a multi-purpose organ that manages a business *and* manages managers *and* manages worker and work. If one of these were omitted, we would not have management any more—and we also would not have a business enterprise or an industrial society.

CHAPTER 3

THE CHALLENGE TO MANAGEMENT

The new industrial revolution—Automation: science fiction and reality—What is Automation?—Conceptual principles, not techniques or gadgets—Automation and the worker—Automation, planning and monopoly—The demands on the manager.

MANAGEMENT faces the first great test of its competence and its hardest task in the imminent industrial revolution which we call "Automation."

A lot of rather lurid "science fiction" is being written today about Automation. The "push-button factory" is the least fantastic of them (though it, too, is largely nonsense). The coming of the new technology has revived all the slogans of the "planners" of the thirties. It is producing a new crop of penny-dreadfuls purporting to give us a glimpse of that nightmare, the technocrat's paradise, in which no human decisions, no human responsibility, no human management is needed, and in which the push button run by its own "electronic brain" produces and distributes abundant wealth.

Specifically we are being told in these mathematical romances that the new technology will require such capital investments as to make impossible all but the giant business. We are told—in Europe even more than here—that it will make almost inevitable the elimination of competition and will make both possible and necessary the nationalization of the resulting giant monopolies. We are told that the push-button factory of the future will have practically no workers (though who will buy the unlimited supply of goods it will spew out if everyone lives in enforced idleness we are not being told). And those people that are still needed will be pure technicians—electronics engineers, theoretical physicists, mathematicians—or janitors. But managers will not be needed. Indeed, however much the prophets disagree on other points, they seem to be in emphatic agreement that managers will not be needed.

It is no accident that so much of this speculation comes from the advocates of controlled economy and central planning—especially in Europe. For every item in the present prediction of things to come is straight out of the prescription the planners urged us to swallow yesterday. Now that we in the free world no longer accept the planners' remedies as good for us, an attempt is being made to make us swallow the same nostrums under the pretext that they are inevitable.

What Is Automation?

Yet every one of these assertions, conclusions and fears is the direct opposite of what the new technology really means. Indeed, we have enough examples of it around—in an oil refinery, for instance, or in a synthetic rubber plant—so that we do not have to speculate. We can show what Automation is and what its effects will be.

Automation is not "technical" in character. Like every technology it is primarily a system of concepts, and its technical aspects are results rather than causes.

The first concept is a metaphysical one: that there is a basic pattern of stability and predictability behind the seeming flux of phenomena. The second concept is one of the nature of work. The new technology does not, as did early individual production, focus on skill as the integrating principle of work. Nor does it, as did Henry Ford's concept of mass production, focus on the product as the organizing principle. It focuses on the process, which it sees as an integrated and harmonious whole. Its aim is to arrive at the best process—the process that will produce the greatest variety of goods with the greatest stability, at the lowest cost and with the least effort. Indeed the less variety and fluctuation there is in the process, the greater may be the variety of goods that can be produced.

Finally, the new technology has a concept of control to maintain the equilibrium between ends and means, output and effort. Automation requires that what is significant be pre-established, and that it be used as a pre-set and self-activating governor of the process.

The mechanics of control can be extremely simple.

In the claims office of a life-insurance company, policies that require special handling—because the documents are not all there, because data are missing, because the beneficiary is not clearly established, because the title is clouded, etc.—are simply put aside and handed over to a separate clerk for special, individual handling. This anyone can learn to do in a few days (or a machine could be designed to do it). It makes possible the rapid, smooth and continuous processing of the 98 per cent or so of all policies that are routine—even though there are literally thousands of variations in the mode of payment, the distribution among beneficiaries and so on. Simple rejection is adequate control to maintain the process.

Control may also require complicated machinery. It can be exercised as "feed-back," in which the result of the process is fed back into an earlier stage to maintain the process and to adjust it if necessary.

The simplest example is the "safety valve" on a steam engine which is lifted up by steam pressure in the boiler until it opens up a hole through which the excess steam escapes, thus lowering the pressure enough for the safety valve to sink back to its former place and to close the opening again. It is this principle on which glandular body functions operate. And it is feed-back that is used by the electronic control system of an anti-aircraft gun.

The mechanics of control are, however, quite secondary to the technology of Automation. What is essential is that there always be a control built into the process which maintains it either by eliminating what the process cannot handle, or by adjusting the process so as to make it produce the planned result.

Only *after* these concepts have been thought through can machines and gadgets be fruitfully applied.

After this conceptual rethinking, however, mechanization of those operations that are repetitive in character becomes both possible and economical. A machine can be used to feed material into another machine, to change the material's position in the machine and to move it from one machine to the next. All materials handling—which contributes the bulk of unskilled repetitive work under mass production—can be mechanized. So can changes in machine setting and routine judgments (for instance, whether the machine has become too hot or the tool bit too blunt).

This mechanization is not, however, Automation itself. It is only the result of Automation and it is not essential to it. We have plenty of examples of effective mass production without a single conveyor belt; for instance, the sorting of checks in a clearing house. We will see examples of Automation without a single "automatic tool," let alone a single "push button."

Techniques, tools and gadgets are thus in Automation, as in every technology, specific to the task and determined by it. They do not constitute Automation; nor does Automation consist in their application. Automation is a concept of the organization of work. It is therefore as applicable to the organization of distribution or of clerical work as to that of industrial production.

Automation and the Worker

The popular belief that the new technology will replace human labor by robots is utterly false.

"I was in charge of an analogue computer for some time," one of my students told me. "I am still appalled by the number of businessmen who believe that the machine was in charge of me."

Actually the new technology (though there will certainly be problems of displacement) will employ more people and, above all, more people who are highly skilled and highly trained.

A scant twenty years ago, it was widely believed that the mass-production technology—yesterday's industrial revolution—threw people out of work. Today we know that wherever it has been introduced, it has rapidly increased the number of job opportunities in industry. But it is still widely believed that mass production replaces skilled labor by unskilled labor. We know this today to be a fallacy. In the United States, for instance, where mass-production methods have been applied on the broadest scale, the class of employess that has been growing most rapidly in numbers and proportion is that of skilled and trained people. And the truly unskilled laborer of yesterday, who contributed only his brawn, has become the semi-skilled machine operator of today—a man of higher skill and education, producing more wealth, earning a vastly higher standard of living.

The technological changes now occurring will carry the process a big step further. They will not make human labor superfluous. On the contrary, they will require tremendous numbers of highly skilled and highly trained men—managers to think through and plan, highly trained technicians and workers to design the new tools, to produce them, to maintain them, to direct them. Indeed, the major obstacle to the rapid spread of these changes will almost certainly be the lack, in every country, of enough trained men.

It is similarly not true that the new technology demands the giant enterprise, let alone that it squeezes out the small and independent and establishes monopoly. In some industries it may indeed increase the size of the most economical unit. In many others (one example is the production of raw steel) it is likely to make significantly smaller units economically possible, if not necessary.

It is finally not true that the new technology brings a tremendous increase in capital requirements. Investment per *production* worker will, of course, go up. Investment per *employee* may, however, not rise at all, as more technicians and managers will be needed; and there is nothing in our experience to make it appear likely that investment per *unit of output* will increase significantly.

The Demands on Management

Above all, the new technology will not render managers superfluous or replace them by mere technicians. On the contrary, it will demand many more managers. It will greatly extend the management area; many people now considered rank-and-file will have to become capable of doing management work. The great majority of technicians will have to be able to understand what management is and to see and think managerially. And on all levels the demands on the manager's responsibility and competence, his vision, his capacity to choose between alternate risks, his economic knowledge and skill, his ability to manage managers and to manage worker and work, his competence in making decisions, will be greatly increased.

Far from making inevitable, let alone desirable, centralized planning and monopoly—whether nationalized or private cartel—the new technology will demand the utmost in decentralization, in flexibility and in management autonomy. Any society in the era of the new technology would perish miserably were it to attempt to get rid of free management of autonomus enterprise so as to run the economy by central planning. And so would any enterprise that attempted to centralize responsibility and decision-making at the top. It would go under as did the great reptiles of the Saurian age who attempted to control a huge body by a small, centralized nervous system that could not adapt itself to rapid change in the environment.

For all of these reasons, no description of the nature of management will be complete that fails to take Automation into account. I am inclined to believe that Automation will not inundate us in a sudden flood but will seep in gradually though steadily. But there can be little doubt that it is coming. There can be little doubt that the industrial country that first understands Automation and first applies it systematically will lead in productivity and wealth during the second half of the twentieth century, just as the United States, through understanding and applying mass production, came to lead the world during the first half of this century. And there is even less doubt that this leadership position will fall to the country whose managers understand and practice management in its fullest sense.

PART ONE

MANAGING A BUSINESS

CHAPTER 4

THE SEARS STORY

What is a business and how it is managed—Unexplored territory—Sears, Roebuck as an illustration—How Sears became a business—Rosenwald's innovations—Inventing the mail-order plant—General Wood and Sears's second phase—Merchandise planning and manager development—T. V. Houser and the challenges ahead.

How to manage a business would seem to be of such importance as to insure a veritable flood of books on the subject. Actually there are almost none.

There are hundreds, if not thousands, of books on the management of the various functions of a business: production and marketing, finance and engineering, purchasing, personnel, public relations and so forth. But what it is to manage a business, what it requires, what management is supposed to do and how it should be doing it, have so far been neglected.[1]

This oversight is no accident. It reflects the absence of any tenable economic theory of business enterprise. Rather than start out theorizing ourselves, we shall therefore first take a good look at the conduct and behavior of an actual business enterprise. And there is no better illustration of what a business is and what managing it means, that one of America's most successful enterprises: Sears, Roebuck and Company.[2]

[1] The only exception I know of is the short essay by Oswald Knauth: *Managerial Enterprise* (New York: Norton, 1948). See also Joel Dean's *Managerial Economics* (New York: Prentice-Hall, 1951). Though Dean is concerned mainly with the adaptation of the economist's theoretical concepts and tools to business management, the book, especially its earlier, general parts, is required reading for any manager.

[2] For the data on Sears I have drawn heavily on Emmet & Jeuck *Catalogues and Counters: a History of Sears, Roebuck & Co.* (Chicago: University of Chicago

Sears became a business around the turn of the century with the realization that the American farmer represented a separate and distinct market. Separate, because of his isolation which made existing channels of distribution virtually inaccessible to him; distinct, because of his specific needs which, in important respects, were different from those of the city consumer. And while the farmer's purchasing power was individually low, it represented a tremendous, almost untapped, buying potential in the aggregate.

To reach the farmer a new distribution channel had to be created. Merchandise had to be produced to answer his needs and wants. It had to be brought to him in large quantities, at low price, and with a guarantee of regular supply. He had to be given a warranty of reliability and honesty on the part of the supplier, since his physical isolation made it impossible for him to inspect merchandise before delivery or to seek redress if cheated.

To create Sears, Roebuck as a business therefore required analysis of customer and market, and especially of what the farmer considered "value." Furthermore, it required innovation in five distinct areas.

First, it demanded systematic merchandising, that is, the finding and developing of sources of supply for the particular goods the farmer needed, in the quality and quantity he needed them and at a price he could pay. Second, it required a mail-order catalogue capable of serving as adequate substitute for the shopping trips to the big city the farmer could not make. For this reason the catalogue had to become a regular publication rather than an announcement of spectacular "bargains" at irregular intervals. It had to break with the entire tradition of mail-selling and had to learn not to high-pressure the farmer into buying by exaggerated boasts, but to give him instead a factual description of the goods offered. The aim had to be to create a permanent customer by convincing him of the reliability of the catalogue and of the company behind it; the catalogue had to become the "wish book" for the farmer.

Third, the age-old concept of "caveat emptor" had to be changed to "caveat vendor"—the meaning of the famous Sears policy of "your money back and no questions asked." Fourth, a way had to

Press, 1950), one of the best company histories written so far. For the interpretation of these data I am alone responsible, however; and I also bear sole responsibility for the analysis of Sears's present position.

be found to fill large quantities of customer orders cheaply and quickly. Without the mail-order plant, conduct of the business would have been physically impossible.

Finally, a human organization had to be built—and when Sears, Roebuck started to become a business, most of the necessary human skills were not available. There were, for instance, no buyers for this kind of an operation, no accountants versed in the new requirements of inventory control, no artists to illustrate the catalogues, no clerks experienced in the handling of a huge volume of customer orders.

Richard Sears gave the company his name. But it was not he who made it into a modern business enterprise. In fact, Sears's own operations could hardly be called a "business." He was a shrewd speculator, buying up distress-merchandise and offering it, one batch at a time, through spectacular advertising. Every one of his deals was a complete transaction in itself which, when finished, liquidated itself and the business with it. Sears could make a lot of money for himself. But his way of operation could never found a business, let alone perpetuate it. In fact, he would have been forced out of business within a few years, as all the many people before him had been who operated on a similar basis.

It was Julius Rosenwald who made a business enterprise out of Sears in the ten years between 1895 when he took control, and 1905 when the Chicago mail-order plant was opened. He made the analysis of the market. He began the systematic development of merchandise sources. He invented the regular, factual mail-order catalogue and the policy of "satisfaction guaranteed or your money back." He built the productive human organization. He early gave to management people the maximum of authority and full responsibility for results. Later he gave every employee an ownership stake in the company bought for him out of profits. Rosenwald is thus the father not only of Sears, Roebuck but of the "distribution revolution" which has made over twentieth-century America and which is so vital a factor in our economic growth.

Only one basic contribution to the early history of Sears was not made by Rosenwald. The Chicago mail-order plant was designed by Otto Doering in 1903. It was, five years before Henry Ford, the first modern mass-production plant, complete with breakdown of all work into simple repetitive operations, assembly line, conveyor belt, standardized, interchangeable parts—and, above all, with planned plant-wide scheduling.[3]

It was on these foundations that Sears had grown by the end of World War I into a national institution with its "wish-book" the only literature, outside of the Bible, to be found in many farm homes.

The second phase in the Sears story begins in the mid-twenties. Just as the first chapter was dominated by one man, Julius Rosenwald, the second chapter was dominated by another: General Robert E. Wood.

By the mid-twenties, when Wood joined Sears, the original Sears market was changing rapidly. The farmer was no longer isolated; the automobile had enabled him to go to town and to shop there. He was no longer a distinct market but was, largely thanks to Sears, rapidly assimilating his way of life and his standard of living to those of the urban middle classes.

At the same time a vast urban market had come into being that was, in its way, as isolated and as badly supplied as the farmer had been twenty-five years earlier. The low-income groups in the cities had outgrown both their subsistence standards and their distinct "lower-class" habits. They were fast acquiring both the money and the desire to buy the same goods as the middle and upper classes. In other words, the country was rapidly becoming one big homogeneous market—but the distribution system was still one of separate and distinct class markets.

Wood had made this analysis even before he joined Sears. Out of it came the decision to switch Sears's emphasis over to retail stores—equipped to serve both the motorized farmer and the city population.

Again a whole series of innovations had to be undertaken to make this decision possible. To the finding of sources of supply and to the purchase of goods from them, merchandising had to add two new major functions: the design of products and the development of manufacturers capable of producing these products in large quan-

[3] There is indeed a persistent legend at Sears that Henry Ford, before he built his own first plant, visited and carefully studied the then brand-new Sears mail-order plant.

tity. "Class market" products—for instance, refrigerators in the twenties—had to be redesigned for a "mass market" with limited purchasing power. Suppliers had to be created—often with Sears money and Sears-trained management—to produce these goods. This also required another important innovation: a basic policy for the relations between Sears and its suppliers, especially those who depended on the company's purchases for the bulk of their business. Merchandise planning and research and the systematic building of hundreds of small suppliers capable of producing for a mass market had to be invented—largely by T. V. Houser, for many years the company's merchandising vice-president. They are as basic to mass distribution in Sears's second phase as mail-order house and catalogue were in its first. And they are as distinct a contribution to the American economy.

But to go into retail selling also meant getting store managers. Mail-order selling did not prepare a man for the management of a retail store. The greatest bottleneck for the first ten or fifteen years of Sears's retail operation, that is almost until World War II, was the shortage of managers. The most systematic innovations had to be in the field of manager development; and the Sears policies of the thirties became the starting point for all the work in manager development now going on in American industry.

Expansion into retail selling also meant radical innovations in organization structure. Mail-order selling is a highly centralized operation—or at least it has always been so in Sears. But retail stores cannot be run from headquarters two thousand miles away. They must be managed locally. Also only a few mail-order plants were needed to supply the country; but Sears today has seven hundred stores, each with its own market in its own locality. A decentralized organization structure, methods of managing a decentralized company, measuring the performance of store managers and maintaining corporate unity with maximum local autonomy—all these had to be created to make possible retail selling. And new compensation policies had to be found to reward store managers for performance.

Finally, Sears had to turn innovator in respect to location, architecture and physical arrangement of the stores. The traditional retail store was unsuited for the Sears market. It was not just a matter of putting the Sears store on the outskirts of the cities and of providing it with an adequate parking lot. The whole concept of the retail store had to be changed. In fact, few people even at Sears realize how far this innovation has gone and how deeply it has influenced the shopping habits of the American people as well as the physical appearance of our towns. The suburban shopping center, touted today as a radical innovation in retail selling, is really nothing but an imitation of concepts and methods developed by Sears during the thirties.

The basic decisions underlying the expansion into retail stores were taken in the mid-twenties; the basic innovations had been made by the early thirties. This explains why Sears's volume of business and its profits grew right through depression, World War II and postwar boom. And yet, almost thirty years after these basic decisions were taken, they are still not fully carried through into practice.

Merchandise planning—the systematic design of quality goods for mass distribution, the systematic development of mass producers for them—has still to be applied to the women's fashion field. The traditional production organization for women's fashions—the New York "Garment District"—simply does not go with mass-distribution requirements. And while Sears has been able to transform other equally traditional industries to mass production and mass distribution—and is doing so today with singular success in Latin America—it has either been unable or unwilling to change the production system of women's fashion goods.

Another area in which the transition has not yet been completed is that of public relations. Sears, under Julius Rosenwald, pioneered in public relations; and everyone at Sears considers it a vitally important area. Yet although it was basic to the analysis that underlay the expansion into retail stores that the Sears market had become urban, at least in its shopping habits, Sears's public relations are still focused primarily on "Sears, the farmer's friend." In view of the reality of the Sears market, this can only be considered an agrarian nostalgia unsuited to the needs of the business.

General Wood retired from the chairmanship of Sears in the spring of 1954, and T. V. Houser took his place. This well symbolizes the end of an era for Sears, which now faces new problems and new opportunities.

For the automobile that changed Sears's market once seems to be about to change it again. In most of our cities driving has become so unpleasant, and parking so difficult, that the automobile is rapidly ceasing to be an aid to the shopper and is becoming its own worst enemy. At the same time, the typical Sears customer, the housewife, tends more and more to be employed and at work during shopping hours. Or else she has small children and nobody to leave them with when she goes shopping.

If this interpretation is correct, Sears needs as searching an analysis of market and customer as was made in the two earlier turning points in its history. New objectives will have to be developed. A new type of distributive organization might be needed in which the local store becomes headquarters for order-taking salesmen, traveling (perhaps with a sample car) from house to house. Such a development might well be foreshadowed in the growing volume of door-to-door sales during the last few years. This change would almost certainly require new concepts of organization, new compensation policies and new methods. It would create a new problem of finding the right personnel as difficult as was finding retail store managers twenty years ago. Servicing the Sears products in the customer's home might well become of central importance—perhaps eventually as important as was the original money-back warranty of forty years ago. The bulk of customer buying might again shift to catalogue buying—though no longer by mail—either from a traveling salesman or over the telephone. And this in turn would require a technological change in the mail-order plant which, to this day, operates almost unchanged from the basic pattern developed fifty years ago by Otto Doering. The filling of customers' orders, whether received by mail, by telephone or through salesmen, would appear to demand a fully automatic plant based on a radical application of the principles of Automation and feed-back.

Even in merchandising there might be need for new objectives; for today's most important customer—the young married mother and housewife, who often holds down a job as well—is in many ways as distinct a market as the American farmer ever was in the days of his most complete isolation.

Once again, in other words, Sears may have to think through what its business is, where its markets are, and what innovations are needed.

CHAPTER 5

WHAT IS A BUSINESS?

Business created and managed by people, not by forces—The fallacy of "profit maximization"—Profit the objective condition of economic activity, not its rationale—The purpose of a business: to create a customer—The two entrepreneurial functions: marketing and innovation—Marketing not a specialized activity—The General Electric solution—The enterprise as the organ of economic growth—The productive utilization of all wealth-producing resources—What is productive labor?—Time, product mix, process mix and organization structure as factors in productivity—The function of profit—How much profit is required?—Business management a rational activity.

THE first conclusion to be drawn from the Sears story is that a business enterprise is created and managed by people. It is not managed by "forces." Economic forces set limits to what management can do. They create opportunities for management's action. But they, by themselves, do not determine what a business is or what it does. Nothing could be sillier than the oft-repeated assertion that "management only adapts the business to the forces of the market." Management not only finds these "forces"; management creates them by its own action. Just as it took a Julius Rosenwald fifty years ago to make Sears into a business enterprise, and a General Wood twenty-five years ago to change its basic nature and thus insure its growth and success during the depression and World War II, it will take somebody—and probably quite a few people—to make the decisions that will determine whether Sears is going to continue to prosper or will decline, whether it will survive or will eventually perish. And that is true of every business.

The second conclusion is that a business cannot be defined or explained in terms of profit.

The average businessman when asked what a business is, is likely to answer: "An organization to make a profit." And the average economist is likely to give the same answer. But this answer is not only false; it is irrelevant.

Similarly, there is total bankruptcy in the prevailing economic theory of business enterprise and behavior: the theory of the "maximization of profits"—simply a complicated way of phrasing the old saw of "buying cheap and selling dear." This theorem may adequately explain how Richard Sears operated. But it is bankrupt precisely because it cannot explain how Sears, Roebuck—or any other business enterprise—operates, nor how it should operate.

This shows clearly in the attempts the economists themselves must make to salvage the theorem. Joel Dean, the most brilliant and fruitful of the economists analyzing business today, still maintains the theorem as such. But this is how he defines it:

> Economic theory makes a fundamental assumption that maximizing profits is the basic objective of every firm. But in recent years "profit maximization" has been extensively qualified by theorists to refer to the long run; to refer to management's rather than to owners' income; to include non-financial income such as increased leisure for high-strung executives and more congenial relations between executive levels within the firm; and to make allowance for special considerations such as restraining competition, maintaining management control, warding off wage demands, and forestalling anti-trust suits. The concept has become so general and hazy that it seems to encompass most of men's aims in life.
>
> This trend reflects a growing realization by theorists that many firms, and particularly the big ones, do not operate on the principle of profit maximizing in terms of marginal costs and revenues. . . .[1]

Surely a theorem that can be used only when qualified out of existence has ceased to have meaning or usefulness.

This does not mean that profit and profitability are unimportant. It does mean that profitability is not the purpose of business enterprise and business activity, but a limiting factor on it. Profit is not the explanation, cause or rationale of business behavior and business decisions, but the test of their validity. If archangels, instead of

[1] *Managerial Economics* (New York: Prentice-Hall, 1951), page 28.

businessmen, sat in directors' chairs, they would still have to be concerned with profitability despite their total lack of personal interest in making profits. And this applies with equal force to those far from angelic individuals, the Commissars who run Soviet Russia's business enterprises. For the problem of any business is not the maximization of profit but the achievement of sufficient profit to cover the risks of economic activity and thus to avoid loss.

The root of the confusion is the mistaken belief that the motive of a person—the so-called "profit motive" of the businessman—is an explanation of his behavior or his guide to right action. Whether there is such a thing as a profit motive at all is highly doubtful. It was invented by the classical economists to explain economic behavior that otherwise made no sense. Yet there has never been any but negative evidence for the existence of the profit motive. And we have long since found the true explanation of the phenomena of economic change and growth which the profit motive was first put forth to explain.

But it is irrelevant for an understanding of business behavior, including an understanding of profit and profitability, whether there is a profit motive or not. That Jim Smith is in business to make a profit concerns only him and the Recording Angel. It does not tell us what Jim Smith does and how he performs. We do not learn anything about the work of a prospector, hunting for uranium in the Nevada desert, by being told that he is trying to make his fortune. We do not learn anything about the work of a heart specialist by being told that he is trying to make a livelihood, or even that he is trying to benefit humanity. The profit motive and its offspring, maximization of profits, are just as irrelevant to the function of a business, the purpose of a business and the job of managing a business.

In fact, the concept is worse than irrelevant. It does harm. It is a major cause for the misunderstanding of the nature of profit in our society and for the deep-seated hostility to profit which are among the most dangerous diseases of an industrial society. It is largely responsible for the worst mistakes of public policy—in this country as well as in western Europe—which are squarely based on a lack of understanding of the nature, function and purpose of business enterprise.

The Purpose of a Business

If we want to know what a business is we have to start with its *purpose*. And its purpose must lie outside of the business itself. In fact, it must lie in society since a business enterprise is an organ of society. There is only one valid definition of business purpose: *to create a customer.*

Markets are not created by God, nature or economic forces but by businessmen. The want they satisfy may have been felt by the customer before he was offered the means of satisfying it. It may indeed, like the want for food in a famine, have dominated the customer's life and filled all his waking moments. But it was a theoretical want before; only when the action of businessmen makes it effective demand is there a customer, a market. It may have been an unfelt want. There may have been no want at all until business action created it—by advertising, by salesmanship, or by inventing something new. In every case it is business action that creates the customer.

It is the customer who determines what a business is. For it is the customer, and he alone, who through being willing to pay for a good or for a service, converts economic resources into wealth, things into goods. What the business thinks it produces is not of first importance—especially not to the future of the business and to its success. What the customer thinks he is buying, what he considers "value," is decisive—it determines what a business is, what it produces and whether it will prosper.

The customer is the foundation of a business and keeps it in existence. He alone gives employment. And it is to supply the consumer that society entrusts wealth-producing resources to the business enterprise.

The Two Entrepreneurial Functions

Because it is its purpose to create a customer, any business enterprise has two--and only these two—basic functions: marketing and innovation. They are the entrepreneurial functions.

Marketing is the distinguishing, the unique function of the business. A business is set apart from all other human organizations by the fact that it markets a product or a service. Neither Church.

nor Army, nor School, nor State does that. Any organization that fulfils itself through marketing a product or a service, is a business. Any organization in which marketing is either absent or incidental is not a business and should never be run as if it were one.

The first man to see marketing clearly as the unique and central function of the business enterprise, and the creation of a customer as the specific job of management, was Cyrus McCormick. The history books mention only that he invented a mechanical harvester. But he also invented the basic tools of modern marketing: market research and market analysis, the concept of market standing, modern pricing policies, the modern service-salesman, parts and service supply to the customer and installment credit. He is truly the father of business management. And he had done all this by 1850. It was not until fifty years later, however, that he was widely imitated even in his own country.

The economic revolution of the American economy since 1900 has in large part been a marketing revolution caused by the assumption of responsibility for creative, aggressive, pioneering marketing by American management. Fifty years ago the typical attitude of the American businessman toward marketing was still: "The sales department will sell whatever the plant produces." Today it is increasingly: "It is our job to produce what the market needs." But our economists and government officials are just beginning to understand this: only now, for instance, is the U. S. Department of Commerce setting up an Office of Distribution.

In Europe there is still almost no understanding that marketing is the specific business function—a major reason for the stagnation of the European economies of today. For to reach full realization of the importance of marketing requires overcoming a deep-rooted social prejudice against "selling" as ignoble and parasitical, and in favor of "production" as gentlemanly, with its resultant theoretical fallacy of considering production as the main and determining function of a business.

A good example of this historical attitude toward marketing are those big Italian companies which have no domestic sales managers even though the home market accounts for 70 per cent of their business.

Actually marketing is so basic that it is not just enough to have a strong sales department and to entrust marketing to it. Marketing is not only much broader than selling, it is not a specialized activity at all. It encompasses the entire business. It is the whole business seen from the point of view of its final result, that is, from the customer's point of view. Concern and responsibility for marketing must therefore permeate all areas of the enterprise.

One illustration of this concept of marketing is the policy worked out by the General Electric Company over the last ten years, which attempts to build customer and market appeal into the product from the design stage on. It considers the actual act of selling but the last step in a sales effort that began before the first engineer put pencil to drawing paper. This, according to a statement in the company's 1952 annual report, "introduces the marketing man at the beginning rather than the end of the production cycle and would integrate marketing into each phase of the business. Thus marketing, through its studies and research, will establish for the engineer, the designer and the manufacturing man what the customer wants in a given product, what price he is willing to pay, and where and when it will be wanted. Marketing would have authority in product planning, production scheduling and inventory control, as well as in the sales distribution and servicing of the product."

The Enterprise as the Organ of Economic Growth

But marketing alone does not make a business enterprise. In a static economy there are no "business enterprises." There are not even "businessmen." For the "middleman" of a static society is simply a "broker" who receives his compensation in the form of a fee.

A business enterprise can exist only in an expanding economy, or at least in one which considers change both natural and desirable. And business is the specific organ of growth, expansion and change.

The second function of a business is therefore *innovation,* that is, the provision of better and more economic goods and services. It is not enough for the business to provide just any economic goods and services; it must provide better and more economic ones. It is not necessary for a business to grow bigger; but it is necessary that it constantly grow better.

Innovation may take the form of lower price—the form with which the economist has been most concerned, for the simple reason that it is the only one that can be handled by his quantitative tools. But it may also be a new and better product (even at a higher price), a new convenience or the creation of a new want. It may be finding new uses for old products. A salesman who succeeded in selling refrigerators to the Eskimos to prevent food from freezing would be an "innovator' quite as much as if he had developed brand-new processes or invented a new product. To sell the Eskimos a refrigerator to keep food cold, is finding a new market; to sell a refrigerator to keep food from getting too cold is actually creating a new product. Technologically there is, of course, only the same old product; but economically there is innovation.

Innovation goes right through all phases of business. It may be innovation in design, in product, in marketing techniques. It may be innovation in price or in service to the customer. It may be innovation in management organization or in management methods. Or it may be a new insurance policy that makes it possible for a businessman to assume new risks. The most effective innovations in American industry in the last few years were probably not the much publicized new electronic or chemical products and processes but innovations in materials handling and in manager development.

Innovation extends through all forms of business. It is as important to a bank, an insurance company or a retail store as it is to a manufacturing or engineering business.

In the organization of business enterprise innovation can therefore no more be considered a separate function than marketing. It is not confined to engineering or research but extends across all parts of the business, all functions, all activities. It is not, to repeat, confined to manufacturing business alone. Innovation in distribution has been as important as innovation in manufacturing; and so has been innovation in an insurance company or in a bank.

The leadership in innovation with respect to product and service can normally be focused in one functional activity which is responsible for nothing else. This is always true in a business with a strong engineering or chemical flavor. In an insurance company, too, a special department charged with leadership responsibility for the development of new kinds of coverage is in order; and there might well be another such department charged with innovation in the organization of sales, the administration of policies and the settling of claims. For both together are the insurance company's business.

or go bankrupt, dependent on the product mix. Obviously this represents a considerable difference in the productivity of the same resources—but not one that shows itself in cost or can be detected by cost analysis.

There is also an important factor I would call "process mix." Is it more productive for a company to buy a part or to make it, to assemble its product or to contract out the assembly process, to market under its own brand name through its own distributive organization or to sell to independent wholesalers using their own brands? What is the company good at? What is the most productive utilization of its specific knowledge, ability, experience, reputation?

Not every management can do everything, nor should any business necessarily go into those activities which are objectively most profitable. Every management has specific abilities and limitations. Whenever it attempts to go beyond these it is likely to fail, no matter how inherently profitable the venture. People who are good at running a highly stable business will not be able to adjust to a mercurial or a rapidly growing business. People who have grown up in a rapidly expanding company will, as everyday experience shows, be in danger of destroying the business should it enter upon a period of consolidation and rest. People good at running a business with a foundation in long-range research are not likely to do well in high-pressure selling of novelties or fashion goods. Utilization of the specific abilities of the company and its management, observance of their specific limitations, is an important productivity factor.

Finally, productivity is vitally affected by organization structure and by the balance between the various activities within the business. If, for lack of clear organization, managers waste their time trying to find out what they are supposed to do rather than doing it, the company's scarcest resource is being wasted. If top management is interested only in engineering (perhaps because that's where all the top men came from) while the company needs major attention to marketing, it lacks productivity; and the end result is likely to be more serious than a drop in output per man-hour.

We therefore need not only to define productivity so as to embrace all these factors affecting it, but also to set objectives that take all these factors into account. And we must develop yardsticks measuring the impact on productivity of the substitution of capital for labor, and of overhead expense for both—with some way to distinguish between creative and parasitical overhead; the impact on productivity of time utilization, product mix, process mix, organization structure and the balance of activities.

Not only does individual management need a real measurement of productivity, the whole country needs it. Its absence is the biggest gap in our economic statistics and seriously weakens all attempts of economic policy to forecast, anticipate and fight a business depression.

The Function of Profit

Only now are we ready to talk of profit and profitability with which discussions of the nature of a business usually begin. For profit is not a cause. It is the result—the result of the performance of the business in marketing, innovation and productivity. It is at the same time the test of this performance—the only possible test, as the Communists in Russia soon found out when they tried to abolish it in the early twenties. Indeed, profit is a beautiful example of what today's scientists and engineers mean when they talk of the feed-back that underlies all systems of automatic production: the self-regulation of a process by its own product.

But profit has a second function, equally important. Economic activity, because it is activity, focuses on the future; and the one thing certain about the future is its uncertainty, its risks. It is no accident that the word "risk" itself in the original Arabic meant "earning one's daily bread"; it is through risk-taking that any businessman earns his daily bread. Because business activity is economic, it always attempts to bring about change. It always saws off the limb on which it sits, always on purpose making existing risks riskier or creating new ones. As the Sears story showed, this "future" of economic activity is a long one; it took fifteen or twenty years for basic Sears decisions to become fully effective, and for major investments to pay off. "Lengthening the economic detour" has been known for fifty years to be a necessity of economic advance. Yet, while we know nothing about the future, we know that its risks increase in geometric progression the further ahead we try to predict or to foreordain it.

It is the first duty of a business to survive. The guiding principle of business economics, in other words, is not the maximization of profits; *it is the avoidance of loss.* Business enterprise must produce the premium to cover the risks inevitably involved in its operation. And there is only one source for this risk premium: profits.[3] Indeed, business enterprise must provide not only for its own risks. It must contribute toward covering the losses of those businesses that operate unprofitably. For society has a real interest in an active economic metabolism in which some businesses always incur losses and disappear. This is a main safeguard of a free, flexible and "open" economy. The enterprise must also make a contribution to the social cost—the schools, the armament, etc.—of a society; that is, it must earn enough to pay taxes. Finally, it must produce capital for future expansion. But first and foremost it must have enough profit to cover its own risks.

To summarize, whether it is the motive of the businessman to maximize profits is debatable. But it is an absolute necessity for the business enterprise to produce at the very least the profit required to cover its own future risks, the profit required to enable it to stay in business and to maintain intact the wealth-producing capacity of its resources. This "required minimum profit" affects business behavior and business decisions—both by setting rigid limits to them and by testing their validity. Management, in order to manage, needs a profit objective at least equal to the required minimum profit, and yardsticks to measure its profit performance against this requirement.

What then is "managing a business"? It follows from the analysis of business activity as the creation of a customer through marketing and innovation that managing a business must always be entrepreneurial in character. It cannot be a bureaucratic, an administrative or even a policy-making job.

It also follows that managing a business must be a creative rather than an adaptive task. The more a management creates economic conditions or changes them rather than passively adapts to them, the more it manages the business.

But our analysis of the nature of a business also shows that

[3] For a detailed discussion of this, see my *The New Society* (New York: Harper & Bros., 1950) page 52 ff. where the various risks are discussed in detail.

management, while ultimately tested by performance alone, is a rational activity. Concretely this means that a business must set objectives that express what is desirable of attainment rather than (as the maximization-of-profit theorem implies) aim at accommodation to the possible. The objectives should therefore be set by fixing one's sights at the desirable. Only then should the question be raised what concessions to the possible have to be made. This requires management to decide what business the enterprise is engaged in, and what business it should be engaged in.

CHAPTER 6

WHAT IS OUR BUSINESS—AND WHAT SHOULD IT BE?

What is our business, neither easy nor obvious—The Telephone Company example—Failure to answer the question a major source of business failure—Success in answering it a major reason for business growth and results—Question most important when business is successful—Who is the customer?—What does the customer buy?—Cadillac and Packard—What is value to the customer?—What will our business be?—What should our business be?—Profitability as an objective.

NOTHING may seem simpler or more obvious than to answer what a company's business is. A steel mill makes steel, a railroad runs trains to carry freight and passengers, an insurance company underwrites fire risks. Indeed, the question looks so simple that it is seldom raised, the answer seems so obvious that it is seldom given.

Actually "what is our business" is almost always a difficult question which can be answered only after hard thinking and studying. And the right answer is usually anything but obvious.

One of the earliest and most successful answers to the question was the one that Theodore N. Vail worked out for American Telephone and Telegraph almost fifty years ago: "Our business is service." This sounds obvious once it has been said. But first there had to be the realization that a telephone system, being a natural monopoly, was susceptible to nationalization, that indeed a privately owned telephone service in a developed and industrialized country was exceptional and needed community support for its survival. Secondly there had to be the realization that community support could not be obtained by propaganda campaigns or by attacking critics as "un-American" or "socialistic." It could only be obtained by creating customer-satisfaction. This realization meant radical innovations in business policy. It meant constant indoctrination in dedication to service for all employees; and public relations which stressed service. It meant emphasis on research and technological leadership; and a financial policy which assumed that the company had to give service wherever there was a demand, and that it was management's job to find the needed capital and to earn a return on it. In retrospect all these things are obvious; but it took well over a decade to work them out. Yet would we have gone through the New Deal period without a serious attempt at telephone nationalization but for the careful analysis of its business that the Telephone Company made around 1905?

What is our business is not determined by the producer but by the consumer. It is not defined by the company's name, statutes or articles of incorporation but by the want the consumer satisfies when he buys a product or a service. The question can therefore be answered only by looking at the business from the outside, from the point of view of the customer and the market. What the consumer sees, thinks, believes and wants at any given time must be accepted by management as an objective fact deserving to be taken as seriously as the reports of the salesman, the tests of the engineer or the figures of the accountant—something few managements find it easy to do. And management must make a conscious effort to get honest answers from the consumer himself rather than attempt to read his mind.

It is, then, the first responsibility of top management to ask the question "what is our business?" and to make sure that it is carefully studied and correctly answered. Indeed, the one sure way to tell whether a particular job is top management or not is to ask whether its holder is expected to be concerned with, and responsible for, that answer.

That the question is so rarely asked—at least in a clear and sharp form—and so rarely given adequate study and thought, is perhaps the most important single cause of business failure. Conversely, wherever we find an outstandingly successful business we will almost always find, as we did in the case of the Telephone Company or in that of Sears, that its success rests to a large extent on raising the question clearly and deliberately, and on answering it thoughtfully and thoroughly.

"What Is Our Business?" Most Important in Successful Business

The example of Sears also shows that it is not a question that needs to be raised only at the ineeption of a business or when the company is in trouble. On the contrary: to raise the question and to study it thoroughly is most needed when a business is successful. For then failure to raise it may result in rapid decline.

At the very inception of a business, the question often cannot be raised meaningfully. The man who mixes up a new cleaning fluid and peddles it from door to door need not know more than that his mixture does a superior job taking stains out of rugs and upholstery fabrics. But when the product catches on; when he has to hire people to mix it and to sell it; when he has to decide whether to keep on selling it directly or through retail stores, whether through department stores, supermarkets, hardware stores or through all three; what additional products he needs for a full "line"—then he has to ask and to answer the question: "what is my business?" If he fails to answer it when successful, he will, even with the best of products, soon be back wearing out his own shoe leather peddling from door to door.

It is as important a question in a business that appears to have little control over what it produces physically—a copper mine, for instance, or a steel mill—as in a business such as a retail store or an insurance company, that seems to have a great deal of control. To be sure, a copper mine produces copper. If there is no demand for copper, it will have to shut down. But whether there is demand for copper depends substantially on management's action in creating markets, in finding new uses, and in spotting, well in advance, market or technological developments that might create opportunities for copper or threaten existing uses.

The product-determined or process-determined industries—steel making, petroleum chemistry, mining or railroading—differ from the rest only in their being, inevitably, in many businesses rather than in one. This means that they have a much more difficult task deciding which of the wants that customers satisfy with their products are most important or most promising.

What failure to do so can mean is shown by the fate of the American anthracite coal industry and by the steady decline of the railroads' competitive position in the freight and passenger business. Neither industry, it can be asserted with confidence, *need* have tumbled from the high estate it occupied less than a generation ago had managements thought through what business they were in, instead of considering the question so obvious as to answer itself.

Who Is the Customer?

The first step toward finding out what our business is, is to raise the question: "Who is the customer?"—the actual customer and the potential customer? Where is he? How does he buy? How can he be reached?

One of the companies that had come into existence during World War II decided after the war to go into the production of fuse boxes and switch boxes for residential use. Immediately it had to decide whether its customer should be the electric contractor and builder or the homeowner making his own electric installations and repairs. To reach the first would require a major effort at building a distributive organization; the homeowner could be reached through the mail-order catalogues and retail stores of such existing distributive organizations as Sears, Roebuck and Montgomery Ward.

Having decided in favor of the electrical contractor as the larger as well as the stabler (though the more difficult and much more competitive) market, the company had to decide where the customer was. This innocent-sounding question required major analysis of population and market trends. In fact, to go by past experience would have meant disaster to the company. It would have led them to look for their customer in the big cities—and the postwar housing boom was primarily suburban. That the company foresaw this and built a marketing organization centering in the suburbs—unprecedented in the industry—was the first major reason for its success.

The question "how does the customer buy?" was fairly easy to answer in this case: the electrical contractor buys through specialty wholesalers. But the question of how best to reach him was hard—indeed, today, after almost ten years of operations, the company is still undecided and is still trying out various methods such as salesmen or manufacturer's agents. It has tried to sell direct to the contractor—by mail or out of central sales warehouses of its own. It has tried something never attempted before in the industry: to advertise its products directly to the public so as to build up ultimate-consumer demand. These experiments have been successful enough to warrant the suspicion that the first supplier who finds a way lowest manufacturer's price would be a serious mistake. On the contrary, "cheap" for the contractor means a product that has a fairly high manufacturer's price: a product that (a) costs the least money finally installed in the home, (b) achieves this low ultimate cost by requiring a minimum of time and skill for installation, and (c) has a high enough manufacturer's cost to give the contractor a good profit. Wages for skilled electrical labor being very high, low installation costs go a very long way to offset high manufacturer's price. Furthermore under the billing tradition of the trade, the contractor makes little money out of the labor required for installation. If he is not his own skilled worker, he bills his customer for little more than his actual wage costs. He makes his profit traditionally by charging double the manufacturer's price for the product he installs. That product that will give him the lowest cost to the homeowner, with the lowest installation cost and the highest mark-up on the product—that is, the highest manufacturer's price—is therefore the cheapest to him. And if price is value, then high manufacturer's price is better value for the electrical contractor.

This may appear to be a complicated price structure. Actually I know few others as simple. In the American automobile industry, where most new cars are sold in trade against a used car, the "price" is actually a constantly shifting configuration of differentials between the manufacturer's price for a new car, a second-hand and third-hand used car, a third-hand and fourth-hand used car, and so on. And the whole is complicated on the one hand by constantly changing differentials between the amount a dealer will allow on a used car and the price he will ask for it, and on the other hand by the differences in running costs between various makes and sizes. Only advanced mathematics can actually calculate the real automobile "price."

And, secondly, price is only a part of value. There is the whole range of quality considerations: durability, freedom from breakdown, the maker's standing, purity,.etc High price may actually be value—as in expensive perfumes, expensive furs or exclusive gowns.

Finally, what about such concepts of value on the part of the customer as the service he receives? There is little doubt, for instance, that the American housewife today buys appliances largely on the basis of the service experience she or her friends and neighbors have had with other appliances sold under the same brand name. The speed with which she can obtain service if something goes wrong, the quality of the service and its costs have become major determinants in the buyer's decision.

Indeed, what the customer considers value is so complicated that it can only be answered by the customer himself. Management should not even try to guess at it—it should always go to the customer in a systematic quest for the answer.

What Will Our Business Be?

So far all questions regarding the nature of "our business" have been concerned with the present. But management must also ask: "What will our business be?" This involves finding out four things.

The first is market potential and market trend. How large can we expect the market for our business to be in five or ten years—assuming no basic changes in market structure or technology? And what are the factors that will determine this development?

Second, what changes in market structure are to be expected as the result of economic developments, changes in fashion or taste, or moves by competition? And "competition" must always be defined according to the customer's concept of what product or service he buys and must include indirect as well as direct competition.

Third, what innovations will change the customer's wants, create new ones, extinguish old ones, create new ways of satisfying his wants, change his concepts of value or make it possible to give him greater value satisfaction? This has to be studied not only in respect to engineering or chemistry, but on respect to all activities of the business. There is a technology in the mail-order business, in banking, in insurance, in office management, in warehousing, etc., as well as in metallurgy, or in fuels. And innovation is not only a servant of the marketing goals of the business but is in itself a dynamic force to which the business contributes and which in turn affects it. Not that "pure research" is a function of the business enterprise—though in many cases business enterprises have found it a productive way to obtain marketable results. But the "advancement of the arts"—the constant improvement of our ability to *do* by applying to it our increased *knowledge*—is one of the tasks of the business enterprise and a major factor in its survival and prosperity.

Finally, what wants does the consumer have that are not being adequately satisfied by the products or services offered him today?

prises in the engineering and chemical fields have largely grown by projecting innovation into new businesses. The same is true of insurance companies; the growth of the successful ones is largely traceable to their ability to develop new business on the basis of innovations in insurance coverage. The recent almost explosive growth of health, hospitalization and medical expense insurance is an example.

Productivity considerations, too, may demand a change in the nature of the business.

A small wholesaler of Christmas toys added an entirely different business, the wholesaling of beachwear, to employ all year round his major economic resource: his trained sales force. Here utilization of time demanded adding a new business.

To improve the productive utilization of his resources another small manufacturer decided to give up making machine tool parts entirely, and instead confines himself to being a consultant on welding problems and techniques. His manufacturing, while profitable, was no more so than that of hundreds of other small companies. But as a welding consultant he was in a class by himself. As long as he kept on manufacturing he used his really productive resource, his welding expertise, at a very low rate of productivity and return.

Another illustration also shows a change of business to utilize productively the managerial resources of the business. A successful, though still fairly small, manufacturer of patent medicines decided some twenty years ago that he did not get full productivity out of his highly trained and highly paid management group. To attain higher productivity he decided to switch from supplying a certain line of products to managing businesses engaged in the mass-distribution of branded packaged and nationally advertised goods. The company still runs its original business successfully. But its has systematically acquired small branded-goods companies that, for lack of management, had not been too successful: a company making dog food, a company making toiletries for men; a company making cosmetics and perfumes, etc. In each case it has supplied a management that raised the business to a substantial and highly profitable position.

Profitability considerations alone should not, however, normally lead to changes in the nature of the business. Of course, a business can become so unprofitable as to be abandoned. But almost always market standing, innovation or productivity would have counseled its abandonment much earlier. Certainly profitability considerations limit the businesses an enterprise might go into. In fact, it is one of the main uses of a profitability yardstick to warn against such businesses and to prevent management from pouring money and energy into bolstering the weak, ailing and declining, rather than into strengthening the strong and growing, among its ventures. At the least a good profitability yardstick should block that most dangerous and most deceptive of all alibis for following the line of least resistance: the argument that an otherwise unprofitable venture pays for itself by "absorbing overhead" (the accountant's translation of "two can live as cheaply as one," and as irrational and questionable as the original).

But if the decision to go into a business is sound on the basis of market standing, innovation and productivity, if it is sound according to what makes a business, it is the responsibility of management to make it produce the needed minimum profit. That, bluntly, is what managements are being paid for. And if a management cannot, over a reasonable period of time, produce the minimum profit needed, it is in duty bound to abdicate so as to let another management try to do the job properly.

This is simply another way of saying that a business must be managed by setting objectives for it. These objectives must be set according to what is right and desirable for the enterprise. They must not be based on the expedient or on adaptation to the economic tides. Managing a business cannot, in other words, depend on "intuition." In fact, in the modern industrial economy with its long time-span between a decision and the ripening of its fruits, the intiuitive manager is a luxury few companies, large or small, can afford. And profit in a well-managed business is not what one happens to make. It is what one sets out to make because one has to make it.

Of course, objectives are not a railroad time-table. They can be compared to the compass bearing by which a ship navigates. The compass bearing itself is firm, pointing in a straight line toward the desired port. But in actual navigation the ship will veer off its course for many miles to avoid a storm. She will slow down to a walk in a fog and heave to altogether in a hurricane. She may even change destination in mid-ocean and set a new compass bearing toward a new port—perhaps because war has broken out, perhaps only because her cargo has been sold in mid-passage. Still, four fifths of all voyages end in the intended port at the originally scheduled time. And without a compass bearing, the ship would neither be able to find the port nor be able to estimate the time it will take to get there.

Similarly, to reach objectives, detours may have to be made around obstacles. Indeed, the ability to go around obstacles rather than charge them head-on is a major requirement for managing by objectives. In a depression progress toward the attainment of the objectives may be slowed down considerably; there may even be standstill for a short time. And new developments—for instance, the introduction by a competitor of a new product—may change objectives. This is one reason why all objectives have to be reexamined continually. Yet, setting objectives enables a business to get where it should be going rather than be the plaything of weather, winds and accidents.

CHAPTER 7

THE OBJECTIVES OF A BUSINESS

The fallacy of the single objective—The eight key areas of business enterprise—"Tangible" and "intangible" objectives—How to set objectives—The low state of the art and science of measurement—Market standing, Innovation, Productivity and "Contributed Value"—The physical and financial resources—How much Profitability?—A rational capital-investment policy—The remaining key areas.

Most of today's lively discussion of management by objectives is concerned with the search for the one right objective. This search is not only likely to be as unproductive as the quest for the philosopher's stone; it is certain to do harm and to misdirect.

To emphasize only profit, for instance, misdirects managers to the point where they may endanger the survival of the business. To obtain profit today they tend to undermine the future. They may push the most easily saleable product lines and slight those that are the market of tomorrow. They tend to short-change research, promotion and the other postponable investments. Above all, they shy away from any capital expenditure that may increase the invested-capital base against which profits are measured; and the result is dangerous obsolescence of equipment. In other words, they are directed into the worst practices of management.

To manage a business is to balance a variety of needs and goals. This requires judgment. The search for the one objective is essentially a search for a magic formula that will make judgment unnecessary. But the attempt to replace judgment by formula is always irrational; all that can be done is to make judgment possible by narrowing its range and the available alternatives, giving it clear focus, a sound foundation in facts and reliable measurements of the effects and validity of actions and decisions. And this, by the very nature of business enterprise, requires multiple objectives.

What should these objectives be, then? There is only one answer: *Objectives are needed in every area where performance and results directly and vitally affect the survival and prosperity of the business.* These are the areas which are affected by every management decision and which therefore have to be considered in every management decision. They decide what it means concretely to manage the business. They spell out what results the business must aim at and what is needed to work effectively toward these targets.

Objectives in these key areas should enable us to do five things: to organize and explain the whole range of business phenomena in a small number of general statements; to test these statements in actual experience; to predict behavior; to appraise the soundness of decisions when they are still being made; and to enable practicing businessmen to analyze their own experience and, as a result, improve their performance. It is precisely because the traditional theorem of the maximization of profits cannot meet any of these tests—let alone all of them—that it has to be discarded.

At first sight it might seem that different businesses would have entirely different key areas—so different as to make impossible any general theory. It is indeed true that different key areas require different emphasis in different businesses—and different emphasis at different stages of the development of each business. But the areas are the same, whatever the business, whatever the economic conditions, whatever the business's size or stage of growth.

There are eight areas in which objectives of performance and results have to be set:

Market standing; innovation; productivity; physical and financial resources; profitability; manager performance and development; worker performance and attitude; public responsibility.

There should be little dispute over the first five objectives. But there will be real protest against the inclusion of the intangibles: manager performance and development; worker performance and attitude; and public responsibility.

Yet, even if managing were merely the application of economics, we would have to include these three areas and would have to demand that objectives be set for them. They belong in the most purely formal economic theory of the business enterprise. For neglect of manager performance and development, worker performance and public responsibility soon results in the most practical and tangible loss of market standing, technological leadership, productivity and profit—and ultimately in the loss of business life. That they look so different from anything the economist—especially the modern economic analyst—is wont to deal with, that they do not readily submit to quantification and mathematical treatment, is the economist's bad luck; but it is no argument against their consideration.

The very reason for which economist and accountant consider these areas impractical—that they deal with principles and values rather than solely with dollars and cents—makes them central to the management of the enterprise, as tangible, as practical—and indeed as measurable—as dollars and cents.

For the enterprise is a community of human beings. Its performance is the performance of human beings. And a human community must be founded on common beliefs, must symbolize its cohesion in common principles. Otherwise it becomes paralyzed, unable to act, unable to demand and to obtain effort and performance from its members.

If such considerations are intangible, it is management's job to make them tangible by its deeds. To neglect them is to risk not only business incompetence but labor trouble or at least loss of worker productivity, and public restrictions on business provoked by irresponsible business conduct. It also means risking lack-luster, mediocre, time-serving managers—managers who are being conditioned to "look out for themselves" instead of for the common good of the enterprise, managers who become mean, narrow and blind for lack of challenge, leadership and vision.

How To Set Objectives

The real difficulty lies indeed not in determining what objectives we need, but in deciding how to set them.

There is only one fruitful way to make this decision: by determining what shall be measured in each area and what the yardstick of measurement should be. For the measurement used determines wh[illegible] ays attention to. It makes things visible and tangible. The [illegible] uded in the measurement become relevant; the things omitted are out of sight and out of mind. "Intelligence is what the Intelligence Test measures"—that well-worn quip is used by the psychologist to disclaim omniscience and infallibility for his gadget. Parents or teachers, however, including those well aware of the shakiness of its theory and its mode of calculation, sometimes tend to see that precise-looking measurement of the "I.Q." every time they look at little Susie—to the point where they may no longer see little Susie at all.

Unfortunately the measurements available to us in the key areas of business enterprise are, by and large, even shakier than the I.Q. We have adequate concepts only for measuring market standing. For something as obvious as profitability we have only a rubber yard-stick, and we have no real tools at all to determine how much profitability is necessary. In respect to innovation and, even more, to productivity, we hardly know more than what ought to be done. And in the other areas—including physical and financial resources—we are reduced to statements of intentions rather than goals and measurements for their attainment.

For the subject is brand new. It is one of the most active frontiers of thought, research and invention in American business today. Company after company is working on the definition of the key areas, on thinking through what should be measured and on fashioning the tools of measurement.

Within a few years our knowledge of what to measure and our ability to do so should therefore be greatly increased. After all, twenty-five years ago we knew less about the basic problems in market standing than we know today about productivity or even about the efficiency and attitudes of workers. Today's relative clarity concerning market standing is the result not of anything inherent in the field, but of hard, concentrated and imaginative work.

In the meantime, only a "progress report" can be given, outlining the work ahead rather than reporting accomplishment.

Market Standing

Market standing has to be measured against the market potential, and against the performance of suppliers of competing products or services—whether competition is direct or indirect.

"We don't care what share of the market we have, as long as our sales go up," is a fairly common comment. It sounds plausible enough; but it does not stand up under analysis. By itself, volume of sales tells little about performance, results or the future of the business. A company's sales may go up—and the company may actually be headed for rapid collapse. A company's sales may go down—and the reason may not be that its marketing is poor but that it is in a dying field and had better change fast.

A maker of oil refinery equipment reported rising sales year after year. Actually new refineries and their equipment were being supplied by the company's competitors. But because the equipment it had supplied in the past was getting old and needed repairs, sales spurted; for replacement parts for equipment of this kind have usually to be bought from the original supplier. Sooner or later, however, the original customers were going to put in new and efficient equipment rather than patch up the old and obsolescent stuff. Then almost certainly they were going to go to the competitors designing and building the new equipment. The company was thus threatened with going out of business—which is what actually happened.

Not only are absolute sales figures meaningless alone, since they must be projected against actual and potential market trends, but market standing itself has intrinsic importance. A business that supplies less than a certain share of the market becomes a marginal supplier. Its pricing becomes dependent on the decisions of the larger suppliers. In any business setback—even in a slight one—it stands in danger of being squeezed out altogether. Competition becomes intense. Distributors in cutting back inventories tend to cut out slow-moving merchandise. Customers tend to concentrate their purchases on the most popular products. And in a depression the sales volume of the marginal supplier may become too low to give the needed service. The point below which a supplier becomes marginal varies from industry to industry. It is different in different price classes within the same industry. It has marked regional variations. But to be a marginal producer is always dangerous, a minimum of market standing always desirable.

Conversely, there is a maximum market standing above which it may be unwise to go—even if there were no anti-trust laws. Leadership that gives market dominance tends to lull the leader to sleep; monopolists have usually foundered on their own complacency rather than on public opposition. For market dominance creates tremendous internal resistance against any innovation and thus makes adaptation to change dangerously difficult. Also it almost always means that the enterprise has too many of its eggs in one basket and is too vulnerable to economic fluctuations There is, in other words, an upper as well as a lower margin—though for most businesses the perils of the former may appear a good deal more remote.

To be able to set market-standing objectives, a business must first find out what its market is—who the customer is, where he is, what he buys, what he considers value, what his unsatisfied wants are. On the basis of this study the enterprise must analyze its products or services according to "lines," that is, according to the wants of the customers they satisfy.

All electric condensers may look the same, be the same technically and come off the same production line. Market-wise, condensers for new radios may, however, be an entirely different line from condensers for radio repair and replacement, and both again quite different from the physically indistinguishable condensers that go into telephones. Condensers for radio repair may even be different lines if customers in the South judge their value by their resistance to termites, and customers in the Northwest by their resistance to high humidity.

For each line the market has to be determined—its actual size and its potential, its economic and its innovating trends. This must be done on the basis of a definition of the market that is customer-oriented and takes in both direct and indirect competition. Only then can marketing objectives actually be set.

In most businesses not one but seven distinct marketing goals are necessary:

1. The desired standing of existing products in their present market, expressed in dollars as well as in percentage of the market, measured against both direct and indirect competition.

2. The desired standing of existing products in new markets set both in dollars and percentage points, and measured against direct and indirect competition.

3. The existing products that should be abandoned—for technological

reasons, because of market trend, to improve product mix or as a result of management's decision concerning what its business should be.

4. The new products needed in existing markets—the number of products, their properties, the dollar volume and the market share they should gain for themselves.

5. The new markets that new products should develop—in dollars and in percentage points.

6. The distributive organization needed to accomplish the marketing goals and the pricing policy appropriate to them.

7. A service objective measuring how well the customer should be supplied with what he considers value by the company, its products, its sales and service organization.

At the least the service objective should be in keeping with the targets set for competitive market standing. But usually it is not enough to do as well as the competition in respect to service; for service is the best and the easiest way to build customer loyalty and satisfaction. Service performance should never be appraised by management guesses or on the basis of occasional chats the "big boss" has with important customers. It should be measured by regular, systematic and unbiased questioning of the customer.

In a large company this may have to take the form of an annual customer survey. The outstanding job here has probably been done by General Motors; and it explains the company's success in no small degree. In the small company the same results can be achieved by a different method.

In one of the most successful hospital-supply wholesalers, two of the top men of the company—president and chairman of the Board—visit between them two hundred of the company's six hundred customers every year. They spend a whole day with each customer. They do not sell—refuse indeed to take an order. They discuss the customer's problems and his needs, and ask for criticism of the company's products and service. In this company the annual customer survey is considered the first job of top management. And the company's eighteen-fold growth in the last twelve years is directly attributed to it.

Innovation

There are two kinds of innovation in every business: innovation in product or service; and innovation in the various skills and activities needed to supply them. Innovation may arise out of the needs of market and customer; necessity may be the mother of innovation. Or it may come out of the work on the advancement of skill and knowledge carried out in the schools and the laboratories, by researchers, writers, thinkers and practitioners.

The problem in setting innovation objectives is the difficulty of measuring the relative impact and importance of various innovations. Technological leadership is clearly desirable, especially if the term "technology" is used in its rightful sense as applying to the art, craft or science of any organized human activity. But how are we to determine what weighs more: one hundred minor but immediately applicable improvements in packaging the product, or one fundamental chemical discovery which, after ten more years of hard work, may change the character of the business altogether? A department store and a pharmaceutical company will answer this question differently; but so may two different pharmaceutical companies.

Innovating objectives can therefore never be as clear and as sharply focused as marketing objectives. To set them, management must first obtain a forecast of the innovations needed to reach marketing goals—according to product lines, existing markets, new markets and, usually, also according to service requirements. Secondly, it must appraise developments arising or likely to arise out of technological advancement in all areas of the business and in all of its activities. These forecasts are best organized in two parts: one looking a short time ahead and projecting fairly concrete developments which, in effect, only carry out innovations already made; another looking a long time ahead and aiming at what might be.

Here are the innovation goals for a typical business:

1. New products or services that are needed to attain marketing objectives.

2. New products or services that will be needed because of technological changes that may make present products obsolete.

3. Product improvements needed both to attain market objectives and to anticipate expected technological changes.

4. New processes and improvements in old processes needed to satisfy market goals—for instance, manufacturing improvements to make possible the attainment of pricing objectives.

5. Innovations and improvements in all major areas of activity—in accounting or design, office management or labor relations—so as to keep up with the advances in knowledge and skill.

Management must not forget that innovation is a slow process. Many companies owe their position of leadership today to the activity of a generation that went to its reward twenty-five years or so ago. Many companies that are unknown to the public will be leaders in their industry tomorrow because of their innovations today. The successful company is always in danger of living smugly off the accumulated innovating fat of an earlier generation. An index of activity and success in this field is therefore indicated.

An appraisal of performance during the last ten years serves well for this purpose. Has innovation in all the major areas been commensurate with the market standing of the company? If it has not, the company is living off past achievements and is eating up its innovating capital. Has the company developed adequate sources of innovation for the future? Or has it come to depend on work done on the outside—in the universities, by other businesses, maybe abroad—which may not be adequate to the demands of the future?

Deliberate emphasis on innovation may be needed most where technological changes are least spectacular. Everybody in a pharmaceutical company or in a company making synthetic organic chemicals knows that the company's survival depends on its ability to replace three quarters of its products by entirely new ones every ten years. But how many people in an insurance company realize that the company's growth—perhaps even its survival—depends on the development of new forms of insurance, the modification of existing forms and the constant search for new, better and cheaper ways of selling policies and of settling claims? The less spectacular or prominent technological change is in a business, the greater is the danger that the whole organization will ossify; the more important therefore is the emphasis on innovation.

It may be argued that such goals are "big-company stuff" suitable for General Electric or for General Motors, but unnecessary in the small business. But although the small company may be less in need of a complete and detailed analysis of its needs and goals, this means only that it is easier to set innovation objectives in the smaller business—not that the need for objectives is less. In fact, the managements of several small companies I know assert that the comparative simplicity of planning for innovation is one of the main advantages of small size. As the president of one of them—a container manufacturer with sales of fewer than ten million dollars—puts it: "When you are small, you are sufficiently close to the market to know fairly fast what new products are needed. And your engineering staff is too small to become ingrown. They know they can't do everything themselves and therefore keep their eyes and ears wide open for any new development that they could possibly use."

Productivity and "Contributed Value"

A productivity measurement is the only yardstick that can actually gauge the competence of management and allow comparison between managements of different units within the enterprise, and of different enterprises. For productivity includes all the efforts the enterprise contributes; it excludes everything it does not control.

Businesses have pretty much the same resources to work with. Except for the rare monopoly situation, the only thing that differentiates one business from another in any given field is the quality of its management on all levels. And the only way to measure this crucial factor is through a measurement of productivity that shows how well resources are utilized and how much they yield.

The Wall Street exercise of comparing the profit margin of Chrysler and General Motors is actually meaningless. General Motors manufactures most of the parts of the car; it buys only the frame, the wheels and the brake. Chrysler until recently was an assembler; it made nothing but the engine which is but a fraction of the value of the car. The two companies are entirely different in their process mix. Yet both sell a complete car. In the case of G.M. the bulk of the sales price is compensation for work done by G.M.; in the case of Chrysler the bulk of the sales price is paid out again to independent suppliers. The profit G.M. shows is for 70 per cent of the work and risk, the profit Chrysler shows is for 30 or 40 per cent of the work and risk. Obviously General Motors must show a much bigger profit margin—but how much bigger? Only an analysis of productivity which would show how the two companies utilize their respective resources and how much profit they get out of them, would show which company did the better managing job.

But such a yardstick is needed also because the constant improvement of productivity is one of management's most important jobs. It is also one of the most difficult; for productivity is a balance between a great variety of factors, few of which are easily definable or clearly measurable.

We do not as yet have the yardstick we need to measure productivity. Only within the last few years have we found a basic concept that even enables us to define what we have to measure—the economist calls it "Contributed Value."

Contributed Value is the difference between the gross revenue received by a company from the sale of its products or services, and the amount paid out by it for the purchase of raw materials and for services rendered by outside suppliers. Contributed Value, in other words, includes all the costs of all the efforts of the business and the entire reward received for these efforts. It accounts for all the resources the business itself contributes to the final product and the appraisal of their efforts by the market.

Contributed Value is not a panacea. It can be used to analyze productivity only if the allocation of costs which together make up the figures is economically meaningful. This may require major reforms in the accountant's traditional concepts, figures and methods. We have to give up such time-honored practices as the allocation of "overhead" on a percentage basis "across the board" which makes realistic cost analysis impossible. We have to think through what depreciation charges are supposed to do—charge for the use of capital, measure the shrinkage in value of the equipment, or provide for its eventual replacement; we cannot be satisfied with a "rule of thumb" percentage depreciation allowance. In short, we have to focus accounting data on management's needs in running a business, rather than on the requirements of tax collector and banker, or on the old wives' tales so many investors imbibe at their security analyst's knee and forever after mistake for financial wisdom.

Contributed Value will not measure productivity resulting from balance of functions or from organization structure, for these are qualitative factors rather than quantitative ones, and Contributed Value is strictly a quantitative tool. Yet, the qualitative factors are among the biggest factors in productivity.

Within these limitations, however, Contributed Value should make possible, for the first time, a rational analysis of productivity and the setting of goals for its improvement. In particular it should make possible the application to the systematic study of productivity of new tools such as the mathematical methods known as "Opera

retailer, public utility or transportation business needs to think through the problem of its physical resources, and spell out basic decisions.

Should the company depend on one supplier for an important material, part or product? There may be a price advantage because of bulk purchases; in times of shortage a big and constant buyer may get priority; and the close relationship may result in a better design or in closer quality control. Or should the company find several suppliers for the same resource? This may make it independent; it minimizes the danger of being forced to close down because of a strike at a single supplier; it may even lead to lower purchase prices as a result of competition between several suppliers. A cotton-textile manufacturer has to decide whether he should attempt to outguess the cotton market or try, in his buying policy, to average out fluctuations in cotton price, and so forth.

Whatever the decision, objectives should aim at providing the physical supplies needed to attain the goals set for market standing and innovation.

Equally important is good facilities planning. And it is even rarer. Few industrial companies know when to stop patching up an old plant and start building a new one, when to replace machines and tools, when to build a new office building. The costs of using obsolete facilities are usually hidden. Indeed, on the books the obsolete plant or machine may look very profitable; for it has been written down to zero so that it looks as if running it involved no cost at all. Most managers know, of course, that this is pure fallacy; but it is not easy to free ourselves completely from the spell of arithmetical sleight of hand.

Yet, clearly, both undersupply of facilities and their oversupply are extremely dangerous. Physical facilities cannot be improvised; they must be planned.

The tools for the job are available today. They have been developed above all by Joel Dean, the Columbia business economist.[1] They are simple enough to enable every business, large or small, to decide what physical facilities and equipment it needs to attain its basic goals, and to plan for them.

[1] See especially his *Capital Budgeting* (New York: Columbia University Press, 1951) and his brilliant article: "*Measuring the Productivity of Capital,*" in the January 1954 issue of the *Harvard Business Review.*

This, of course, requires a capital budget. And this raises the questions: How much capital will we need, and in what form; and where will it come from?

The life-insurance companies have had capital objectives for a long time. They know that they have to obtain a certain amount of money each year to pay off their claims. They know that this money has to come from the income earned on their invested reserves. Accordingly they plan for a certain minimum rate of return on these investments. Indeed "profit" in a life-insurance company is essentially nothing but the excess of investment earnings over the planned minimum return.

Other examples of capital-supply planning are those of General Motors, DuPont and the Chesapeake and Ohio Railroad. And the American Telephone and Telegraph Company, as already mentioned, considers this so important a job as to justify the full-time attention of a senior member of top management.

But, on the whole, managements do not worry over capital supply until the financial shoe pinches. Then it is often too late to do a good job. Such vitally important questions as: should new capital be raised internally by self-financing, borrowed long-term or short-term, or through stock issue, not only need careful thought and study; they largely determine what kinds of capital expenditure should be undertaken. Decisions on these questions lead to conclusions regarding such vital matters as pricing, dividend, depreciation and tax policy. Also, unless answered in advance, the company may well fritter away its available capital on the less important investments only to find itself unable to raise the capital for vital investments. In far too many companies—including some big and reputedly well-managed ones—failure to think through capital supply and to set capital objectives has stunted growth and nullified much of the management's brilliant work on marketing, innovation and productivity.

How Much Profitability?

Profit serves three purposes. It measures the net effectiveness and soundness of a business's efforts. It is indeed the ultimate test of business performance.

It is the "risk premium" that covers the costs of staying in business—replacement, obsolescence, market risk and uncertainty.[2] Seen from this point of view, there is no such thing as "profit"; there are only "costs of being in business" and "costs of staying in business." And the task of a business is to provide adequately for these "costs of staying in business" by earning an adequate profit —which not enough businesses do.

Finally, profit insures the supply of future capital for innovation and expansion, either directly, by providing the means of self-financing out of retained earnings, or indirectly, through providing sufficient inducement for new outside capital in the form in which it is best suited to the enterprise's objectives.

None of these three functions of profit has anything to do with the economist's maximization of profit. All the three are indeed "minimum" concepts—the minimum of profit needed for the survival and prosperity of the enterprise. A profitability objective therefore measures not the maximum profit the business can produce, but the minimum it must produce.

The simplest way to find this minimum is by focusing on the last of the three functions of profit: a means to obtain new capital. The rate of profit required is easily ascertainable; it is the capital-market rate for the desired type of financing. In the case of self-financing, there must be enough profit both to yield the capital-market rate of return on money already in the business, and to produce the additional capital needed.

It is from this basis that most profitability objectives in use in American business today are derived. "We shoot for a return on capital of 25 per cent before taxes," is accountant's shorthand way of saying: "A return of 25 per cent before taxes is the minimum we need to get the kind of capital we want, in the amounts we need and at the cost we are willing to pay."

This is a rational objective. Its adoption by more and more businesses is a tremendous step forward. It can be made even more serviceable by a few simple but important refinements. First, as Joel Dean has pointed out,[3] profitably must always include the time factor. Profitability as such is meaningless and misleading un-

[2] For a discussion of these terms see my *New Society*, (New York: Harper & Bros., 1950), especially Chapter 4.

[3] Most effectively in the *Harvard Business Review* article mentioned above.

less we know for how many years the profit can be expected. We should therefore always state anticipated total profits over the life of the investment discounted for present cash value, rather than as an annual rate of return. This is the method the capital market uses when calculating the rate of return of a bond or similar security; and, after all, this entire approach to profit is based on capital-market considerations. This method also surmounts the greatest weakness of conventional accounting: its superstitious belief that the calendar year has any economic meaning or reality. We can never have rational business management until we have freed ourselves from what one company president (himself an ex-accountant) calls "the unnecessary tyranny of the accounting year."

Second, we should always consider the rate of return as an average resulting from good and bad years together. The business may indeed need a profit of 25 per cent before taxes. But if the 25 per cent are being earned in a good year they are unlikely to be earned over the life time of the investment. We may need a 40 per cent return in good years to average 25 per cent over a dozen years. And we have to know how much we actually need to get the desired average.

The tool for this is also available today. It is the "break-even point analysis" (best described by Rautenstrauch and Villiers in their book *The Economics of Industrial Management,* (New York: Funk and Wagnall's, 1949). This enables us to predict with fair accuracy the range of returns under various business conditions—especially if the analysis is adjusted to express both changes in volume and in price.

For small and simple businesses this capital-market concept of the minimum profitability required is probably adequate. For the large business it is not sufficient, however, for the rate of return expected is only one factor. The other is the amount of risk involved. An investment may return 40 per cent before taxes but there may be a 50 per cent risk of failure. Is it a better investment than one returning 20 per cent with practically no risk?

Shooting for a 25 per cent return before taxes may be good enough for existing investments, investments that have already been made irrevocably. But for new decisions management needs to be able to say: "We aim at a ratio of 1.5 to 1, 1.33 to 1, or 1.25 to 1 between anticipated return after all costs (including those of capital) and estimated risk." Otherwise a rational capital investment policy cannot be worked out.

And without a rational capital-investment policy, especially in the big business, no real budget is possible. It is a necessity for effective decentralization of management; for without it central management will always manage its components by arbitrarily granting or withholding capital and arbitrarily centralizing the management of cash. It is a prerequisite of the spirit of management; without it lower management will always feel that its best ideas get lost in the procedural maze of the Appropriations Committee "upstairs."

A rational capital-investment policy sets the range for management decisions. It indicates which of the alternative ways of reaching marketing, innovation and productivity goals should be preferred. Above all, it forces management to realize what obligations it assumes when making decisions. That our business managers have for so long been able to manage without such a policy is as amazing a feat of navigation as Leif Erickson's feat in finding his way back to Vineland across the Atlantic without map, compass or sextant.

A capital-investment policy must be based on a reasonably reliable assessment of the ratio between return and risks. These risks are not statistical risks like the odds at the roulette table or the life expectancies of the actuary, which can always be calculated. Only one of the four "costs of staying in business" is a statistical risk: replacement. It is no accident that it is the only one that is being handled as a cost, called variously depreciation, amortization or replacement reserve. The other three—each of which is a more serious risk than replacement—are essentially not predictable by what happened in the past; that is, they are not predictable statistically. They are the risks of some new, different, unprecedented occurrence in the future.

Still we can today reduce even these risks to probability forecasts—though only with a fairly large margin of error. Several of the large companies are apparently doing work in the field; but the systematic job has yet to be done.

The real problem concerning profitability is not however what we should measure. It is what to use for a yardstick.

Profit as percentage of sales—lately very popular in American business—will not do, for it does not indicate how vulnerable a product or a business is to economic fluctuations. Only a "break-even point" analysis will do that.

"Return on invested captial" makes sense, but it is the worst of all yardsticks—pure rubber of almost infinite elasticity. What is "invested capital"? Is a dollar invested in 1920 the same thing as a dollar invested in 1950? Is capital to be defined with the accountant as original cash value less subsequent depreciation? Or is it to be defined with the economist as wealth-producing capacity in the future, discounted at capital-market interest rates to current cash value?

Neither definition gets us far. The accountant's definition makes no allowance for changes in the purchasing power of the currency nor for technological changes. It does not permit any appraisal of business performance for the simple reason that it does not take the varying risks of different businesses into account, does not allow comparison between different businesses, between different components of the same company, between the old plants and the new plants, etc. Above all, it tends to encourage technological obsolescence. Once equipment is old enough to have been written down to zero, it tends to look much more profitable on the books than new equipment that actually produces at much lower cost. This holds true even during a deflationary period.

The economist's concept of invested capital avoids all this. It is theoretically perfect. But it cannot be used in practice. It is literally impossible to figure out how much future wealth-producing capacity any investment made in the past represents today. There are too many variables for even the best "electronic brain." There are far too many unknowns and unknowables. To find out even what would be knowable would cost more than could possibly be gained.

For these reasons a good many management people and accountants now incline toward a compromise. They would define "invested capital" as the amount it would cost today to build a new organization, a new plant, new equipment with the same productive capacity as the old organization, plant and equipment. Theoretically this, too, has weaknesses—it would, for instance, greatly distort profitability in a depression period when new equipment prices and building costs are low. But the main difficulties are practical. For replacement assumptions, besides being not too reliable, are difficult to make; and even minor changes in the assumed basis will lead to wide divergences in the end results.

There is, in other words, no really adequate method as yet. Perhaps the most sensible thing is not to search for one but to accept the simplest way, to realize its shortcomings and to build safeguards against its most serious dangers.

I have therefore come to advocate a method which has little in theory to commend it: to measure profitability by projecting net profit—after depreciation charges but before taxes—against original investment at original cost, that is, before depreciation. In inflationary periods the original investment figures are adjusted roughly for the rise in costs. In deflationary periods (this method has still to be tested in one) original investment figures would similarly be adjusted downward. In this way a uniform investment figure can be arrived at in roughly comparable dollars every three or five years, regardless of the date of the original investment or the purchasing power of the original money. This is admittedly crude; and I cannot defend it against the argument advanced by a friend that it is no better than painting over a badly rusted spot. But at least the method is simple; and it is so crude that it will not fool any manager into mistaking for precision what, like all "return on invested capital" figures, no matter how obtained, is at best a rough guess.

The Remaining Key Areas

Little needs to be said here about the three remaining key areas: manager performance and development, worker performance and attitude, and public responsibility. For each is dealt with in later parts of this book.

However, it should be clear that performance and results in these areas cannot be fully measured quantitatively. All three deal with human beings. And as each human being is unique, we cannot simply add them together, or subtract them from one another. What we need are qualitative standards, judgment rather than data, appraisal rather than measurements.

It is fairly easy to determine what objectives are needed for *manager performance and development.* A business—to stay in business and remain profitable—needs goals in respect to the direction of its managers by objectives and self-control, the setting up of their jobs, the spirit of the management organization, the structure of management and the development of tomorrow's managers. And once the goals are clear, it can always be determined whether they are being attained or not. Certainly the examination of the spirit of management, proposed in Chapter 13 below, should bring out any significant shortfall.

No one but the management of each particular business can decide what the objectives in the area of *public responsibility* should be. As discussed in the Conclusion of this book, objectives in this area, while extremely tangible, have to be set according to the social and political conditions which affect each individual enterprise and are affected by it, and on the basis of the beliefs of each management. It is this that makes the area so important; for in it managers go beyond the confines of their own little world and participate responsibly in society. But the overriding goal is common for every business: to strive to make whatever is productive for our society, whatever strengthens it and advances its prosperity, a source of strength, prosperity and profit for the enterprise.

We are in a bad way, however, when we come to setting objectives for *worker performance and attitude.* It is not that the area is "intangible." It is only too tangible; but we know too little about it so far, operate largely by superstitions, omens and slogans rather than by knowledge.

To think through the problems in this area and to arrive at meaningful measurements is one of the great challenges to management.

The objectives in this area should include objectives for union relations.

If this were a book on industrial society, the union would figure prominently (as it does indeed in my *New Society*). In a book on the *Practice of Management* the union is only one of many outside groups and forces management deals with—suppliers, for instance. But it is a powerful outside force. It can through wage demands wreck the business, and through a strike deprive management of control. The management of any unionized company therefore needs definite long-range objectives for its union relations. If it leaves the initiative in labor relations entirely to the union, it can be said not to manage at all.

Unfortunately that has been precisely the way too many of our managements have conducted their labor relations in the last fifteen or twenty years. They have left the initiative to the union. They have usually not even known what to expect in the way of union demands. They have, by and large, not known what the union is, how it behaves and why it behaves as it does. When first told that certain union demands are about to be made, the typical management refuses to listen. It is sure that the demand will not be made—for the simple reason that it does not consider it justified. Then, when the demand is made, management tends to turn it down as "impossible" and as "certain to ruin the business," if not our free enterprise system. Three days to three years later management caves in, accepts the demand, and in a joint statement with the union leader hails the agreement as a "milestone in democratic labor relations." This is not management; it is abdication.

What union-relations objectives should be concretely goes beyond the scope of this book. But they should first focus on returning the initiative to management. This requires that management must know how a union operates and why. It must know what demands the union will make and why; indeed it must be able to anticipate these demands so as to make their eventual acceptance beneficial to the enterprise or, at the least, harmless to it. Above all, it must learn to make demands itself; as long as the union alone makes demands, management will remain the passive, the frustrated, the ineffectual partner in the relationship.

Union relations, no matter how important, are however only a small and peripheral part of the management of work and worker. Yet, in the main areas we simply do not even know whether the things we can measure—turnover, absenteeism, safety, calls on the medical department, suggestion system participation, grievances, employee attitudes, etc.,—have anything at all to do with employee performance. At best they are surface indications. Still they can be used—in some companies are being used—to build an Employee Relations Index. And though we can only guess what such an index measures, at least the systematic attempt to find out what goes on in the work force focuses management's attention on what it could and should do. While no more than the merest palliative it serves at least to remind managers of their responsibility for the organization of the worker and his work. Admittedly this is hardly even a stopgap, perhaps only an acknowledgment of ignorance. The goal must be to replace it by real objectives which are based on knowledge.

The Time-Span of Objectives

For what time-span should objectives be set? How far ahead should we set our targets?

The nature of the business clearly has a bearing here. In certain parts of the garment business next week's clearance sale is "long-range future." It may take four years to build a big steam turbine and two more to install it; in the turbine business six years may be "immediate present" therefore. And Crown Zellerbach is forced to plant today the trees it will harvest fifty years hence.

Different areas require different time-spans. To build a marketing organization takes at least five years. Innovations in engineering and chemistry made today are unlikely to show up in marketing results and profits for five years or longer. On the other hand a sales campaign, veteran sales managers believe, must show results within six weeks or less; "Sure, there are sleepers," one of these veterans once said, "but most of them never wake up."

This means that in getting objectives management has to balance the immediate future—the next few years—against the long range: five years or longer. This balance can best be found through a "managed-expenditures budget." For practically all the decisions that affect the balance are made as decisions on what the accountant calls "managed expenditures"—those expenditures that are determined by current management decision rather than by past and irrevocable decisions (like capital charges), or by the requirements of current business (like labor and raw material costs). Today's managed expenditures are tomorrow's profit; but they may also be today's loss.

Every second-year accountancy student knows that almost any "profit" figure can be turned into a "loss" by changing the basis of depreciation charges; and the new basis can usually be made to appear as rational as the old. But few managements—including their accountants—realize how many such expenditures there are that are based, knowingly or not, on an assessment of short-range versus long-range needs, and that vitally affect both. Here is a partial list:

Depreciation charges; maintenance budgets; capital replacement, modernization and expansion costs; research budgets; expenditures on product development and design; expenditures on the management group, its compensation and rewards, its size, and on developing tomorrow's managers; cost of building and maintaining a marketing organization; promotion and advertising budgets; cost of service to the customer; personnel management, especially training expenditures.

Almost any one of these expenditures can be cut back sharply, if not eliminated; and for some time, perhaps for a long time, there will be no adverse effect. Any one of these expenditures can be increased sharply and for good reasons, with no resulting benefits visible for a long time. By cutting these expenditures immediate results can always be made to look better. By raising them immediate results can always be made to look worse.

There are no formulas for making the decisions on managed expenditures. They must always be based on judgment and are almost always a compromise. But even a wrong decision is better than a haphazard approach "by bellows and meat ax": inflating appropriations in fair weather and cutting them off as soon as the first cloud appears. All managed expenditures require long application; short spurts of high activity do not increase their effectiveness. Sudden cuts may destroy in one day what it took years to build. It is better to have a modest but steady program of employee activities than to splurge on benefits, lush company papers and plant baseball teams when times are good, only to cut down to the point of taking out the soap in the washrooms when orders drop 10 per cent.[4] It is better to give the customer minimum service than to get him used to good service only to lay off half the service force when profits go down. It is more productive to spend 50,000 dollars each year for ten years on research than to spend, say, two millions one year and nothing the next nine. Where managed expenditures are concerned,

[4] Lest this be considered hyperbole, it actually happened, in this country, and in 1951.

one slice of bread every day is better than half a loaf today and none tomorrow.

Almost every one of these expenditures requires highly skilled people to be effective. Yet, first-rate people will not remain with a business if their activity is subject to sudden, unpredictable and arbitrary ups and downs. Or if they stay, they will cease to exert themselves—for "what's the use of my working hard if management will kill it anyhow." And if the meat ax cuts off trained people during an "economy wave," replacements are hard to find or take a long time to train when management, applying the bellows, suddenly decides to revive the activity.

Decisions concerning managed expenditures themselves are of such importance for the business as a whole—over and above their impact on individual activities—that they must not be made without careful consideration of every item in turn and of all of them jointly. It is essential that management know and consciously decide what it is doing in each area and why. It is essential that management know and consciously decide which area to give priority, which to cut first and how far, which to expand first and how far. It is essential finally that management know and consciously decide what risks to take with the long-run future for the sake of short-term results, and what short-term sacrifices to make for long-run results.

A managed-expenditures budget for a five-year period should show the expenditure considered necessary in each area to attain business objectives within the near future—up to five years or so. It should show the additional expenditure considered necessary in each area to maintain the position of the business beyond the five-year period for which concrete objectives are being set. This brings out the areas where expenditures are to be raised first if business gets better, and those where they are to be cut first if business turns down; it enables management to plan what to maintain even in bad times, what to adjust to the times, and what to avoid even in a boom. It shows the total impact of these expenditures on short-range results. And finally it shows what to expect from them in the long range.

Balancing the Objectives

In addition to balancing the immediate and the long-range future, management also has to balance objectives. What is more important: an expansion in markets and sales volume, or a higher rate of return? How much time, effort and energy should be expended on improving manufacturing productivity? Would the same amount of effort or money bring greater returns if invested in new-product design?

There are few things that distinguish competent from incompetent management quite as sharply as the performance in balancing objectives. Yet, there is no formula for doing the job. Each business requires its own balance—and it may require a different balance at different times. The only thing that can be said is that balancing objectives is not a mechanical job, is not achieved by "budgeting." The budget is the document in which balance decisions find final expression; but the decisions themselves require judgment; and the judgment will be sound only if it is based on a sound analysis of the business. The ability of a management to stay within its budget is often considered a test of management skill. But the effort to arrive at the budget that best harmonizes the divergent needs of the business is a much more important test of management's ability. The late Nicholas Dreystadt, head of Cadillac and one of the wisest managers I have ever met, said to me once: "Any fool can learn to stay within his budget. But I have seen only a handful of managers in my life who can draw up a budget that is worth staying within."

Objectives in the key areas are the "instrument panel" necessary to pilot the business enterprise. Without them management flies by the "seat of its pants"—without landmarks to steer by, without maps and without having flown the route before.

However, an instrument panel is no better than the pilot's ability to read and interpret it. In the case of management this means ability to anticipate the future. Objectives that are based on completely wrong anticipations may actually be worse than no objectives at all. The pilot who flies by the "seat of his pants" at least knows that he may not be where he thinks he is. Our next topic must therefore be the tools that management needs to make decisions today for the results of tomorrow.

CHAPTER 8

TODAY'S DECISIONS FOR TOMORROW'S RESULTS

Management must always anticipate the future—Getting around the business cycle—Finding the range of fluctuations—Finding economic bedrock—Trend analysis—Tomorrow's managers the only real safeguard.

An objective, a goal, a target serves to determine what action to take today to obtain results tomorrow. It is based on anticipating the future. It requires action to mold the future. It always balances present means and future results, results in the immediate future and results in the more distant future.

This is of particular importance in managing a business. In the first place, practically every basic management decision is a long-range decision—with ten years a rather short time-span in these days. Whether on research or on building a new plant, on designing a new marketing organization or a new product, every major management decision takes years before it is really effective. And it takes years for it to be productive, that is, to pay off the investment of men or money.

Management has no choice but to anticipate the future, to attempt to mold it and to balance short-range and long-range goals. It is not given to mortals to do either of these well. But lacking divine guidance, business management must make sure that these difficult repsonsibilities are not overlooked or neglected but taken care of as well as is humanly possible.

Predictions concerning five, ten or fifteen years ahead are always "guesses." Still, there is a difference between an "educated guess" and a "hunch," between a guess that is based upon a rational appraisal of the range of possibilities and a guess that is simply a gamble.

Getting around the Business Cycle

Any business exists as a part of a larger economic context; a concern with "general business conditions" is mandatory to any plan for the future. However, what management needs is not the "business forecast" in the usual sense, that is, a forecast that attempts to read tomorrow's weather and to predict what business conditions will be like three, five or ten years ahead. What management needs are tools that enable it to free its thinking and planning from dependence on the business cycle.

At first sight this may look like a paradox. Certainly the business cycle is an important factor; whether a decision will be carried out in a period of boom or in a period of depression may make all the difference in its validity and success. The standard advice of the economists to make capital investments at the trough of the depression and to refrain from expansion and new investments at the peak of a boom seems to be nothing but the most elementary common sense.

Actually it is no more useful and no more valid than the advice to buy cheap and sell dear. It is good advice; but how is it to be followed? Who knows in what stage of the cycle we are? The batting average of the economists has not been impressive—and the forecasting success of businessmen has not been much more so. (Remember the all but general prediction back in 1944 or 1945 of a major postwar slump?) Even if it were sound, to play the business cycle would be unusable advice.

If people could act according to this advice, we would not have boom and depression to begin with. We have extreme fluctuations only because it is psychologically impossible to follow such advice. In a boom almost everybody is convinced that this time even the sky will not be the limit. At the bottom of a depression everybody is equally convinced that this time there will be no recovery but that we will keep on going down or stay at the bottom forever. As long as businessmen focus their thinking on the business cycle they will be dominated by the business-cycle psychology. They will therefore make the wrong decision no matter how good their intentions and how good the economists' analytical ability.

Moreover, economists doubt more and more whether there is a real "cycle." There are ups and downs, no doubt; but do they have any periodicity, any inherent predictability? The greatest of modern economists, the late Joseph A. Schumpeter, labored mightily for twenty-five years to find the "cycle." But at best, his "business cycle" is the result of so many different cyclical movements that it can only be analyzed *in retrospect*. And a business-cycle analysis that only tells where the cycle has been but not where it will go, is of little use in managing a business.

Finally, the business cycle is too short a period for a good many business decisions—and for the most important ones. A plant expansion program in heavy industry, for instance, cannot be founded on a forecast for the next four or five or six years. It is a fifteen- or twenty-year program. And the same is true of a basic change in product or marketing organization, of a decision to build a new store or to develop a new type of insurance policy.

What business needs therefore are tools which will enable it to make decisions without having to try to guess in what stage of the cycle the economy finds itself. These tools must enable business to plan and develop for more than the next three or even the next seven years, regardless of the economic fluctuations to be expected over the cyclical period.

We have today three such tools. In managing a business all three are useful.

In the first place, we can assume that there will always be fluctuaions, without attempting to guess what stage of the cycle the economy is currently passing through. We can, in other words, free decisions from cyclical guesswork by testing the business decision against the worst possible and the sharpest possible setback that past experience could lead us to expect.[1]

This method does not indicate whether a decision is right or

[1] For most American manufacturing industries this was not the "Great Depression" of 1929-32, but the much shorter "recession" of 1937-38. The rate of decline during the eight months of that depression was the sharpest ever witnessed in an industrial country other than the collapse following total defeat in war such as that of Germany or Japan.

not. It indicates, however, the extremes of cyclical risk involved. It is therefore the most important forecasting tool in the determination of the minimum necessary profit.

The second tool—more difficult to handle but also more productive—consists of basing a decision on events which are likely to have heavy impact upon future economic conditions but which have already happened. Instead of forecasting the future, this method focuses on past events—events which, however, have not yet expressed themselves economically. Instead of attempting to guess economic conditions, this method tries to find the "bedrock" underlying economic conditions.

We have mentioned before the case of the company which decided during World War II to turn to the production of fuse boxes and switch boxes after the war. This decision was based on such an analysis of the bedrock underlying the economy, namely, the pattern of family formation and population structure that had emerged in the United States between 1937 and 1943.

By 1943 it had become clear that something fundamental was happening to population trends. Even if the population statisticians had turned out to be right in their forecast that the high birthrate was a wartime phenomenon and would come to an end with the conclusion of the war (one of the most groundless, if not frivolous, forecasts ever made), it would not have altered the fact that from a low point in 1937 the rate of family formation had risen to where it was significantly above the rate of the depression years. These new families would need houses, even if the rate of family formation and the birthrate were to decline again after the end of the war. In addition, there had been almost twenty years of stagnation in residential building, so that there was a tremendous pent-up demand for houses. From this it could be concluded that there would be substantial residential building activity in the postwar period. The only thing that could have prevented it would have been America's losing the war.

If the postwar period had brought a sizable depression, this housing activity would have been a government project. In fact, population trends and the housing situation indicated that housing would have to be the major depression-fighting tool of governmental policy. If the postwar period were to be a boom period, as it turned out to be, there should be substantial private housing activity. In other words, housing would be at a high level in depression as well as in boom. (In fact, building would probably have been on a higher level than the one we actually experienced in the postwar period, had the much-heralded postwar depression actually come to pass.)

It was on the basis of this analysis of a development that had already happened and that could be expected to shape the economy regardless of business conditions, that the company's management decided to move into its new business. Management could justifiably claim that, even though it planned long-range, no forecast regarding the future was actually involved.

Of course, population structure is only one of the bedrock factors. In the period immediately following World War II it was probably a dominant factor in the American economy. In other times, however, it might well be secondary, if not irrelevant.

However, the basic method used is universally applicable: to find events that have already occurred, events that lie outside of economic conditions, but in turn shape those conditions, thus basing a decision for the future on events that have already happened.

But though the best tool we have, bedrock analysis is far from perfect. Exactly the same bedrock analysis of population trends with the same conclusion for a postwar housing boom could have been made in 1944 for France. The analysis would have been right; but the French housing boom never occurred. Of course, the reasons may be totally outside of the economic system proper. Perhaps they are to be found in strangulation by rent controls and by a vicious tax system. The boom may only be delayed and may still be "just around the corner." And the lack of any appreciable postwar residential building in France may be a major cause of the French political and economic sickness, and therefore should not have been allowed to happen. This would have been cold comfort to the businessman, however. In France the decision to go into fuse boxes and switch boxes, though based on rational premises, would still have been the wrong decision.

In other words, one cannot say that anything will "inevitably" happen in the future. Even if the inevitable does happen, one does not know when. Bedrock analysis should therefore never be used alone. It should always be tested by the third and final method of limiting the risks of making prediction: Trend analysis—the most widely used of the three tools in this country today. Where bedrock analysis tries to find the "why" of future events, trend analysis asks "how likely" and "how fast."

Trend analysis rests on the assumption that economic phenomena—say, the use of electric power by a residential customer or the amount of life insurance per dollar of family income—have a long-term trend that does not change quickly or capriciously. The trend may be confused by cyclical fluctuations; but over the long run it will reassert itself. To express it in the terms of the statistician: the "trend line" will tend to be a "true curve" over a ten-, fifteen- or twenty-year period.

Trend analysis thus tries to find the specific trends that pertain to the company's business. It then projects them in such a form that decisions can be taken for the long term without too much attention to the business cycle.

As a check of the results of bedrock analysis, trend analysis is invaluable. But it, too, should never be used by itself lest it become blind reliance on the past or on a rather mythical "law of social inertia." In fact, though quite different in techniques, the two analyses are really the two jaws of the same vise with which we attempt to arrest fleeting time long enough to get a good look at it.

Despite their shortcomings, the three methods sketched here, if used consistently, skillfully and with full realization of their limitations, should go a long way toward converting management decisions from "hunch" into "educated guess." At least they will enable management to know on what expectations it founds its objectives, whether the expectations are reasonable, and when to review an objective because the expected has not happened or has happened when not expected.

Tomorrow's Managers the Only Real Safeguard

But even with these improved methods, decisions concerning the future will always remain anticipations; and the odds will always be against their being right. Any management decision must therefore contain provision for change, adaptation and salvage. Management must with every decision make provision for molding the future as far as possible toward the predicted shape of things to come. Otherwise, despite all technical brilliance in forecasting, management decisions will be merely wishful thinking—as all decisions based on long-range prediction alone inevitably are.

Concretely this means that today's managers must systematically provide for tomorrow's managers. Tomorrow's managers alone can adapt today's decision to tomorrow's conditions, can convert the "educated guess" into solid achievement. They alone can mold tomorrow's conditions to conform to the decisions made today.

In our discussions of manager development we tend to stress that provision must be made for managers capable of making the decisions of tomorrow. This is true; but systematic manager development is first needed for the sake of the decisions made today. It must, above all, provide for men who know and understand these decisions and the thinking behind them, so that they can act intelligently when the decisions of today will have become the headaches of tomorrow.

In the last analysis, therefore, managing a business always comes back to the human element—no matter how sound the business economics, how careful the analysis, how good the tools.

CHAPTER 9

THE PRINCIPLES OF PRODUCTION

Ability to produce always a determining and a limiting factor—Production is not the application of tools to materials but the application of logic to work—Each system of production has its own logic and makes its own demands on business and management—The three systems of production—Is mass production "new style" a fourth?—Unique-product production—Mass production, "old style" and "new style"—Process production—What management should demand of its production people—What production systems demand of management—"Automation"; revolution or gradual change?—Understanding the principles of production required of every manager in the decades ahead.

MANUFACTURING management, as the term is commonly understood, is not the concern of this book any more than the management of selling, finance, engineering or insurance-company investments. But the principles of production must be a serious concern of top management in any business that produces or distributes physical goods. For in every such business the ability to attain performance goals depends on the ability of production to supply the goods in the required volume, at the required price, at the required quality, at the required time or with the required flexibility. In any manufacturing enterprise, ability to produce physically has to be taken into account when setting business objectives. Management's job is always to push back the limitations set by the hard reality of physical production facts. It must so manage its business as to convert these physical limitations into opportunities.

There is, of course, nothing new in this. But traditionally management reacts to the physical limitations of production by putting pressure on its manufacturing function: there are few areas in which "management by drives" is as common. And production people themselves see the answer in a number of techniques and tools, ranging from machine design to industrial engineering.

Neither, however, is the key. To push back the physical limitations or to convert them into opportunities requires first that management understand what system of production its operations require and what the principles of that system are; and second that it apply these principles consistently and thoroughly. Production is not the application of tools to materials. *It is the application of logic to work.* The more clearly, the more consistently, the more rationally the right logic is applied, the less of a limitation and the more of an opportunity production becomes.

Each system of production makes its own demands on the management of the business—in all areas and on all levels. Each requires different competence, skill and performance. One set of demands is not necessarily "higher" than another, any more than non-Euclidian geometry is higher than Euclidian geometry. But each is different. And unless management understands the demands of its system of production, it will not manage well.

This is particularly important today when many businesses are moving from one system of production into another. If this move is considered a mere matter of machines, techniques and gadgets, the business will inevitably reap only the difficulties of the new system. To reap its benefits management must realize that the new system involves new principles, and must understand what these are.

The Three Systems of Production

There are three basic systems of industrial production known to us so far: unique-product production, mass production and process production. We may perhaps count four systems; for mass production "old style," that is, the production of uniform products, is different from mass production "new style," which manufactures uniform parts but assembles them into diversified products.

Each of these systems has its own basic principles; and each makes specific demands on management.

There are two general rules for advancing production performance and pushing back limitations: 1) The limitations of production are pushed back further and faster, the more consistently and thoroughly the principles pertaining to the system in use are applied. 2) The systems themselves represent a distinct order of advance, with unique-product production the least advanced, process production the most advanced. They represent different stages of control over physical limitations. This does not mean that opportunities for advance lie everywhere in moving from the unique-product system to the process-production system. Each system has its specific applications, requirements and limitations. But it does mean that we advance to the extent to which we can organize parts of production on the principles of a more advanced system and learn, at the same time, how to harmonize the two systems within the business.

There are also two general rules concerning the demands on management competence made by each system.

1) The systems differ not just in the difficulty of their demands, but in the variety of competence and the order of performance. Management, in moving from one system to another, has to learn how to do new things rather than learn to do the old things better.

2) The more we succeed in applying consistently the principles of each system, the easier it becomes for management to satisfy its demands.

Each management has to meet the demands of the system it ought to have according to the nature of its product and production, rather than those of the system it actually has. Being unable or unwilling to apply what would be the most appropriate system only results in lack of performance; it does not result in lower demands on management. Indeed, it inevitably increases the difficulties of managing the business.

One case in point is basic steel making, which has—in the "batch process"—primarily a unique-product system. There is probably no industry that has worked harder or more successfully on perfecting a unique-product system. Yet, the problems the managements of basic-steel companies face are all process-production problems: high fixed capital requirements and the need for continuous production resulting together in high break-even points, the need for a high and constant level of business, the need to make basic investment decisions for a long time ahead, etc. At the same time the basic-steel industry enjoys few of the benefits of process production.

It is, in summary, of major importance in managing a business to know which system applies; to carry its principles through as far as possible; to find out which parts of production can be organized in a more advanced system and to organize them accordingly; to know what demands each system makes on management. And where, as in the basic-steel industry, historical and technological obstacles have barred the organization of production in the appropriate system, it is a major challenge to management to work systematically on overcoming these obstacles. Indeed, emphasis in such a situation should not be given to working a little more effectively what is basically the wrong system. I am convinced that a great deal of the tremendous technological effort in the steel industry has been misdirected. Focused on improving the traditional process, it will turn out to have been wasted when steel making will finally become process production—which is in all probability not too far off any more. A business using the wrong system has to satisfy all the demands that the appropriate and more advanced system would make on management. Yet, it does not have the wherewithal to pay for them, for this can come only out of the increased ability to produce which the more advanced system provides.

Unique-Product Production

What, then, concretely are these three systems of production and their principles?

In the first, the production of a unique product, each product is self-contained. Of course, strictly speaking, there is no such thing as manufacturing unique products—they are produced only by the artist. But building a battleship, a big turbine or a skyscraper comes close to turning out a unique product. So does the building of a house, and in most cases "batch production" in a job shop.

Under this system the basic principle is organization into homogeneous stages. In the building of the traditional one-family house—one of the simplest examples of unique-product production—we can distinguish four such stages. First, digging the foundation and pouring concrete for the foundation walls and the basement floor. Second, putting up the frame and the roof. Third, installing plumbing and wiring equipment in the inside walls. Finally, interior finishing. What makes each of these a distinct stage is that work on the house can stop after each is completed, without any damage—even for a fairly long time. On the other hand, within each stage, work has to be carried right through; or else what has been done already will be damaged and may even have to be done again. Each stage can be varied from house to house without too much trouble or adjustment and without delaying the next stage. Each of these stages by the inner logic of the product, that is, of the house, is an entity in itself.

Unique-product production, with its organization of the work by homogeneous stages, is radically different from craft organization, in which a carpenter does all the carpentry, a plumber all the plumbing, etc. Properly organized, unique-product production does not go by craft skills but by stage skills. The model is the telephone installation man who, without being a skilled electrician, carpenter, plumber or roofer, installs electric wiring, saws through boards, makes a ground connection and can take up a roof shingle and replace it. In other words, either every man engaged in the work of a particular stage must be able to do everything needed within that stage; or, as in the building of a big turbine, there must be an integrated team for each stage which contains within itself all the stage skills needed. No skill is needed by individual or team that goes beyond the requirement of the particular stage.

This is largely how we succeeded in building ships at such a tremendous rate during the war. It was not mass production that resulted in the unprecedented output of ships. It was the division of the work into homogeneous stages; the systematic organization of the work group for the specific requirements of each stage; and the systematic training of a large number of people to do all the work required within one stage. This in turn made possible the progressive scheduling of the work flow which was the greatest time saver.

Mass Production "Old Style" and "New Style"

Mass production is the assembly of varied products—in large numbers or small—out of uniform and standardized parts.

In the manufacturing industry mass production is today the prevailing system. It is, and with good reason, considered to be the typical system of an industrial society—though process production may soon become a strong contender.

So universal is mass production today that it might be assumed that we know all about it, certainly that we know all about its basic principles. This is far from true. After forty years we are only now beginning to understand what we should be doing. The reason for this is that the man who ushered in mass production as a universal system misunderstood and misapplied it—so often the fate of the pioneer.

When Henry Ford said that "the customer can have any color car as long as it's black," he was not joking. He meant to express the essence of mass production as the manufacture of uniform products in large quantity. Of course, he knew that it would have been easy to give his customer a choice of colors; all that was needed was to give the painter at the end of the assembly line three or four spray guns instead of one. But Ford also realized, rightly, that the uniformity of the product would soon be gone altogether once he made any concession to diversity. And to him the uniformity of the product was the key to mass production.

This old-style mass production is, however, based on a misunderstanding. It is the essence of genuine mass production that it can create a greater diversity of products than any method ever designed by man. It does not rest on uniform products. It rests on *uniform parts* which can then be mass-assembled into a large variety of different products.

The model of mass production is therefore not the old Ford assembly line. It is rather the farm equipment manufacturer in Southern California who designs and makes specialized cultivating machines for large-scale farming on irrigated land. Every one of his designs is unique. He makes, for instance, a machine that performs, with various attachments, all operations needed in large-scale cucumber growing—from preparing the hills in the spring, to harvesting cucumbers at the right stage of their growth, to pickling them. He rarely makes more than one of each machine at a time. Yet every one of his more than seven hunderd different machines is made up entirely of mass-produced, uniform, standardized parts, which someone in the American economy turns out by the thousands. His biggest job is not to solve the problem of designing a machine that will identify cucumbers of the right ripeness for pickling, but to find a mass producer of a part that, though originally designed for an entirely different purpose, will, when put on the cucumber cultivator, do whatever is needed.

The specific technique for applying this principle is the systematic analysis of products to find the pattern that underlies their multiplicity. Then this pattern can be organized so that the minimum number of manufactured parts will make possible the assembly of the maximum number of products. The burden of diversity, in other words, is taken out of manufacturing and shifted to assembly.

One large manufacturer of electric implements produced, ten years ago, 3,400 different models, each composed of 40 to 60 parts. The analysis of this line of products first made it possible to reduce the number by about one third; 1,200 models were found to be duplications. The analysis still left 2,200 products—and to make them the company was making or buying well over 100,000 different parts.

After the products had been analyzed, their pattern established and the parts determined, it was found that almost all of the 2,200 models fell into 4 categories, according to the voltage they were supposed to carry. Only 40 products did not fit into this pattern. This made it possible to reduce the number of parts for all the other products. Then the number of variations for each part could be cut down to the minimum. Only one part now requires as many as 11 variations; the average today is 5 variations per part.

Production in this company is production of parts—even though the final products are widely different. The burden of variety is thrown on assembly. The parts themselves can be produced continuously against a schedule determined by the size of the inventory rather than by customer orders. And the size of the inventory is again determined by the time needed for assembly and delivery.

This new-style mass production is the most immediately useful production concept that we have in our possession today. It is still understood only by a minority of production people, and applied only in a fairly small number of companies. Also the techniques and methods to take full advantage of the concept have only now become available. It is above all the logical methods of "Operations Research" that allow us to make the complicated analyses of products and parts that are necessary to put the correct mass-production principle into effect.

Wherever this new principle has actually been applied cost

reductions have been spectacular—sometimes reaching 50 or 60 per cent. Nor is its application confined to the production process itself. By making it possible to keep an inventory in parts instead of in finished products, it often enables a company to cut its cost and yet give the customer better service.

This new principle does achieve, in other words, what Henry Ford was after; the continuous production of uniform things without interruption because of an irregular flow of customer orders, or the need to change tools, styles or models. But it does this not by producing uniform products but by producing standardized parts. Uniformity in manufacturing is coupled with diversity in assembly.

Obviously the application of the mass-production principle, is not simple. It goes well beyond manufacturing and requires hard and extensive work on the part of the marketing people, engineers, financial people, personnel people, purchasing agents and so forth. It carries risks, as it must be based on a fairly long production cycle at a constant rate of machine utilization—three, six, in some cases, eighteen months. It requires new accounting tools.

New-style mass production can also not be put in overnight—the development in the electrical implement company took all of three years. But so great are the savings that the company recovered the expense of a virtually complete redesign of its products and manufacturing facilities in less than two years.

Process Production

The third system is process production. Here process and product become one.

The oldest example of a process industry is the oil refinery. The end products that a refinery will obtain out of crude oil are determined by the process it uses. It can produce only the oil distillates for which it is built and only in definite proportions. If new distillates have to be added, or if the proportion between the various distillates is to be changed significantly, the refinery has to be rebuilt. Process production is the rule in the chemical industries. It is, with minor variations, the basic system of a milk-processing or a plate-glass plant.

And both mass production "new style" and process production are ready for Automation.

What Management Should Demand of Its Production People

Management must demand that those responsible for production know what system of production is appropriate, and apply the principles of that system consistently and to the limit. These are the first and decisive steps in pushing back the limitations of production on business performance.

Only when these steps have been taken can the next one be made: the organization of parts of production on the basis of a more advanced system.

The result of doing this without first analyzing the production process and organizing it properly is shown by the failure of the prefabricated house. It would seem the most obvious thing in the world to build a house from prefabricated, standardized parts. Yet the attempt, when made after World War II, proved abortive.

The reason was that uniform, standardized parts—mass production, in other words—were superimposed on a badly disorganized unique-product system. Instead of homogeneous stages, the organizing principle was craft organization. The use of prefabricated parts in a craft system proved more expensive and slower than the old methods. When, however, the Levitts in Long Island organized home building by homogeneous stages, they could immediately use uniform standardized prefabricated parts with conspicuous savings in time and money

Similarly, standardized parts brought no savings in a locomotive repair shop as long as it was craft-organized. When the work was organized in teams, each containing all the skills needed in a particular stage of the work, when, in other words, craft organization was replaced by stage organization, standardized parts brought tremendous savings.

This is of particular importance in a mass-production industry, which produces diversified products. For there the great opportunity lies in the application of Automation; and this can only be achieved if production is properly understood and organized as the manufacture of unform parts and their assembly into diversified products.

The electrical instrument maker mentioned above could fairly easily put his production of parts on an automatic basis, approaching closely the continuous flow and automatic self-control of an oil refinery or a plate-glass plant. There are other illustrations.

The U.S. Bureau of Standards has recently worked out, for the U.S. Navy, a method of automatic production of electronic circuits. This process does away with the soldering of individual circuits; it eliminates, in other words, the traditional "production by assembly" of the electronics industry. At the same time it makes possible the use of a large number of different circuits and their combinations without redesign of the process and without change in production. It does this by replacing the wiring in a radio or television set with a fairly small number of predesigned parts that can be plugged together in assembly to give many circuits or combinations of circuits.

My favorite example is a shirt manufacturer who faced the problem of an almost infinite variety of sizes, styles and colors, seemingly making impossible any production planning. He found, however, that three quarters of his production were in white shirts; and that there were only three basic qualities of fabric used in making white shirts, and in fairly predictable proportions. He then found that all shirts were made of seven parts: front, back, shoulder yoke, collars, right sleeve, left sleeve, cuffs. Size adjustments could all be made in assembly where the finished shirt is sewn together by cutting off excess length or width; for it is cheaper to sacrifice a few inches of material than to turn out parts of different size. Style adjustments could be made by using different collars and cuffs and different buttons. As a result all parts except collars and cuffs could be produced in the three grades of cloth without variation; cuffs required three variations; collars six. Only collars, which are simple to produce, are therefore made according to customers' orders today. And a job that, twenty years ago, was still almost entirely run by hand on individual sewing machines, is now done as a continuous automatic process, controlled by inventory standards. The result has been a sharp cut in cost, a tremendous increase in the variety of final products—sizes and styles—and greater customer satisfaction.

What Production Systems Demand of Management

But management must also know what the various systems of production demand of its own competence and performance.

In unique-product production, management's first job, it might be said, is to get an order. In mass production, the job is to build an effective distributive organization and to educate the customer to adapt his wants to the range of product variety. In process production, the first task is to create, maintain and expand a market and to find new markets. To distribute kerosene lamps free to the Chinese peasants to create a market for kerosene—the famous

Standard Oil story of fifty years ago—is a good example of what this means.

Unique-product production has high costs for the individual product but great flexibility in the plant. Mass production "new style" has the ability to supply wants cheaply and within a wide and flexible range of products. But it requires much higher capital investment than unique-product production and a much higher level of continuous activity; it involves inventory risks; and it needs a distributive organization that can sell continuously rather than one that goes after a specialized, individual order. Process production requires the highest capital investment—in absolute dollars—and the most nearly continuous operation. Also, since products and process have, so to speak, become one, new products will be created by changes in the process even if there is no demand for them in the existing market—a common occurrence in the chemical industry. Management must therefore develop new markets for any new products as well as maintain a steady market for the old. Indeed, under Automation it is a major responsibility of management both in mass production and in process production to maintain a steadier level of economic activity and to prevent extreme economic fluctuations, whether of boom or of depression.

Under the unique-product system the time-span of decisions is short. Under mass production it becomes longer: a distributive organization, for instance, may take ten years to build, as the Kaiser-Frazer Automobile Company found out after World War II. But under a process system decisions are made for an even longer future. Once built, the production facilities are relatively inflexible and can be changed only at major expense; the total investment may be large; and the development of a market is long-range. The marketing systems of the big oil companies are good examples. The more advanced the production organization, the more important are decisions for the future.

Each system requires different management skills and organization. Unique-product production requires people good at a technical function. Mass production—"old style" and "new"—requires management trained in analytical thinking, in scheduling and in planning. New-style mass production as well as process production requires management trained in seeing a business as a whole in conceptual synthesis and in decision-making.

Under unique-product production management can be centralized at the top. Co-ordination between the various functions is needed primarily at the top. Selling, design, engineering and production can all be distinct and need only come together where company policy is being determined. It is this pattern of unique-product production that is still largely assumed in our organization theory—even though unique-product production may well be the exception rather than the rule in the majority of American industry today.

Mass production "old style" can still maintain this pattern, though with considerable difficulty and at a high price in efficiency. It does better with a pattern that establishes centers of decision and integration much further down. For it requires close co-ordination between the engineers who design the product, the production people who make it, the sales people who market it, and so forth.

In both mass production "new style" and process production, functional centralization is impossible. They require the closest co-operation of people from all functions at every stage. They require that design, production, marketing and the organization of the work be tackled simultaneously by a team representing all functions. They require that every member of the team both know his own functional work and see the impact on the whole business all the time. And decisions affecting the business as a whole have to be taken at a decentralized level—sometimes at a level not even considered "management" today.

There are significant differences with respect to the work force and its management. Unique-product production can usually adjust its work force to economic fluctuations, keeping in bad times only foremen and a nucleus of the most highly skilled. It can, as a rule, find what other skills it needs on the labor market. Precisely because they have limited skill, the workers in old-style mass production must increasingly demand employment stability from the enterprise. And in any business that uses Automation—whether new-style mass production or process production—the enterprise itself must make efforts to stabilize employment. For the work force needed for Automation consists largely of people trained both in skill and in theoretical understanding. It not only represents too great an investment to be disbanded; it can normally only be created within the company and with years of effort. It is neither accident nor philanthropy that the oil companies—typical process businesses—have tried so hard to keep employment steady even in bad depression years.

Under Automation there are few "workers." As said before, Automation will not (in the traditional sense of the word) cut down the total number of people employed—just as mass production did not do so. What we can see so far in the process industries shows clearly that the total work force does not shrink. On the contrary, it tends to expand. But Automation requires totally different workers who are actually much closer to the professional and technical specialist than to today's production worker. This creates a problem of managing people that is quite different from any "personal management problem" businessmen are normally familiar with.

Automation—Revolution or Gradual Change?

I have learned to be extremely skeptical of any prediction of imminent revolution or of sweeping changes in technology or business organization. After all, today, two hundred years since the first Industrial Revolution, there still flourishes in our midst the New York garment industry, a large industry organized on the "putting-out" system which, the textbooks tell us, had become obsolete by 1750. It would not be difficult to find other examples of such living ancestors who are blissfully (indeed profitably) unaware that they died a long time ago.

Certainly the obstacles to the Automation revolution are great—above all, the lack of men properly trained in the new concepts and skills. Also it has been estimated that only one tenth of America's industries could readily benefit from Automation at the present state of its technology. Even a real "Automation revolution" would be a gradual and highly uneven process.

Still revolutions do happen. And in the American economy there will be one powerful force pushing toward an Automation revolution in the next decade: the shortage of workers. As a result mainly of the lean birth years of the thirties, our labor force will increase only 11 per cent until 1965. Yet, our total population will go up much faster, even if present record birth rates should not be maintained.

To reach minimum growth objectives indicated by population figures, technological progress and economic trends would require, in many companies, a doubling of the labor force were production to continue on the present system.

Even without a revolution, the most significant, the most promising and the most continuous opportunity to improve the performance of business enterprise will not lie, for decades to come, in new machines or new processes. *It will lie first in the consistent application of the new mass-production principle* and secondly in the *application of the principles of Automation.* The techniques and tools of production management will continue to be a specialized subject with which only production people need to be familiar. But every manager will have to acquire an understanding of the principles of production—above all, an understanding that efficient production is a matter of principles rather than of machines or gadgets. For without it he will not, in the decades ahead, adequately discharge his job.

PART TWO

MANAGING MANAGERS

CHAPTER 10

THE FORD STORY

Managers the basic resources of a business, the scarcest, the most expensive and most perishable—Henry Ford's attempt to do without managers—The near-collapse of the Ford Motor Company—Rebuilding Ford management—What it means to manage managers—Management not by delegation—The six requirements of managing managers.

THE fundamental problems of order, structure, motivation and leadership in the business enterprise have to be solved in the managing of managers. Managers are the basic resource of the business enterprise and its scarcest. In a fully automatic factory there may be almost no rank-and-file employees at all. But there will be managers—in fact, there will be many times the number of managers there are in the factory of today.

Managers are the most expensive resource in most businesses—and the one that depreciates the fastest and needs the most constant replenishment. It takes years to build a management team; but it can be destroyed in a short period of misrule. The number of managers as well as the capital investment each manager represents are bound to increase steadily—as they have increased in the past half century. Parallel with this will go an increase in the demands of the enterprise on the ability of its managers. These demands have doubled in every generation; there is no reason to expect a slowing down of the trend during the next decades.

How well managers are managed determines whether business goals will be reached. It also largely determines how well the enterprise manages worker and work. For the worker's attitude reflects, above all, the attitude of his management. It directly mirrors management's competence and structure. The worker's effectiveness is determined largely by the way he himself is managed. That "personnel management" confines itself by and large today to the rank-and-file employee and all but excludes managers from its purview, can be explained historically. But it is nonetheless a serious mistake. The common practice expressed recently by a large company in setting up a Department of Human Relations—"The Department will of course confine itself to the relations between the company and employees earning less than $5,000 a year"—almost guarantees in advance the failure of the new department and of its efforts.

Managing managers is the central concern of every manager. During the last ten or fifteen years American managers have subjected themselves to a steady barrage of exhortations, speeches and programs in which they tell each other that their job is to manage the people under them, urge each other to give top priority to that responsibility and furnish each other with copious advice and expensive gadgets for "downward communications." But I have yet to sit down with a manager, whatever his level or job, who was not primarily concerned with his upward relations and upward communications. Every president I know, be the company large or small, worries more about his relations with his Board of Directors than with his vice-presidents. Every vice-president feels that relations with the president are the real problem. And so on down to the first-line supervisor, the production foreman or chief clerk, who is quite certain that he could get along with his men if only the "boss" and the personnel department left him alone.

This is not, as personnel people seem inclined to think, a sign of the perversity of human nature. Upward relations are properly a manager's first concern. To be a manager means sharing in the responsibility for the performance of the enterprise. A man who is not expected to take this responsibility is not a manager. And a manager who does not take it as his first responsibility is a poor manager, if not untrue to his duty.

These problems of upward relations that worry the manager—the relationship to his own boss; his doubts as to what is expected of him; his difficulty in getting his point across, his program accepted, his activity given full weight; the relations with other departments and with staff people, and so forth—are all problems of managing managers.

The starting point of the discussion of the human organization of the enterprise cannot therefore be the rank-and-file employees and their work, no matter how numerous they are; it must be managing managers.

Henry Ford's Attempt To Do Without Managers

The basic challenges as well as the basic concepts in managing managers are again best illustrated by an example. And the best example is the story of the Ford Motor Company.[1]

There is no more dramatic story than that of the fall of Ford from unparalleled success to near-collapse in fifteen short years—unless it is the equally swift and dramatic revival of the company in the last ten years.

In the early twenties Ford's share of the automobile market had climbed to two thirds. Fifteen years later, by the time World War II started, Ford's market share had fallen to 20 per cent. The Ford Motor Company, being privately owned, publishes no financial figures. But it is widely (though probably mistakenly) believed in the automobile industry that the company did not make a profit in any one of these fifteen years.

How close the company had come to ruin was shown by the near-panic in the automobile industry when Edsel Ford, Henry Ford's only son, suddenly died during World War II. For almost twenty years everybody in the industry had been saying: "The old man can't last much longer; wait till Edsel takes over." That he died while the old man was still alive forced the industry to face the reality of the Ford situation. And the reality was such that the survival of the company seemed improbable—some people said impossible.

The best indication of the seriousness with which these chances of survival were viewed was a scheme proposed in responsible circles during those days in Detroit. The U. S. Government, it was said, should lend enough money to Studebaker—the fourth largest auto-

[1] The history of the Ford Motor Company is still to be written, Allan Nevins' *Ford*. (New York: Scribner's, 1954), though definitive, carries the story only to 1915. But the main facts are common knowledge. For their interpretation I alone bear the responsibility.

mobile producer but still less than one sixth the size of Ford—to buy out the Ford family and to take over the company. In this way, and this way alone, Ford would have a chance to survive. Otherwise, it was agreed, the company might well have to be nationalized lest its collapse seriously endanger the country's economy and its war effort.

What brought Ford to this crisis? The story of Henry Ford's personal misrule has been told in lurid and not too accurate detail several times. People in American management—if not the public at large—have become familiar with his secret-police methods and his one-man tyranny. What is not understood, however, is that these things were not pathological aberration or senility—though both may have played a part. Fundamental to Henry Ford's misrule was a systematic, deliberate and conscious attempt *to run the billion-dollar business without managers.* The secret police that spied on all Ford executives served to inform Henry Ford of any attempt on the part of one of his executives to make a decision. When they seemed to acquire managerial authority or responsibility of their own, they were generally fired. And one of the chief reasons why Harry Bennett, Ford's police chief, rose during these years to almost supreme power in the organization was that he could never be anything but the old man's creature, and totally lacked the experience and competence to hold any managerial position.

This refusal to allow anyone to be a manager goes back to the early days of the Ford Motor Company. Even then it had been the old man's practice, for instance, to demote first-line supervisors regularly every few years or so lest they "become uppity" and forget that they owed their job to Mr. Ford's will. Technicians Henry Ford wanted; and he was willing to pay them generously. But management was his personal job as owner. Just as, early in his career, he decided not to share ownership with anybody, he apparently decided not to share management. His executives had to be his personal assistants, doing what he told them to do; they had at most to execute, never to manage. From this concept followed everything else: the secret police, Ford's fear of a conspiracy against him among his closest associates, his basic insecurity.

The concept of the executive as an extension of the owner and as his delegate has parallels in the development of many institutions. The army officer started out as the personal vassal of his lord. As late as the eighteenth century, commissions in many European armies were still considered the personal property of the regimental commander, to be sold by him to the highest bidder; and, our military titles—lieutenant, especially—recall to this day the origin of officership in personal delegation. Similarly, the public servant was at first his sovereign's delegate if not his body-servant. Louis XI of France, who may have conceived the modern idea of a staff of full-time lay administrators, used the same man as his personal barber, secret-police chief and chief minister. And the ministers of government are "secretaries" to this day.

Henry Ford's concept was not even unique in industry. It was widely held in the early years of the century. He shared it, for instance, with one of his most distinguished contemporaries: Lenin. It is no accident that the early Bolshevik leaders were such fervent admirers of Ford. "Fordism" seemed to offer the key to rapid industrialization in a country lacking in skilled labor. Above all, it seemed to make possible industrialization without management, in which the "owner," represented by the political dictatorship, would control all business decisions while business itself would employ only technicians. That this proved an idle dream early in the first Five-Year Plan was among the major causes of the bloody "purge" of the mid-thirties which liquidated practically all industrial managers. And that the successors to the "purged" executives have in turn had to be allowed to become managers, rather than remain mere technicians, represents a defeat of the entire theory of the Communist Revolution. One does not need the gift of prophecy to predict that the emergence of a managerial class insures, over the long run, the downfall of the Communist regime in Russia.

Certainly it was the absence of a management that caused the fall of the Ford Motor Company. Even at its lowest point—just before World War II—it still had a strong distributive and service organization. The automobile industry believed that Ford's financial resources after fifteen years of losses were fully equal to those of General Motors, even though Ford sales were hardly more than one third those of General Motors.

But Ford had few managers (except in sales). Most of the good
ie had either been fired or had left; there was a mass exodus of
:ecutives as soon as World War II created job opportunities
n years of depression. And few of the Ford executives who
vere good enough to find other jobs. When the company

was revived a few years later, not many of the old-timers were found to be competent to hold a management job much above the lowest.

Rebuilding Ford Management

Whether Ford could have survived at all had there been a postwar depression is debatable. But the company might have collapsed even in the postwar boom had Henry Ford's idea of managing without managers not been reversed radically by his grandson and successor, Henry Ford II. The story of the revival of the Ford Motor Company since 1944 is one of the epics of American business. Many of the details are not known outside the company; it is high time that the whole story was published. But enough is known to make it clear that the key to Ford's revival has been the building and organization of management—just as the stifling and destruction of management had been the key to the earlier decline.

Henry Ford II was in his mid-twenties when responsibility suddenly fell on his shoulders, with his father dead and his grandfather rapidly failing. He had no business experience at all. And there were few executives of stature left in the company to help or guide him. Yet he obviously understood what the real problem was; for his first act was to establish as basic policy that there would be a real management. Most of the men constituting this management had to be found on the outside. But before he could bring in anyone he had first to clean house. And he had to establish the basic principles on which the company would operate in the future. All this he had to do alone—with his grandfather still alive and his grandfather's henchmen still on the job. Only then could he pick new people to help him manage, people who could run their activities themselves, take full responsibility for them and be given full authority over them. In fact, the first appointment, that of Ernest R. Breech as executive vice-president, announced that Breech would have full operating authority. And this concept has been observed in setting up all management jobs throughout the organization.

Management has become management by objectives. Where Ford executives under the old regime were never told anything, the new regime has been trying to supply every manager with the information he needs to do his own job, and with as much information about the company as is feasible. The concept of the executive as a personal delegate of the owner has been replaced by the concept of the manager whose authority is grounded in the objective responsibility of the job. Arbitrary orders have been replaced by performance standards based on objectives and measurements.

The greatest change perhaps—certainly the most visible—is in organization structure.

The old Ford Motor Company was rigidly centralized. Not only was all power and decision in the hands of old Henry Ford; but there was only one set of figures for the whole, complex operation.

The Ford Motor Company owns its own steel mill, for instance. With a capacity of 1.5 million tons a year, it is one of the country's largest. Yet it was an open secret in Detroit that the cost figures of the steel mill disappeared in the over-all cost figures for the company. The mill superintendent for instance, did not know what price the company paid for the coal he used. Purchase contracts under the old regime were usually "top secret."

By contrast Ford today is decentralized into fifteen autonomous divisions, each with its own complete management fully responsible for the performance and results of its business and with full authority to make all decisions to attain these results. The steel mill, incidentally, is among these divisions, along with major automobile-producing divisions like Ford and Mercury-Lincoln, parts and equipment divisions and one division in charge of international and export business.

Henry Ford II did not, of course, invent his concepts of management and organization. He took most of them—along with his top managers—from his big competitor, General Motors. They are the concepts on which General Motors was built,[2] and which underlay General Motors' rise to the position of largest manufacturing enterprise in the country. But Henry Ford II is unique in that he started out with a complete set of principles rather than develop them imperceptibly as he went along. His experience is therefore of particular significance as a test of these concepts. Here was a company that seemed headed for almost certain decay, if not ruin, a

[2] For full description of General Motors' management concepts and practice see my book *The Concept of the Corporation* (New York, John Day, 1946). This book presents the results of a two-year analysis undertaken at the request of General Motors' top management.

company without any management, demoralized and leaderless Ten years later, Ford's share of the market is climbing steadily. It has joined battle with General Motors' Chevrolet car for first place in the automobile market. From being moribund it has become a major growth company. And the miracle—for miracle it is—has been brought about by a complete change in the principles of the management of managers.

What It Means to Manage Managers

The Ford story enables us to say dogmatically that the enterprise cannot do without managers. One cannot argue that management does the owner's job by delegation. Management is needed not only because the job is too big for any one man to do himself, but because running an enterprise is something essentially different from running one's own property.

The older Ford ran his company quite consciously as a single proprietorship. His experience proves that, whatever the legal rules, the modern business enterprise cannot be run this way. The resources entrusted to it can produce wealth only if they are maintained beyond the life-span of one man. The enterprise must therefore be capable of perpetuating itself; and to do this it must have managers. The complexity of the task is such, even in a small business, that it cannot be discharged by one man working with helpers and assistants. It requires an organized and integrated team, each member of which does his own managerial job.

It is therefore the definition of modern business enterprise that it requires a management—that is, an organ which rules and runs the enterprise. The functions and duties of this organ are determined by only one thing: the objective needs of the enterprise. Owners may legally be the "employers" of management; they may even be omnipotent in a given situation. But the nature, functions and responsibilities of management are always determined by the task rather than by delegation.

It is true that in its genetic origin management grows out of the delegation to assistants of those tasks which the owner of a small but growing business can no longer discharge himself. But while growth in size, that is quantitative change, makes management necessary the change itself is qualitative in its effects. Once there is a business enterprise, management's function is no longer definable in terms of delegation by the owners. Management has a function because of the objective requirements of the enterprise. To deny or to slight this function is to ruin the enterprise.

Management is not an end in itself. It is an organ of the business enterprise. And it consists of individuals. The first requirement in managing managers is therefore that the vision of the individual managers be directed toward the goals of the business, and that their wills and efforts be bent toward reaching these goals. The first requirement in managing managers is *management by objectives and self-control.*

But the individual manager must also be able to make the needed efforts and produce the required results. His job must be set up so as to allow maximum performance. The second requirement of managing managers is therefore the *proper structure of the manager's job.*

Though managers are individuals, they have to work together in a team, and such an organized group always has a distinct character. Though made by individuals, their vision, their practices, their attitudes, and behavior, this character is a common character. It survives long after the men are gone who originally created it. It molds the behavior and attitudes of newcomers. It decides largely who will succeed in the organization. It determines whether the organization will recognize and reward excellence or scuttle into the shallow harbor of placid mediocrity. Indeed, it controls whether men will grow or become stunted, whether they will stand straight and erect or become crooked and misshapen. A mean spirit in the organization will produce mean managers, a great spirit great managers. A major requirement in managing managers is therefore the creation of the *right spirit in the organization.*

A business enterprise must have a government. In fact it needs both an organ of overall leadership and final decision, and an organ of overall review and appraisal. It needs both a *chief executive* and a *board of directors.*

The business enterprise must make provision for its own survival and growth. It must make *provision for tomorrow's managers.*

An organized group needs a structure. Arriving at *sound structural principles of management organization* is therefore the final necessity in managing managers.

These are not things that "should" be done; they are things that are done in every enterprise whether its managers realize it or not. In every enterprise managers are either guided in the right direction or are misdirected; but their vision and efforts are always focused on something. In every business enterprise managers' jobs are set up either properly or improperly; they cannot be left unorganized. Every business enterprise has either an effective or an ineffective organization structure; but it always has an organization structure. It has either a spirit that killeth or one that giveth life. People are always being developed. The only choice is whether they are to be developed equal to their potential and to tomorrow's demands or are to be misdeveloped.

Henry Ford wanted no managers. But the only result was that he misdirected managers, set up their jobs improperly, created a spirit of suspicion and frustration, misorganized his company and misdeveloped management people. The only choice management has in these six areas is therefore whether it will do the jobs right or not. But the jobs themselves cannot be evaded. And whether they are being done right or not will determine largely whether the enterprise will survive and prosper or decline and ultimately fall.

CHAPTER 11

MANAGEMENT BY OBJECTIVES AND SELF-CONTROL

The forces of misdirection—Workmanship: a necessity and a danger—Misdirection by the boss—What should the objectives be?—Management by "drives"—How should managers' objectives be set and by whom?—Self-control through measurements—The proper use of reports and procedures—A philosophy of management.

ANY business enterprise must build a true team and weld individual efforts into a common effort. Each member of the enterprise contributes something different, but they must all contribute toward a common goal. Their efforts must all pull in the same direction, and their contributions must fit together to produce a whole—without gaps, without friction, without unnecessary duplication of effort.

Business performance therefore requires that each job be directed toward the objectives of the whole business. And in particular each manager's job must be focused on the success of the whole. The performance that is expected of the manager must be derived from the performance goals of the business, his results must be measured by the contribution they make to the success of the enterprise. The manager must know and understand what the business goals demand of him in terms of performance, and his superior must know what contribution to demand and expect of him—and must judge him accordingly. If these requirements are not met, managers are misdirected. Their efforts are wasted. Instead of team work, there is friction, frustration and conflict.

Management by objectives requires major effort and special instruments. For in the business enterprise managers are not automatically directed toward a common goal. On the contrary, business, by its very nature, contains three powerful factors of misdirection: in the specialized work of most managers; in the hierarchical structure of management; and in the differences in vision and work and the resultant insulation of various levels of management.

A favorite story at management meetings is that of the three stonecutters who were asked what they were doing. The first replied: "I am making a living." The second kept on hammering while he said: "I am doing the best job of stonecutting in the entire county." The third one looked up with a visionary gleam in his eyes and said: "I am building a cathedral."

The third man is, of course, the true "manager." The first man knows what he wants to get out of the work and manages to do so. He is likely to give a "fair day's work for a fair day's pay." But he is not a manager and will never be one.

It is the second man who is a problem. Workmanship is essential; without it no work can flourish; in fact, an organization demoralizes if it does not demand of its members the most scrupulous workmanship they are capable of. But there is always a danger that the true workman, the true professional, will believe that he is accomplishing something when in effect he is just polishing stones or collecting footnotes. Workmanship must be encouraged in the business enterprise. But it must always be related to the needs of the whole.

The majority of managers in any business enterprise are, like the second man, concerned with specialized work. True, the number of functional managers should always be kept at a minimum, and there should be the largest possible number of "general" managers who manage an integrated business and are directly responsible for its performance and results. Even with the utmost application of this principle the great bulk of managers will remain in functional jobs, however. This is particularly true of the younger people.

A man's habits as a manager, his vision and his values, therefore, will as a rule be formed while he does functional and specialized work. And it is essential that the functional specialist develop-high standards of workmanship, that he strive to be "the best stonecutter in the county." For work without high standards is dishonest. It corrupts the man himself. It corrupts those under him. Emphasis on, and drive for, workmanship produces innovations and advances in every area of management. That managers strive to do "professional personnel management," to run "the most up-to-date plant," to do "truly scientific market research," to "put in the most modern accounting system," or to do "perfect engineering" must be encouraged.

But this striving for professional workmanship in functional and specialized work is also a danger. It tends to direct a man's vision and efforts away from the goals of the business. The functional work becomes an end in itself. In far too many instances the functional manager no longer measures his performance by its contribution to the enterprise, but only by his own professional criteria of workmanship. He tends to appraise his subordinates by their craftsmanship, to reward and to promote them accordingly. He resents demands made on him for the sake of business performance as interference with "good engineering," "smooth production," or "hard-hitting selling." The functional manager's legitimate desire for workmanship becomes, unless counterbalanced, a centrifugal force which tears the enterprise apart and converts it into a loose confederation of functional empires, each concerned only with its own craft, each jealously guarding its own "secrets," each bent on enlarging its own domain rather than on building the business.

This danger will be greatly intensified by the technological changes now under way. The number of highly educated specialists working in the business enterprise is bound to increase tremendously. And so will the level of workmanship demanded of these specialists. The tendency to make the craft or function an end in itself will therefore be even more marked than it is today. But at the same time the new technology will demand much closer co-ordination between specialists. And it will demand that functional men even at the lowest management level see the business as a whole and understand what it requires of them. The new technology will need both the drive for excellence in workmanship and the consistent direction of managers at all levels toward the common goal.

Misdirection by the Boss

The hierarchical structure of management aggravates the danger. What the "boss" does and says, his most casual remarks, his habits, even his mannerisms, tend to appear to his subordinates as calculated, planned and meaningful.

"All you ever hear around the place is human-relations talk; but when the boss calls you on the carpet it is always because the burden figure is too high; and when it comes to promoting a guy, the plums always go to those who do the best job filling out accounting-department forms." This is one of the most common tunes, sung with infinite variations on every level of management. It leads to poor performance—even in cutting the burden figure. It also expresses loss of confidence in, and absence of respect for, the company and its management.

Yet the manager who so misdirects his subordinates does not intend to do so. He genuinely considers human relations to be the most important task of his plant managers. But he talks about the burden figure because he feels that he has to establish himself with his men as a "practical man," or because he thinks that he shows familiarity with their problems by talking their "shop." He stresses the accounting-department forms only because they annoy him as much as they do his men—or he may just not want to have any more trouble with the comptroller than he can help. But to his subordinates these reasons are hidden; all they see and hear is the question about the burden figure, the emphasis on forms.

The solution to this problem requires a structure of management which focuses both the manager's and his boss's eyes on what the job—rather than the boss—demands. To stress behavior and attitudes—as does a good deal of current management literature—cannot solve the problem. It is likely instead to aggravate it by making managers self-conscious in their relationships. Indeed, everyone familiar with business today has seen situations in which a manager's attempt to avoid misdirection through changing his behavior has converted a fairly satisfactory relationship into a nightmare of embarrassment and misunderstanding. The manager himself has become so self-conscious as to lose all easy relationship with his men. And the men in turn react with: "So help us, the old man has read a book; we used to know what he wanted of us, now we have to guess."

Differences in Levels of Management

The misdirection that can result from the difference in concern and function between various levels of management is illustrated by this story. I call it "the mystery of the broken washroom door."

The newly appointed comptroller of a railroad in the Northwest noticed, when going through the accounts, that extraordinarily large sums were spent each year for the replacement of broken doors in passenger stations. He found that washroom doors in small stations were supposed to be kept locked, with the key obtainable from the ticket agent on request. For economy reasons the agent was only issued one key per door—a long-defunct president had decreed this economy measure and had preened himself on thus saving the company two hundred dollars at one stroke. Hence when a customer walked off without returning the key—as happened all the time—the agent had a locked door on his hands and no means of opening it. To get a new key made—cost twenty cents—was, however regarded as a "capital expenditure"; and agents could make capital expenditures only with the approval of the Superintendent of Passenger Service at company headquarters, which it took six months to obtain. "Emergency repairs," however, an agent could make on his own and pay for out of his cash account. There could be no clearer emergency than a broken washroom door—and every small station has an ax!

This may seem the height of absurdity. But every business has its "broken washroom doors," its misdirections, its policies, procedures and methods that emphasize and reward wrong behavior, penalize or inhibit right behavior. In most cases the results are more serious than an annual twenty-thousand-dollar bill for washroom doors.

This problem, too, cannot be solved by attitudes and behavior; for it is rooted in the structure of the enterprise. Nor can it be solved by "better communications"; for communications presuppose common understanding and a common language, and it is precisely that which is usually lacking.

It is no accident that the old story of the blind men meeting up with an elephant on the road is so popular among management people. For each level of management sees the same "elephant"—the business—from a different angle of vision. The production foreman, like the blind man who felt the elephant's leg and decided that a tree was in his way, tends to see only the immediate production problems. Top management—the blind man feeling the trunk and deciding a snake bars his way—tends to see only the enterprise as a whole; it sees stockholders, financial problems, altogether a host of highly abstract relations and figures. Operating management—the blind man feeling the elephant's belly and thinking himself up against a landslide—tends to see things functionally. Each level needs its particular vision; it could not do its job without it. Yet, these visions are so different that people on different levels talking about the same thing often do not realize it—or, as frequently happens, believe that they are talking about the same thing, when in reality they are poles apart.

An effective management must direct the vision and efforts of all managers toward a common goal. It must insure that the individual manager understands what results are demanded of him. It must insure that the superior understands what to expect of each of his subordinate managers. It must motivate each manager to maximum efforts in the right direction. And while encouraging high standards of workmanship, it must make them the means to the end of business performance rather than ends in themselves.

What Should the Objectives of a Manager Be?

Each manager, from the "big boss" down to the production foreman or the chief clerk, needs clearly spelled-out objectives. These objectives should lay out what performance the man's own managerial unit is supposed to produce. They should lay out what contribution he and his unit are expected to make to help other units obtain their objectives. Finally, they should spell out what contribution the manager can expect from other units toward the attainment of his own objectives. Right from the start, in other words, emphasis should be on teamwork and team results.

These objectives should always derive from the goals of the business enterprise. In one company, I have found it practicable and effective to provide even a foreman with a detailed statement of not only his own objectives but those of the company and of the manufacturing department. Even though the company is so large as to make the distance between the individual foreman's production and the company's total output all but astronomical, the result has been a significant increase in production. Indeed, this must follow if we mean it when we say that the foreman is "part of management." For it is the definition of a manager that in what he does he takes responsibility for the whole—that, in cutting stone, he "builds the cathedral."

The objectives of every manager should spell out his contribution to the attainment of company goals in *all areas* of the business. Obviously, not every manager has a direct contribution to make in every area. The contribution which marketing makes to productivity, for example, may be very small. But if a manager and his unit are not expected to contribute toward any one of the areas that significantly affect prosperity and survival of the business, this fact should be clearly brought out. For managers must understand that business results depend on a balance of efforts and results in a number of areas. This is necessary both to give full scope to the craftsmanship of each function and specialty, and to prevent the empire-building and clannish jealousies of the various functions and specialties. It is necessary also to avoid overemphasis on any one key area.

To obtain balanced efforts the objectives of all managers on all levels and in all areas should also be keyed to both short-range and long-range considerations. And, of course, all objectives should always contain both the tangible business objectives and the intangible objectives for manager organization and development, worker performance and attitude and public responsibility. Anything else is shortsighted and impractical.

Management by "Drives"

Proper management requires balanced stress on objectives, especially by top management. It rules out the common and pernicious business malpractice: management by "crisis" and "drives."

There may be companies in which management people do not say: "The only way we ever get anything done around here is by making a drive on it." Yet, "management by drive" is the rule rather than the exception. That things always collapse into the *status quo ante* three weeks after the drive is over, everybody knows and apparently expects. The only result of an "economy drive" is likely to be that messengers and typists get fired, and that $15,000 executives are forced to do $50-a-week work typing their own letters. And yet many managements have not drawn the obvious conclusion that drives are, after all, not the way to get things done.

But over and above its ineffectiveness, management by drive nisdirects. It puts all emphasis on one phase of the job to the inevitable detriment of everything else.

"For four weeks we cut inventories," a case-hardened veteran of management by crisis once summed it up. "Then we have four weeks of cost-cutting, followed by four weeks of human relations. We just have time to push customer service and courtesy for a month. And then the inventory is back where it was when we started. We don't even try to do our job. All management talks about, thinks about, preaches about, is last week's inventory figure or this week's customer complaints. How we do the rest of the job they don't even want to know."

In an organization which manages by drives people either neglect their job to get on with the current drive, or silently organize for collective sabotage of the drive to get their work done. In either event they become deaf to the cry of "wolf." And when the real crisis comes, when all hands should drop everything and pitch in, they treat it as just another case of management-created hysteria.

Management by drive, like management by "bellows and meat ax," is a sure sign of confusion. It is an admission of incompetence. It is a sign that management does not know how to plan. But, above all, it is a sign that the company does not know what to expect of its managers—that, not knowing how to direct them, it misdirects them.

How Should Managers' Objectives Be Set and by Whom?

By definition, a manager is responsible for the contribution that his component makes to the larger unit above him and eventually to the enterprise. His performance aims upward rather than downward. This means that the goals of each manager's job must be defined by the contribution he has to make to the success of the larger unit of which he is a part. The objectives of the district sales manager's job should be defined by the contribution he and his district sales force have to make to the sales department, the objectives of the project engineer's job by the contribution he, his engineers and draftsmen make to the engineering department The objectives of the general manager of a decentralized division should be defined by the contribution his division has to make to the objectives of the parent company.

This requires each manager to develop and set the objectives of his unit himself. Higher management must, of course, reserve the power to approve or disapprove these objectives. But their development is part of a manager's responsibility; indeed, it is his first responsibility. It means, too, that every manager should responsibly participate in the development of the objectives of the higher unit of which his is a part. To "give him a sense of participation" (to use a pet phrase of the "human relations" jargon) is not enough. Being a manager demands the assumption of a genuine responsibility. Precisely because his aims should reflect the objective needs of the business, rather than merely what the individual manager wants, he must commit himself to them with a positive act of assent. He must know and understand the ultimate business goals, what is expected of him and why, what he will be measured against and how. There must be a "meeting of minds" within the entire management of each unit. This can be achieved only when each of the contributing managers is expected to think through what the unit objectives are, is led, in others words, to participate actively and responsibly in the work of defining them. And only if his lower managers participate in this way can the higher manager know what to expect of them and can make exacting demands.

This is so important that some of the most effective managers I know go one step further. They have each of their subordinates write a "manager's letter" twice a year. In this letter to his superior, each manager first defines the objectives of his superior's job and of his own job as he sees them. He then sets down the performance standards which he believes are being applied to him. Next, he lists the things he must do himself to attain these goals—and the things within his own unit he considers the major obstacles. He lists the things his superior and the company do that help him and the things that hamper him. Finally, he outlines what he proposes to do during the next year to reach his goals. If his superior accepts this statement, the "manager's letter" becomes the charter under which the manager operates.

This device, like no other I have seen, brings out how easily the unconsidered and casual remarks of even the best "boss" can confuse and misdirect. One large company has used the "manager's letter" for ten years. Yet almost every letter still lists as objectives and standards things which completely baffle the superior to whom the letter is addressed. And whenever he asks: "What is this?" he gets the answer: "Don't you remember what you said last spring going down with me in the elevator?"

The "manager's letter" also brings out whatever inconsistencies there are in the demands made on a man by his superior and by the company. Does the superior demand both speed and high quality when he can get only one or the other? And what compromise is needed in the interest of the company? Does he demand initiative and judgment of his men but also that they check back with him before they do anything? Does he ask for their ideas and suggestions but never uses them or discusses them? Does the company expect a small engineering force to be available immediately whenever something goes wrong in the plant, and yet bend all its efforts to the completion of new designs? Does it expect a manager to maintain high standards of performance but forbid him to remove poor performers? Does it create the conditions under which people say: "I can get the work done as long as I can keep the boss from knowing what I am doing?"

These are common situations. They undermine spirit and performance. The "manager's letter" may not prevent them. But at least it brings them out in the open, shows where compromises have to be made, objectives have to be thought through, priorities have to be established, behavior has to be changed.

As this device illustrates: managing managers requires special efforts not only to establish common direction, but to eliminate misdirection. Mutual understanding can never be attained by "communications down," can never be created by talking. It can result only from "communications up." It requires both the superior's willingness to listen and a tool especially designed to make lower managers heard.

Self-control through Measurements

The greatest advantage of management by objectives is perhaps that it makes it possible for a manager to control his own performance. Self-control means stronger motivation: a desire to do the best rather than just enough to get by. It means higher performance goals and broader vision. Even if management by objectives were not necessary to give the enterprise the unity of direction and effort of a management team, it would be necessary to make possible management by self-control.

So far in this book I have not talked of "control" at all; I have talked of "measurements." This was intentional. For "control" is an ambiguous word. It means the ability to direct oneself and one's work. It can also mean domination of one person by another. Objectives are the basis of "control" in the first sense; but they must never become the basis of "control" in the second, for this would defeat their purpose. Indeed, one of the major contributions of management by objectives is that it enables us to substitute management by self-control for management by domination.

That management by self-control is highly desirable will hardly be disputed in America or in American business today. Its acceptance underlies all the talk of "pushing decisions down to the lowest possible level," or of "paying people for results." But to make management by self-control a reality requires more than acceptance of the concept as right and desirable. It requires new tools and far reaching changes in traditional thinking and practices.

To be able to control his own performance a manager needs to know more than what his goals are He must be able to measure his performance and results against the goal. It should indeed be an invariable practice to supply managers with clear and common measurements in all key areas of a business. These measurements need not be rigidly quantitative; nor need they be exact. But they have to be clear, simple and rational. They have to be relevant and direct attention and efforts where they should go. They have to be reliable—at least to the point where their margin of error is acknowledged and understood. And they have to be, so to speak, self-announcing, understandable without complicated interpretation or philosophical discussion

Each manager should have the information he needs to measure his own performance and should receive it soon enough to make any changes necessary for the desired results. And this information should go to the manager himself, and not to his superior. It should be the means of self-control, not a tool of control from above.

This needs particular stress today, when our ability to obtain such information is growing rapidly as a result of technological progress in information gathering, analysis and synthesis. Up till now information on important facts was either not obtainable at all, or could be assembled only so late as to be of little but historical interest. This former inability to produce measuring information was not an unmixed curse. For while it made effective self-control difficult, it also made difficult effective control of a manager from above; in the absence of information with which to control him, the manager had to be allowed to work as he saw fit.

Our new ability to produce measuring information will make possible effective self-control; and if so used, it will lead to a tremendous advance in the effectiveness and performance of management. But if this new ability is abused to impose control on managers from above, the new technology will inflict incalculable harm by demoralizing management, and by seriously lowering the effectiveness of managers.

That information can be effectively used for self-control is shown by the example of General Electric:

General Electric has a special control service—the traveling auditors. The auditors study every one of the managerial units of the company thoroughly at least once a year. But their report goes to the manager of the unit studied. There can be little doubt that the feeling of confidence and trust in the company that even casual contact with General Electric managers reveals is directly traceable to this practice of using information for self-control rather than for control from above.

But the General Electric practice is by no means common or generally understood. Typical management thinking is much closer to the practice exemplified by a large chemical company.

In this company a control section audits every one of the managerial units of the company. The results of the audits do not go, however, to the managers audited. They go only to the president who then calls in the managers to confront them with the audit of their operations. What this has done to morale is shown in the nickname the company's managers have given the control section: "the president's Gestapo." Indeed, more and more managers are now running their units not to obtain the best performance but to obtain the best showing on the control-section audits.

This should not be misunderstood as advocacy of low performance standards or absence of control. On the contrary, management by objectives and self-control is primarily a means to obtain standards higher than are to be found in most companies today. And every manager should be held strictly accountable for the results of his performance.

But what he does to reach these results he—and only he—should control. It should be clearly understood what behavior and methods the company bars as unethical, unprofessional or unsound. But within these limits every manager must be free to decide what he has to do. And only if he has all the information regarding his operations can he fully be held accountable for results.

The Proper Use of Reports and Procedures

Management by self-control requires complete rethinking concerning our use of reports, procedures and forms.

Reports and procedures are necessary tools. But few tools can be so easily misused, and few can do as much damage. For reports and procedures, when misused, cease to be tools and become malignant masters.

There are three common misuses of reports and procedures. The first is the all too common belief that procedures are instruments of morality. They are not; their principle is exclusively that of economy. They never decide what should be done, only how it might be done most expeditiously. Problems of right conduct can never be "proceduralized" (surely the most horrible word in the bureaucrat's jargon); conversely, right conduct can never be established by procedure.

The second misuse is to consider procedures a substitute for judgment. Procedures can work only where judgment is no longer required, that is, in the repetitive situation for whose handling the judgment has already been supplied and tested. Our civilization suffers from a superstitious belief in the magical effect of printed forms. And the superstition is most dangerous when it leads us into trying to handle the exceptional, non-routine situation by procedure. In fact, it is the test of a good procedure that it quickly identifies the situations that, even in the most routine of processes, do not fit the pattern but require special handling and decision based on judgment.

But the most common misuse of reports and procedures is as an instrument of control from above. This is particularly true of those that aim at supplying information to higher management—the "forms" of everyday business life. The common case of the plant manager who has to fill out twenty forms to supply accountants, engineers or staff people in central office with information he himself does not need, is only one of thousands of examples. As a result the man's attention is directed away from his own job. The things he is asked about or required to do for control purposes, come to appear to him as reflections of what the company wants of him, become to him the essence of his job; while resenting them, he tends to put effort into these things rather than into his own job. Eventually, his boss, too, is misdirected, if not hypnotized, by the procedure.

A large insurance company, a few years ago, started a big program for the "improvement of management." To this end it built up a strong central-office organization concerned with such things as renewal ratios, claim settlement, selling costs, sales methods, etc. This organization did excellent work—top management learned a lot about running an insurance company. But actual performance has been going down ever since. For the managers in the field spend more and more time filling out reports, less and less doing their work. Worse still, they soon learned to subordinate performance to a "good showing." Not only did performance go to pieces—spirit suffered ever more. Top management and its staff experts came to be viewed by the field managers as enemies to be outsmarted or at least kept as far away as possible.

Similar stories exist *ad infinitum*—in every industry and in companies of every size. To some extent the situation is caused by the fallacy of the "staff" concept which will be discussed later on in this book. But, above all, it is the result of the misuse of procedures as control.

Reports and procedures should be kept to a minimum, and used only when they save time and labor. They should be as simple as possible.

One of our leading company presidents tells the following story on himself. Fifteen years ago he bought for his company a small independent plant in Los Angeles. The plant had been making a profit of $250,000 a year; and it was purchased on that basis. When going through the plant with the owner—who stayed on as plant manager—the president asked: "How do you determine your pricing?" "That's easy," the former owner answered; "we just quote ten cents per thousand less than your company does." "And how do you control your costs?" was the next question. "That's easy," was the answer; "we know what we pay for raw materials and labor and what production we ought to get for the money." "And how do you control your overhead?" was the final question. "We don't bother about it."

Well, thought the president, we can certainly save a lot of money here by introducing our thorough controls. But a year later the profit of the plant was down to $125,000; sales had remained the same and prices had remained the same; but the introduction of complex procedures had eaten up half the profit.

Every business should regularly find out whether it needs all the reports and procedures it uses. At least once every five years every form should be put on trial for its life. I once had to recommend an even more drastic measure to clear up a situation in which reports and forms, luxuriating like the Amazon rain forest, threatened to choke the life out of an old established utility company. I suggested that all reports be suspended simultaneously for two months, and only those be allowed to return which managers still demanded after living without them. This cut reports and forms in the company by three quarters.

Reports and procedures should focus only on the performance needed to achieve results in the key areas. To "control" everything is to control nothing. And to attempt to control the irrelevant always misdirects.

Finally, reports and procedures should be the tool of the man who fills them out. They must never themselves become the measure of his performance. A man must never be judged by the quality of the production forms he fills out—unless he be the clerk in charge of these forms. He must always be judged by his production performance. And the only way to make sure of this is by having him fill out no forms, make no reports, except those he needs himself to achieve performance.

A Philosophy of Management

What the business enterprise needs is a principle of management that will give full scope to individual strength and responsibility, and at the same time give common direction of vision and effort, establish team work and harmonize the goals of the individual with the common weal.

The only principle that can do this is management by objectives and self-control. It makes the common weal the aim of every manager. It substitutes for control from outside the stricter, more exacting and more effective control from the inside. It motivates the manager to action not because somebody tells him to do something or talks him into doing it, but because the objective needs of his task demand it. He acts not because somebody wants him to but because he himself decides that he has to—he acts, in other words, as a free man.

The word "philosophy" is tossed around with happy abandon these days in management circles. I have even seen a dissertation, signed by a vice-president, on the "philosophy of handling purchase requisitions" (as far as I could figure out "philosophy" here meant that purchase requisitions had to be in triplicate). But management by objectives and self-control may legitimately be called a "philosophy" of management. It rests on a concept of the job of management. It rests on an analysis of the specific needs of the management group and the obstacles it faces. It rests on a concept of human action, human behavior and human motivation. Finally, it applies to every manager, whatever his level and function, and to any business enterprise whether large or small. It insures performance by converting objective needs into personal goals. And this is genuine freedom, freedom under the law.

CHAPTER 12

MANAGERS MUST MANAGE

What is a manager's job?—Individual tasks and team tasks—The span of managerial responsibility—The manager's authority—The manager and his superior.

What Is a Manager's Job?

A manager's job should be based on a task to be performed in order to attain the company's objectives. It should always be a real job—one that makes a visible and, if possible, clearly measurable contribution to the success of the enterprise. It should have the broadest rather than the narrowest scope and authority; everything not expressly excluded should be deemed to be within the manager's authority. Finally, the manager should be directed and controlled by the objectives of performance rather than by his boss.

What managerial jobs are needed and what each of them is should always be determined by the activities that have to be performed, the contributions that have to be made to attain the company's objectives. A manager's job exists because the task facing the enterprise demands its existence—and for no other reason. It has its own necessity; it must therefore have its own authority and its own responsibility.

It should always be a job of managerial proportions. Since a manager is someone who takes responsibility for, and contributes to, the final results of the enterprise, the job must have sufficient scope. It should always embody the maximum challenge, carry the maximum responsibility and make the maximum contribution. And that contribution should be visible and measurable. The manager should be able to point at the final results of the entire business and say: "This part is my contribution."

There are some tasks which are too big for one man and which can still not be cut up into a number of integrated, finite jobs. These should be organized as team tasks.

Outside of business, team organization is widely recognized. Almost any scientific paper, for instance, bears the names of three or four men. Every one of the four—the biochemist, the physiologist, the pediatrician and the surgeon—does a specific kind of work. Yet though each contributes only his own skill, each is responsible for the entire job. There is, of course, always a leader to the team; but though his authority is great, it is guidance rather than supervision or command. It derives from knowledge rather than from rank.

In business, teams are used a good deal more than the literature indicates. They are regularly employed for short-term assignments in every large company. They are common in research work. Team organization, rather than the hierarchy of rank shown on the organization chart, is the reality in the well-run manufacturing plant, especially in respect to the relationship between the plant manager and the heads of the technical functions reporting to him. Many tasks in process manufacturing or in mass production new style can only be done if organized on a team basis.

But the most important team task in any business is the top-management task. In scope, as well as in its requirements of skills, temperaments and kinds of work, it exceeds any one man's capacity. No matter what the textbooks and the organization charts say, well-managed companies do not have a one-man "chief executive." They have an executive team.

It is therefore of genuine importance that management understand what team organization is, when to use it and how. Above all, it is important that management realize that in any real team each member has a clearly assigned and clearly defined role. A team is not just chaos made into a virtue. Teamwork requires actually more internal organization, more co-operation and greater definiteness of individual assignments than work organized in individual jobs.

The Span of Managerial Responsibility

In discussing how big a manager's job should be, the textbooks start out with the observation that one man can *supervise* only a very small number of people—the so-called "span of control." And this in turn leads to that deformation of management: levels upon levels, which impede co-operation and communication, stifle the development of tomorrow's managers and erode the meaning of the management job.

If the manager, however, is controlled by the objective requirements of his own job and measured by his results, there is no need for the kind of supervision that consists of telling a subordinate what to do and then making sure that he does it. There is no span of control. A superior could theoretically have any number of subordinates reporting to him. There is, indeed, a limit set by the "span of managerial responsibility" (the term was coined, I believe, by Dr. H. H. Race of General Electric): the number of people whom one superior can assist, teach and help to reach the objectives of their own jobs. This is a real limit; but it is not fixed.

The span of control, we are told, cannot exceed six or eight subordinates. The span of managerial responsibility, however, is determined by the extent to which assistance and teaching are needed. It can only be set by a study of the concrete situation. Unlike the span of control, the span of managerial responsibility broadens as we move upward in the organization. Junior managers need the most assistance; their objectives are least easy to define sharply, their performance least easy to measure concretely. Senior men, on the other hand, have supposedly learned how to do their job; and their objectives can be defined as directly contributing to the business, their performance measured by the yardsticks of business results.

The span of managerial responsibility is therefore wider than the span of control. (H. H. Race thinks that the theoretical limit is around a hundred.) And where good practice would counsel against stretching the span of control, a manager should always have responsibility for a few more men than he can really take care of. Otherwise the temptation is to supervise them, that is, to take over their jobs or, at least, to breathe down their necks.[1]

[1] This point has been made with a wealth of supporting evidence by James C. Worthy, formerly of Sears, Roebuck and now of the U. S. Department of Commerce.

Whether a manager's subordinates are individuals or teams makes no difference in the span of managerial responsibility. However, a team should always have a small number of members. The largest functioning team I have found in business is the Board of Directors of Standard Oil. It is a Board composed exclusively of full-time officers of the company, and it is actually the top management of one of the world's largest, most extensive, most complicated and most successful businesses. Hence its membership of fourteen does not seem excessive. Still, a team so large can function only if it rigidly disciplines itself. The Standard Oil Board, for instance, never takes any decision except unanimously. For ordinary purposes, however, this procedure is too elaborate. Teams should normally not exceed five or six in number; and they work best, as a rule, if they have three or four members.

A team does not normally make a good superior manager. It should, in other words, have no subordinate managers—though individual members of the team may well have them. Assisting and teaching, the elements of managerial responsibility, are best performed by an individual.

The Manager's Authority

That each manager's job be given the broadest possible scope and authority is nothing but a rephrasing of the rule that decisions be pushed down as far as possible and be taken as close as possible to the action to which they apply. In its effects, however, this requirement leads to sharp deviations from the traditional concept of delegation from above.

What activities and tasks the enterprise requires is indeed worked out from the top down, so to speak. The analysis has to begin with the desired end product: the objectives of business performance and business results. From these the analysis determines step by step what work has to be performed. But in organizing the manager's job we have to work from the bottom up. We have to begin with the activities on the "firing line"—the jobs responsible for the actual output of goods and services, for the final sale to the customer, for the production of blueprints and engineering drawings.

The managers on the firing line have the basic management jobs—the ones on whose performance everything else ultimately rests. Seen this way, the jobs of higher management are derivative, are, in the last analysis, aimed at helping the firing-line manager do his job. Viewed structurally and organically, it is the firing-line manager in whom all authority and responsibility center; only what he cannot do himself passes up to higher management. He is, so to speak, the gene of organization in which all higher organs are prefigured and out of which they are developed.

Quite obviously there are real limits to the decisions the firing-line manager can or should make, and with them to the authority and responsibility he should have.

He is limited as to the extent of his authority. A production foreman has no business changing a salesman's compensation. A regional sales manager has no authority in somebody else's region, etc. He is also limited as to the kind of decision he can make. Clearly he should not make decisions that affect other managers. He should not make decisions that affect the whole business and its spirit. It is only elementary prudence, for instance, not to allow any manager to make by himself and without review a decision on the career and future of one of his subordinates.

The firing-line manager should not be expected to make decisions which he cannot make. A man responsible for immediate performance does not have the time, for instance, to make long-range decisions. A production man lacks the knowledge and competence to work out a pension plan or a medical program. These decisions certainly affect him and his operations; he should know them, understand them, indeed participate as much as is humanly possible in their preparation and formulation. But he cannot make them. Hence he cannot have the authority and responsibility for them; for authority and responsibility should always be task-focused. This applies all the way up the management hierarchy to the chief executive job itself.

There is one simple rule for setting the limitations on the decisions a manager is authorized to make. The management charter of General Electric's Lamp Division in paraphrasing the U. S. Constitution expresses it by saying: "All authority not expressly and in writing reserved to higher management is granted to lower management." This is the opposite of the old Prussian idea of a citizen's rights: "Everything that is not expressly allowed is forbidden." In other words, the decisions which a manager is not entitled to make within the extent of his task should always be spelled out; for all others he should be supposed to have authority and responsibility.

The Manager and His Superior

What then is the job of the manager's superior? What is his authority? What is his responsibility?

If only for aesthetic reasons, I am not over-fond of the term "Bottom-up Management," coined by William B. Given, Jr., of the American Brake Shoe Company.[2]

What it means, however, is important. The relationship between higher and lower manager is not just the downward relationship expressed in the term "supervision." Indeed, it is not even a two-way, up-and-down relationship. It has three dimensions: a relationship up from the lower to the higher manager; a relationship of every manager to the enterprise; and a relationship down from the higher to the lower manager. And every one of the three is essentially a responsibility—a duty rather than a right.

Every manager has the task of contributing what his superior's unit needs to attain its objectives. This is indeed his first duty. From it he derives the objectives of his own job.

He has secondly a duty toward the enterprise. He has to analyze the task of his own unit, and define the activities needed to attain its objectives. He has to establish the management jobs these activities require, and he has to help his managers to work together and to integrate their own interests with those of the enterprise. He has to put men in these jobs. He has to remove managers in his unit who fail to perform, reward those who perform well and see to it that those who perform superbly receive extraordinary return or promotion. He has to help the managers in his unit to develop to the limit of their capacities and prepare themselves for the management tasks of tomorrow.

These are heavy responsibilities. But they are not responsibilities for what somebody else—a subordinate—is doing. They are, as all responsibilities should be, responsibilities for what the manager himself is doing. They are inherent in his own job, not in those of his subordinates.

[2] In his book *Bottom-up Management*, (New York: Harper & Brothers, 1949).

Finally, the manager has responsibilities downward, to his subordinate managers. He has first to make sure that they know and understand what is demanded of them. He has to help them set their own objectives. Then he has to help them to reach these objectives. He is therefore responsible for their getting the tools, the staff, the information they need. He has to help them with advice and counsel. He has, if need be, to teach them to do better.

If a one-word definition of this downward relationship be needed, "assistance" would come closest. Indeed, several successful companies—notably International Business Machines (IBM)—have defined the manager's job in relation to his subordinates as that of an "assistant" to them. Their jobs are theirs—by objective necessity. Their performance and results are theirs, and so is the responsibility. But it is the duty of the superior manager to help them all he can to attain their objectives.

The Catholic Church is customarily considered to exercise authoritarian control over its priests. A Bishop can appoint a priest to a parish (though he cannot remove him except for cause and after a hearing). The Bishop can set up new parishes and abolish or merge existing ones. But he cannot tell a parish priest what to do; that is determined objectively by the nature of the job and laid down in the charter of the Church, Canon Law. Nor can the Bishop himself exercise the functions of the parish priest; as long as the parish has a duly appointed priest the authority and the responsibility of the office are exclusively his. In theology each priest holds office by delegation through Apostolic Succession; in law he has original and sole authority grounded in the objective requirement of his function and limited only by the limits of his function.

The objectives of a managerial unit should always and exclusively consist of the performance and results it has to contribute to the success of the enterprise. They should always and exclusively focus upward. But the objectives of the manager who heads the unit include what he himself has to do to help his subordinate managers attain their objectives. The vision of a manager should always be upward—toward the enterprise as a whole. But his responsibility runs downward as well—to the managers on his team. That his relationship toward them be clearly understood as duty rather than as supervision is perhaps the central requirement for organizing the manager's job effectively.

CHAPTER 13

THE SPIRIT OF AN ORGANIZATION

To make common men do uncommon things: the test of performance—Focus on strength—Practices, not preachments—The danger of safe mediocrity—"You can't get rich but you won't get fired"—"We can't promote him but he has been here too long to get fired"—The need for appraisal—Appraisal by performance and for strengths—Compensation as reward and incentive—Does delayed compensation pay?—Overemphasizing promotion—A rational promotion system—The "life and death" decisions—Managers' self-examination of the spirit of their organization—Whom not to appoint to management jobs—What about leadership?

Two sayings sum up the "spirit of an organization." One is the inscription on Andrew Carnegie's tombstone:

Here lies a man
Who knew how to enlist
In his service
Better men than himself

The other is the slogan of the drive to find jobs for the physically handicapped: "It's the abilities, not the disabilities, that count."

Management by objectives tells a manager what he ought to do. The proper organization of his job enables him to do it. But it is the spirit of the organization that determines whether he will do it. It is the spirit that motivates, that calls upon a man's reserves of dedication and effort, that decides whether he will give his best or do just enough to get by.

It is the purpose of an organization to "make common men do

uncommon things"—this phrasing is Lord Beveridge's. No organization can depend on genius; the supply is always scarce and always unpredictable. But it is the test of an organization that it make ordinary human beings perform better than they are capable of, that it bring out whatever strength there is in its members and use it to make all the other members perform more and better. It is the test of an organization that it neutralize the weaknesses of its members.

Good spirit requires that there be full scope for individual excellence. Whenever excellence appears, it must be recognized, encouraged and rewarded, and must be made productive for all other members of the organization. Good spirit therefore requires that the focus be on the strengths of a man—on what he can do rather than on what he cannot do. It requires constant improvement of the competence and performance of the whole group; yesterday's good performance must become today's minimum, yesterday's excellence today's commonplace.

Altogether the test of good spirit is not that "people get along together"; it is performance, not conformance. "Good human relations" that are not grounded in the satisfaction of good performance and the harmony of proper working relations are actually poor human relations and result in poor spirit. They do not make people grow; they make them conform and contract. I shall never forget the university president who once said to me: "It is my job to make it possible for the first-rate teacher to teach. Whether he gets along with his colleagues or with me—and very few of the really good teachers do either—is irrelevant. We certainly have a collection of problem children here—but, boy, do they teach." And when his successor substituted for this a policy of "peace and harmony," both the performance and the spirit of the faculty rapidly went to pieces.

Conversely, there is no greater indictment of an organization than that the strength and ability of the outstanding man become a threat to the group and his performance a source of difficulty, frustration and discouragement for the others. And nothing destroys the spirit of an organization faster than focusing on people's weaknesses rather than on their strengths, building on disabilities rather than on abilities. The focus must be on strength.

Practice, not Preachments

Good spirit in a management organization means that the energy turned out is larger than the sum of the efforts put in. It means the creation of energy. This, clearly, cannot be accomplished by mechanical means. A mechanical contrivance can at its theoretical best conserve energy intact; it cannot create it. To get out more than is being put in is possible only in the moral sphere.

What is necessary to produce the proper spirit in management must therefore be morality. It can only be emphasis on strength, stress on integrity, and high standards of justice and conduct.

But morality does not mean preachments. Morality, to have any meaning at all, must be a principle of action. It must not be exhortation, serman or good intentions. *It must be practices.* To be effective, morality must, indeed, be independent of the abilities and the attitudes of people. It must be tangible behavior, things everyone can see, do and measure.

Lest I be accused of advocating hypocrisy, let me say that all the organizations in human history that have achieved greatness of spirit have done so through a code of practices. This is true of the United States Supreme Court with its ability to transform hack politicians into great judges. Practices make the famed *esprit de corps* of the U. S. Marines or of the British Navy. Practices—systematic and codified—underlie the spirit of the most successful "staff organization" in the world, the Jesuit Order.

Management therefore needs concrete, tangible, clear practices. These practices must stress building on strength rather than on weakness. They must motivate excellence. And they must express and make tangible that spirit is of the moral sphere, and that its foundation therefore is integrity.

There are five areas in which practices are required to insure the right spirit throughout the management organization.

1. There must be high performance requirements; no condoning of poor or mediocre performance; and rewards must be based on performance.
2. Each management job must be a rewarding job in itself rather than just a step in the promotion ladder.
3. There must be a rational and just promotion system.
4. Management needs a "charter" spelling out clearly who has the

power to make life-and-death decisions affecting a manager; and there should be some way for a manager to appeal to a higher court.

5. In its appointments management must demonstrate that it realizes that integrity is the one absolute requirement of a manager, the one quality that he has to bring with him and cannot be expected to acquire later on.

The Danger of Safe Mediocrity

Few things damn a company and its spirit as thoroughly as to have its managers say: "You can't get rich here but you won't get fired." This puts the emphasis on safe mediocrity. It breeds bureaucrats and penalizes what every business needs the most: entrepreneurs. It does not even, as often believed, encourage people to risk making a mistake; it discourages them altogether from trying anything new. It does not build spirit—only high performance can do that. Indeed, it does not even create a feeling of security. The security a management group needs is one grounded in the consciousness of high performance and its recognition.

The first requirement of management spirit, then, is a high demand on performance. Managers should not be driven, but they should drive themselves. Indeed, one of the major reasons for demanding that management be by objectives and that it be founded in the objective requirements of the job, is the need to have managers set high standards of performance for themselves.

Consistently poor or mediocre performance cannot be condoned, let alone rewarded. The manager who sets his goals low, or who consistently fails in performance, must not be allowed to remain in his job. He must be removed—and moved to a lower job or dismissed rather than "kicked upstairs."

This does not mean that people should be penalized for making mistakes. Nobody learns except by making mistakes. The better a man is the more mistakes will he make—for the more new things he will try. I would never promote a man into a top-level job who has not made mistakes, and big ones at that. Otherwise he is sure to be mediocre. Worse still, not having made mistakes he will not have learned how to spot them early and how to correct them.

That a man who consistently renders poor or mediocre performance should be removed from his job also does not mean that a company should ruthlessly fire people right and left. Management has a strong moral obligation to a man who has served the company long and faithfully. It also, like every other decision-making body, is committed by its own mistakes. If it makes a mistake in promoting a man, it should not fire him because his subsequent performance shows that he should never have been given the promotion. It may not be the fault of the man alone that he performs badly; the requirements of the job may have grown beyond his capacity over the years. Not so long ago the comptroller, for instance, was considered in many companies to be not much more than a senior bookkeeper. Today management is apt to look upon comptrollership as a major policy-making function. A comptroller perfectly adequate to the job ten years ago may well be incompetent to perform under the new concept of his function. Yet, he alone cannot be blamed; the rules of the game have been switched on him.

Whenever a man's failure can clearly be traced to management's mistakes, he has to be kept on the payroll. But, still, people who fail to perform must be removed from their present jobs. Management owes this to the enterprise. It owes it to the spirit of the management group, especially to those who perform well. It owes it to the man himself, for he is likely to be the major victim of his own inadequacy. This decision has to be taken whenever objective performance makes it necessary—regardless of the personal circumstances.

Whether the man should stay in the company's employ, however, is a different matter. While the policy governing the first decision should be strict, the policy governing the second should be considerate and lenient. Strict insistence on standards builds spirit and performance. But decisions on a person demand the greatest consideration for the individual.

One good illustration is the Ford Motor Company. When Henry Ford II took over, none of the nine management people in one department was found to be competent to take on the new jobs created in the course of reorganization. Not one was appointed to these new jobs. Yet, for all the men, jobs as technicians and experts were found within the organization, jobs which they could be expected to perform. It would have been easy to fire most of them. Their incompetence as managers was undisputed. And a new management coming in—especially under such extraordinary conditions—is considered entitled to make pretty drastic personnel changes. Yet, the new Ford management took the line that while no one should be allowed to hold a job without giving superior performance, no one should be penalized for the mistakes of the previous regime. And to the strict observance of this rule the company owes to a considerable extent its rapid revival. (Incidentally, seven of these men did indeed perform in their new jobs—one so well that he has been promoted into a bigger job than the one he originally held. Two men failed; one was pensioned off, one discharged.)

It is fairly easy in practice to combine insistence on superior performance with consideration for the individual. A real job—not "made work"—consonant with the person's capacities can almost always be found with effort and imagination. The frequent excuse: "We can't move him; he has been here too long to be fired," is bad logic and rarely more than a weak-kneed alibi. It does harm to the performance of management people, to their spirit and to their respect for the company.

The Need for Appraisal

Insistence on high goals and high performance requires that a man's ability both to set goals and to attain them be systematically appraised.

Day after day a manager makes decisions based on his appraisal of a man and his performance: in assigning work to him; in assigning people to work under him; in salary recommendations; in promotion recommendations, etc. The manager needs a systematic appraisal. Or else he wastes too much time on these decisions and still goes by hunch rather than by knowledge. The subordinate, too, must demand that these decisions be rational rather than hunch, for they more than anything else spell out what his superior expects and considers important.

For these reasons systematic appraisal of managers has become popular in this country, especially in the larger company. Many of these appraisal procedures require a specialist—often a psychological specialist. They focus on a man's potential. This may be sound psychology. But it is poor management. Appraisal should always be the direct responsibility of a man's manager. It should always focus on proven performance.

To appraise a subordinate and his performance is part of the manager's job. Indeed, unless he does the appraising himself he cannot adequately discharge his responsibility for assisting and teaching his subordinates. Nor can he adequately discharge his responsibility to the company for putting the right man in the job. The appraisal procedure should not be so difficult and complicated that it must be entrusted to the specialist. For this is abdication by the manager and evasion of his responsibility.

Appraisals must be based on performance. Appraisal is judgment; and judgment always requires a definite standard. To judge means to apply a set of values; and value judgments without clear, sharp and public standard are irrational and arbitrary They corrupt alike the judge and the judged. No matter how "scientific," no matter even how many insights it produces, an appraisal that focuses on "potential," on "personality," on "promise"—on anything that is not proven and provable performance—is an abuse.

There is nothing quite so unreliable as a judgment on long-range potential. Not only are few of us reliable judges of a man; nothing, also, may change as much as potential. The world is full of men whose youthful promise of excellence has turned into middle-aged mediocrity. It is full of men who started out as pedestrian plodders only to blossom out into star performers in their forties. To try to appraise a man's long-range potential is a worse gamble than to try to break the bank at Monte Carlo; and the more "scientific" the system, the greater the gamble.

But the greatest mistake is to try to build on weaknesses.

There is an old English anecdote to illustrate the point. The younger Pitt who was Prime Minister before he was out of his teens, and who supplied the courage, the resolution and the leadership for England's firm resistance to Napoleon in those bleak years when she stood alone against the tyrant who had conquered Europe, prided himself on the purity of his personal life. In an age of corruption he was scrupulously honest In an age of immorality he was a perfect husband and father. When he died, still a very young man, he presented himself at the Pearly Gates. St. Peter, the story goes, asked him: "And what makes you, a politician, think you belong up here?" The younger Pitt pointed out how he had not taken bribes, had not had mistresses and so forth. But St. Peter interrupted him rather gruffly: "We aren't a bit interested in what you didn't do; what *did* you do?"

One cannot do anything with what one cannot do. One cannot achieve anything with what one does not do. One can only build on strength. One can only achieve by doing. Appraisal must therefore aim first and foremost on bringing out what a man can do. Only when a man's strengths are known and understood does it make any sense to ask: What weaknesses does he need to overcome to make the progress his strengths would support? Weaknesses as such are of no interest—apart from usually being obvious enough A man's needs for doing better, knowing more, behaving differently, are the important things. They are the things that have to be accomplished for him to become a better, stronger and more effective person.

Compensation as Reward and Incentive

If one can "get fired" for poor performance, one must also be able to "get rich" for extraordinary performance. Rewards should be directly tied in with the objectives set for the manager's job. It is misdirection of the worst kind to tell managers that they have to balance objectives so as to preserve the long-term earning power of the business while basing their pay on immediate short-range profits.

Such misdirection occurred a few years back in a big pharmaceutical company. Management had emphasized that it wanted its senior chemists to work on basic research rather than on immediately saleable products. One year, one of the senior men came up with a discovery of major importance to the whole field of organic chemistry. But the discovery required many years of hard work before it could be turned into commercial products. And when the annual bonus was distributed, the chemist received just about the same sum he had gotten the year before. The big bonus went to a man who had made a large number of small and fairly easy but immediately saleable improvements in existing products. Management thought its behavior completely rational. The major discovery had contributed nothing to yearly profits; and the bonus was clearly based on yearly profits. But the man involved felt that management had convicted itself of dishonesty and double-dealing. He quit; and so did four or five of his colleagues—altogether the best chemists the company had. It still has difficulty recruiting first-rate research men.

Moreover, the salary system should never be so rigid as to exclude special rewards for "performance over and above the call of duty."

In one company I know a member of the engineering department, who himself never climbed beyond the bottom rungs on the promotion ladder, trained for many years all the young engineers that entered the company's employ—including four successive chief engineers. Everybody in the department knew what he was doing. Yet the value of his contribution was not recognized until he retired. Then the company had to hire a training director and two assistants to fill the gap. To the honor of the company, let it be said that it then made good its oversight through a substantial post-retirement gift to the old man.

Contributions of this kind should always be rewarded while they are being made. They may yield no directly measurable business results. But they build spirit and performance. They are rightly valued highly by the people in the organization who are apt to consider it a serious injustice if management fails to recognize and reward them. For it is the willingness of people to give of themselves over and above the demands of the job that distinguishes the great from the merely adequate organization. Any organization that has such a maker of men in its employ should count itself lucky—and forget that the salary limit for his job range is set at $8,500. The reward for such contributions should be rare like the Congressional Medal of Honor or the Victoria Cross. But it should also be as conspicuous and as great.

Financial rewards must not be bribes; they must not create the atmosphere in which executives can neither quit nor be fired. This raises serious doubts regarding the various schemes for delayed compensation that, for tax reasons, have lately become so popular in American business.

One example of their effect is that of the executive who for several years has been wanting to leave his company where his considerable qualities and aptitudes are not fully utilized. The man has had several attractive offers, but in every case he has turned the offer down at the last moment for the simple reason that he has a stake of $50,000 to $75,000 in delayed bonus with the company which he will only receive if he stays the next five years. As a result he is still in his old job but frustrated, bitter, torn in two directions and a source of discontent and dissatisfaction throughout an entire management group.

One cannot buy loyalty; one can only earn it. One must not bribe people into staying; they only blame the company for their own inability to resist the temptation. One must not make the penalty of firing a man so severe that one never imposes it. And one should not make executives security-conscious. Men who look upon their own affairs from the viewpoint of security are not likely to look at their work from a different angle of vision, are not likely to pioneer, to innovate and to reach out for the new.

I am all for offsetting the impact of confiscatory taxes on the executive. I believe it a serious danger to the welfare of our society and of our economy that managers are the only group that receives today conspicuously less income after taxes than it did in 1929. Higher gross pay is no solution; the tax rates would swallow it up, and the only effect would be to infuriate labor (for few workers understand the argument that income before taxes is not the income that counts). But there must be better ways of doing the job than the bribe of delayed compensation—ways that stress the manager's entrepreneurial function and reward him for his performance without making him a bondsman of the company.

Overemphasizing Promotion

Every management job itself should be rewarding and satisfying rather than just the means to the next step up on the promotion ladder. Even in the most rapidly growing business only a minority of management people will be promoted. For the rest, on every level, the job on which they are today is likely to be the job on which they stay till they retire or die. Overemphasis on promotion frustrates and demoralizes three or four out of every five management people. It also leads to the wrong kind of competitive spirit in which a man tries to get ahead at the expense of his fellow-workers.

To prevent overemphasis on promotion, the salary structure should offer rewards for extraordinary performance on the job that are comparable to the financial rewards of promotion. The salary range for every job level might, for instance, make it possible for a man who performs well to earn more than the average salary for the next higher job level and as much as the minimum salary for the job level beyond that. In other words, each man might have the opportunity, without promotion, to advance in salary by the equivalent of two promotional steps if his performance merits it.

But financial rewards alone are not enough. People, whether managers or workers, whether in business or outside, need rewards of prestige and pride.

This is specifically a problem for the large business. For the two areas in which this need is not being met today both lie primarily in the large enterprise: the outward symbols of prestige for the managers of large units within the business, and the outward symbols of prestige for the professional specialist.

A divisional manager in General Motors or in General Electric runs a business that is likely to be the leader in its industry. It is often many times as large or as important as any of the independent companies in the field. Yet his title is "General Manager," whereas the man who heads up the small independent competitor is called a "president" and enjoys all the status and recognition that go to the head of a business. It would seem almost elementary to give the men in the big companies a title that is in keeping with their responsibility and importance. They might be called "presidents" of the division, and their own divisional top management should then carry the title of "vice-president." That this makes no difference in the realities of the relationship within the business has been proven by a number of companies that are using the device—Union Carbide and Carbon and Johnson & Johnson are the best-known. But what a difference it makes to the status of the position, the pride of its holder, his incentive and the spirit of his organization!

Similarly, professional people should be given the incentive and recognition of professional status.

A Rational Promotion System

Even if not overemphasized, promotion will always loom large in the minds and in the ambitions of a management group. Proper spirit and performance therefore require a rational promotion system.

Promotion should always be based on proven performance. Nothing does more harm than the too common practice of promoting a poor man to get rid of him, or of denying a good man promotion because "we don't know what we'd do without him." The promotion system must insure that everybody who is eligible is considered—

and not just the most highly "visible" people. It must insure careful review of all promotional decisions by higher management to make difficult alike "kicking upstairs" and "hoarding good people."

The promotion system should also bring about full utilization of the managerial resources in the company's employ. The situation in which the promotional plums go to engineers, or to salesmen or accountants—or, as on many railroads, to clerks—is not only destructive of the spirit of the groups left out in the cold, but is also wasteful of a scarce and expensive resource. There are businesses where certain functional or technical backgrounds are needed for most of the better jobs. Those businesses should systematically hire lower-grade personnel for the other functions and realistically tell the men in these functions what to expect. But in the great majority of businesses lopsided promotional opportunities reflect nothing but the dead hand of tradition, confused objectives, mental laziness or promotion by "high visibility" rather than by proven competence.

Promotion should not be entirely from within. This should indeed be the norm, but it is important not to let a management become inbred, not to foster smugness and isolation. And the bigger the company, the more desirable is the outsider. It should be clearly understood throughout the company that people from the outside will be brought in periodically even into high management positions, and that once in the company, they are to be given the same treatment as the "old-timers" who came up "the proper way."

The history of Sears, Roebuck shows how important this can be. No one reared in the mail-order business could have brought about the expansion into retail stores which insured the growth of the company. For this General Wood had to be imported. Similarly, the revival of Ford required bringing men from the outside right into the top spots. And only if men are brought in all the time—rather than during a crisis—can the crisis be avoided or anticipated.

The Management Charter

Promotion decisions are what I call "life-and-death" decisions for managers. So are decisions to dismiss or to demote a manager, decisions on his salary and on the scope of his job. Hardly less important to the manager are decisions on the scope and work of his unit—capital investments, for instance. Even the appraisal vitally affects a manager's life and career in the company. These decisions are too important to be left to one man's unaided judgment.

In respect to appraisals this is generally recognized; many appraisal systems demand that a manager review his appraisals of his subordinates with his own superior. In a few companies this principle is extended to all decisions affecting a manager's status, pay or position. General Electric, for instance, requires that all such decisions be approved by the superior of the manager making the decision before they are put into effect. But in most companies such a rule is observed only for appointments to top positions. In respect to lower managers, there is normally neither clear understanding who is responsible, nor any safeguard against the faulty or arbitrary judgment of one man. And decisions other than those directly affecting a man's promotion, demotion, dismissal and salary are commonly left dangling in mid-air.

A manager should know who makes these decisions. He should know whom he has to consult in making them, and know that decisions made in respect to his job and work have been safeguarded against one man's arbitrariness or lack of judgment. He should also have a right of appeal.

The most sensible approach is that of Continental Can. In this company every member of management can appeal against any life-and-death decision affecting him, his job, or his work, all the way up to the president and the chairman of the Board. Appeals to this "final court" have been extremely rare. Most, if not all, appeals are disposed of at the first hearing way down the line. But the fact that there is a right to appeal to the top has had a powerful impact on the whole management group. A manager making a life-or-death decision will give it greater care. A manager affected by such a decision does not feel the helpless victim of spite, bias or stupidity.

Even more potent than these safeguards against mistakes are practices which demonstrate to all men that management sincerely wants to have the right spirit. The simplest practice is one that says in effect to all managers: "The spirit of this organization is the business of every one of us. Find out what you are doing to build the right spirit in the unit you head and tell us, in higher management, what we can do to build the right spirit in the unit of which you are a part."

of his superior's
ajor contribution
to management spirit. It co... management is not content to preach but is determined to act. It creates a desire to improve. And in all matters of the spirit determination and desire to improve are perhaps even more important than the actual level of performance; dynamic growth is more productive than static perfection.

Whom Not to Appoint to Management Jobs

The best practices will fail to build the right spirit unless management bears witness for its own professed beliefs every time it appoints a man to a management job. The final proof of its sincerity and seriousness is uncompromising emphasis on integrity of character. For it is character through which leadership is exercised, it is character that sets the example and is imitated in turn. Character is not something a man can acquire; if he does not bring it to the job, he will never have it. It is not something one can fool people about. The men with whom a man works, and especially his subordinates, know in a few weeks whether he has integrity or not. They may forgive a man a great deal: incompetence, ignorance, insecurity or bad manners. But they will not forgive him lack of integrity. Nor will they forgive higher management for choosing him.

Integrity may be difficult to define, but what constitutes lack of integrity of such seriousness as to disqualify a man for a managerial position is not. A man should never be appointed to a managerial position if his vision focuses on people's weaknesses rather than on their strengths. The man who always knows exactly what people cannot do, but never sees anything they can do, will undermine the spirit of his organization. Of course, a manager should have a clear grasp of the limitations of his people, but he should see these as limitations on what they can do, and as challenges to them to do better. He should be a realist; and no one is less realistic than the cynic.

A man should not be appointed if he is more interested in the question: "Who is right?" than in the question: "What is right?" To put personality above the requirements of the work is corruption and corrupts. To ask "Who is right?" encourage one's subordinates to play safe, if not to play politics. Above all, it encourages them to "cover up" rather than to take corrective action as soon as they find out that they have made a mistake.

Management should not appoint a man who considers intelligence more important than integrity. For this is immaturity. It should never promote a man who has shown that he is afraid of strong subordinates. For this is weakness. It should never put into a management job a man who does not set high standards for his own work. For that breeds contempt for the work and for management's competence.

A man might himself know too little, perform poorly, lack judgment and ability, and yet not do damage as a manager. But if he lack in character and integrity—no matter how knowledgeable, how brilliant, how successful—he destroys. He destroys people, the most valuable resource of the enterprise. He destroys spirit. And he destroys performance.

This is particularly true of the people at the head of an enterprise. For the spirit of an organization is created from the top. If an organization is great in spirit, it is because the spirit of its top people is great. If it decays, it does so because the top rots; as the proverb has it "Trees die from the top." In appointing people to top positions, integrity cannot be overemphasized. In fact, no one should be appointed unless management is willing to have his character serve as the model for all his subordinates.

What about Leadership?

We have defined the purpose of an organization as "making common men do uncommon things." We have not talked, however, about making common men into uncommon men. We have not, in other words, talked about leadership.

This was intentional. Leadership is of utmost importance. Indeed there is no substitute for it. But leadership cannot be created or promoted. It cannot be taught or learned.

The earliest writers on the subject, in ancient Greece or ancient Israel, knew all that has ever been known about leadership. The scores of books, papers and speeches on leadership in the business enterprise that come out every year have little to say on the subject that was not already old when the Prophets spoke and Aeschylus wrote. The first systematic book on leadership: the *Kyropaidaia* of Xenophon—himself no mean leader of men—is still the best book on the subject. Yet three thousand years of study, exhortation, injunction and advice do not seem to have increased the supply of leaders to any appreciable extent nor enabled people to learn how to become leaders.

There is no substitute for leadership. But management cannot create leaders. It can only create the conditions under which potential leadership qualities become effective; or it can stifle potential leadership. The supply of leadership is much too limited and unpredictable to be depended upon for the creation of the spirit the business enterprise needs to be productive and to hold together. Management must work on creating the spirit by other means. These means may be less effective and more pedestrian. But at least they are available and within management's control. In fact, to concentrate an leadership may only too easily lead management to do nothing at all about the spirit of its organization.

Leadership requires aptitude—and men who are good chief engineers or general managers are rare enough even without aptitute for leadership. Leadership also requires basic attitudes. And nothing is as difficult to define, nothing as difficult to change, as basic attitudes (quite apart from the question whether the employment contract confers on management the right to attempt to manipulate what is in effect an employee's basic personality). To talk of leadership as the unique key to spirit therefore only too often means neither action nor results.

But practices, though humdrum, can always be practiced whatever a man's aptitudes, personality or attitudes. They require no genius—only application. They are things to do rather than to talk about.

And the right practices should go a long way toward bringing out, recognizing and using whatever potential for leadership there is in the management group. They should also lay the foundation for the right kind of leadership. For leadership is not magnetic personality—that can just as well be demagoguery. It is not "making friends and influencing people"—that is salesmanship. Leadership is the lifting of a man's vision to higher sights, the raising of a man's performance to a higher standard, the building of a man's personality beyond its normal limitations. Nothing better prepares the ground for such leadership than a spirit of management that confirms in the day-to-day practices of the organization strict principles of conduct and responsibility, high standards of performance, and respect for the individual and his work. For to leadership, too, the words of the savings bank advertisement apply: "Wishing won't make it so; doing will."

CHAPTER 14

CHIEF EXECUTIVE AND BOARD

The bottleneck is at the head of the bottle—How many jobs does the chief executive have?—How disorganized is the job?—Need for work simplification of the chief executive's job—The fallacy of the one-man chief executive—The chief-executive job a team job—The isolation of the top man—The problem of his succession—The demands of tomorrow's top-management job—The crisis of the one-man chief-executive concept—Its abandonment in practice—How to organize the chief-executive team—Team, not committee—No appeal from one member to another—Clear assignment of all parts of chief-executive job—How many on the team?—The Board of Directors—Why a Board is needed—What it should do and what it should be.

"THE bottleneck is at the head of the bottle," goes an old saw. No business is likely to be better than its top management, have broader vision than its top people, or perform better than they do. A business—especially a large one—may coast for a little time on the vision and performance of an earlier top management. But this only defers payment—and usually for a much shorter period than is commonly believed. A business needs a central governing organ and a central organ of review and appraisal. On the quality of these two organs, which together comprise top management, its performance, results and spirit largely depend.

Some time ago I attended a dinner party given by a few men, mostly presidents of sizable companies, for one of the elder statesmen of American business. The guest of honor had built up a large company from small beginnings and had been its president for many years before becoming chairman of the Board of Directors a year earlier. After the dinner he began to reminisce and soon was talking enthusiastically about the work of his successor. For almost an hour he described in detail how the new president did his job. While he spoke I jotted down the various activities as they were brought up. When he finished, saying: "The best thing I ever did for the company was to pick this man as my successor," I had the following list of the activities and duties of a chief executive of a business.

I give it here not because it is necessarily the right analysis of the chief-executive job but because it reflects faithfully the thinking of one of the most successful practitioners.

The chief executive thinks through the business the company is in. He develops and sets over-all objectives. He makes the basic decisions needed to reach these objectives. He communicates the objectives and the decisions to his management people. He educates these managers in seeing the business as a whole and helps them to develop their own objectives from those of the business. He measures performance and results against the objectives. He reviews and revises objectives as conditions demand.

The chief executive makes the decisions on senior management personnel. He also makes sure that future managers are being developed all down the line. He makes the basic decisions on company organization. It is his job to know what questions to ask of his managers and to make sure they understand what the questions mean. He co-ordinates the product businesses within the company and the various functional managers. He arbitrates conflicts within the group and either prevents or settles personality clashes.

Like the captain of a ship, he takes personal command in an emergency.

"One of our main plants had a fire five months ago," the speaker said. "It interrupted all our schedules. Rush work had to be shifted to other plants, and some had to be subcontracted to our closest competitors. Other work had to be postponed. Important customers had to be placated or substitute sources of supply had to be found for them. We had to make an immediate decision whether to repair the plant, one of our older ones, or bu[illegible] a new, modern one from scratch. We could have repaired the [illegible] six months at a cost of two million dollars. Instead, the new president decided to build a new plant which will cost ten million dollars and will take almost two years but will have double the capacity of the old one and significantly lower costs. It was the right decision but it meant changing all our production schedules and all our capital-expenditure planning. It also meant negotiating a six months' bank loan to tide us over until we could float bonds that we had not expected to issue for another year or so. For four weeks the new president spent day and night at the office."

Similarly the new president, the speaker continued, took personal charge when one of the company's businesses got into serious trouble. He himself, with the company's counsel and an outside law firm, worked through the preparation for an important patent-infringement suit brought against the company and spent almost two weeks on the stand as one of the chief witnesses for the defense.

Next on this list of the things which the company president does, and which only he can do, came the responsibility for capital-expenditures planning and for raising capital. Whether it is a bank loan, an issue of bonds or a new stock issue, the president takes an active part in the decision and in the negotiations. He also recommends dividend policy to the board. He is concerned with relations with stockholders. He answers questions at the annual meeting. He must be available to the security analysts of the big institutional investors, such as insurance companies and investment trusts. He must see the financial writers of the major newspapers and business magazines.

He has to prepare the agenda for the monthly meeting of the Board of Directors, present the reports there and be ready to answer questions. And he must relay Board decisions to his managers.

The new president has a host of public-relations duties.

"Once a month he spends two days in Washington to attend meetings of two governmental advisory boards where he succeeded me as a member," the former president reported. "I am still on the hospital committee in our biggest plant-city, and I still serve on the regional Red Cross board. But the new president has taken over as vice-chairman of the Community Chest and serves on the board of the educational foundation we set up for the children of our employees. And he has been elected a member of the Board of Trustees of the engineering school from which he graduated and will be regional chairman of its fund-raising campaign next year. He is cutting down on public-speaking engagements as much as possible. Most of them can be handled by the vice-presidents. But he has to attend one or two trade association meetings each year—usually making one short speech. He appeared last month at a meeting of the American Management Association and spoke about our organization structure. Once a year we have a convention of our dealers which the president has to open with a speech about our new products and our sales plans; there is also a big dinner on the last day which he has to sit through Once a year our "old-timers club" of employees with more than twenty-five years of service has a get-together at which the president introduces the new members and presents them with long-service pins. We also have two or three dinners a year for retiring management people—everybody from foreman to vice-president One of those I still take; the new president takes the others. And we have a custom which I started and which we consider very valuable, of bringing every man who has been promoted into management to headquarters to introduce him to the brass. Of course we bring them in in groups of five or six; but there are eight or nine such groups each year. And it is customary for the president to entertain each at lunch in the executive dining room."

The final item on the list: each year the new president visits personally the company's fifty-two plants in the United States and Canada. And he plans to visit fairly soon the company's seven plants in Europe and Latin America.

"Our plants are quite small," the former president said. "Only one—the one that had the fire—has over two thousand employees. All the others have fewer than a thousand—four hundred or so on average. We intend to keep them small; it makes for better management. And we give the plant manager as much freedom as possible. But that makes it all the more necessary to stress that all the plants are part of the same company, and that all the managers are on the same team. Only a visit from the "big boss" can do that. Also the president himself learns more on these visits than he could ever get reading reports in his office. He usually spends one day at the plant and another one visiting major customers in the area just to find out what complaints they have."

When the old gentleman finished his description of his successor's job, the other people around the table all chimed in and added additional activities. "Doesn't your president," one man asked, "have to see the people who solicit company contributions to the colleges, the hospitals, the charities in your main plant cities? It's one of my most time-consuming chores." Another one said: "Don't you have your president sit in on labor negotiations? My personnel vice-president insists that I do." "What about that strike you had in Chicago last year?" asked a third. "Who handled that?" Not one of the men at the table said: "This or that I don't do but delegate." And it was not until an hour later that one of the company presidents in the room asked the question that had been on my lips ever since the guest of honor had begun to speak: "Tell me, how many heads and hands does this president of yours have?" By that time I had a list of forty-one different activities that experienced company presidents consider to be part of the job which can only be discharged by the chief executive himself.

How Disorganized Is the Job?

There is no job that needs to be organized as carefully and as systematically as that of the chief executive. The president's day has only twenty-four hours like anybody else's. And he certainly needs as many hours for sleep, rest and relaxation as a man burdened with lesser responsibilities. Only the most thorough study of the job can prevent total disorganization. Only the most systematic assignments of priorities can prevent the chief executive from frittering away his time and energy on the less important activities to the neglect of vital matters.

Yet, this careful study, this systematic organization of the job, are almost unknown. The result is that a great many chief executives—in small business or large—are disorganized, do indeed fritter away their time.

The only published study of the way chief executives actually spend their day has been made in Sweden by Professor Sune Carlsson.[1] For several months Carlsson and his associates clocked with a stop watch the working day of twelve leading Swedish industrialists. They noted the time spent on conversations, conferences, visits, telephone calls and so forth. They found that not one of the twelve executives was ever able to work uninterruptedly more than twenty minutes at a time—at least not in the office. Only at home was there some chance of concentration. And the only one of the twelve who did not make important, long-range decisions "off the cuff," and sandwiched in between unimportant but long telephone calls and "crisis" problems, was the executive who worked at home every morning for an hour and a half before coming to the office.

[1] Described in his book *Executive Behavior* (Stockholm: Stromberg, 1952).

We have no such study of American chief executives. But we do not need one to know that far too many let outside pressures and immediate emergencies dictate their day and the utilization of their efforts and energies.

Yet even the chief executive who lets outward pressures manage him is better than some. At least he spends his time on activities that are part of the chief executive's job (albeit the lesser part). Much worse is the chief executive who wastes his time running a function instead of the business: the president who entertains customers when he should be working on the financial policy, the president who corrects details in engineering drawings and neglects a crying problem of malorganization; the president who personally checks the expense account of every salesman, etc. These men not only fail to accomplish their work; they also prevent the operating manager whose job they are doing from accomplishing his. And the number of chief executives who thus cling to the functional work in which they came up and with which they are familiar is uncomfortably large.

The problem is one of systematic conception and organization of the job. Without it even the ablest, most intelligent and best intentioned of chief executives will not succeed in doing his job, and will be forced to manage according to pressures and emergencies. "He who rides the tiger, reaps the whirlwind," I once heard a speaker say. This thoroughly mixed metaphor is not a bad description of the fate of the chief executive who lets the pressure of the job manage himself instead of systematically studying, thinking through and organizing his job, work and time.

A distinguished French industrialist and student of management, Rolf Nordling, recently suggested[2] that the chief executive's job is the biggest and the least explored area for the application of Scientific Management, and especially of "work simplification." The first thing to be done would be what Carlsson did in Sweden: study the work day of the chief executive with a stop watch.

This is certainly sound. But (as Nordling hastened to point out) time study must be accompanied by hard thinking about what the

[2] In his speech accepting the 1954 Wallace Clark Award for Distinguished Contribution to Scientific Management, given before the Council for International Progress in Management (USA) on January 13, 1954.

job should be. What activities must the chief executive do himself? What activities can he leave to others—and to whom? Above all: what activities come first? How much time must be set aside for them, no matter what "crisis" pressures there are?

The intuitive manager, in other words, cannot do the chief executive's job, no matter how brilliant, how quick, how perceptive he is. The job has to be planned. And the work has to be performed according to plan.

The Fallacy of the One-Man Chief Executive

Even if the job is studied most systematically, organized most thoughtfully, and with the maximum of decentralization, it still is not a job one man could or should do. Indeed, 90 per cent of the trouble we are having with the chief executive's job is rooted in our superstition of the one-man chief. We still, as did Henry Ford, model the chief executive of the modern business after the single proprietor of yesterday's economy.

There will always be too many activities in the job for any one man's working day. Half the activities in the list I gave above should probably be taken out of the chief executive's hands and given to other people. The remainder would still be unmanageable for one man; there would still be some fifteen or twenty major activities. Each of them would be of vital importance to the enterprise. Each would be difficult. Each would be time-consuming. And each would require careful planning, thought and preparation. The job, if pared to the bone, would still exceed the span of managerial responsibility of any one man. An unlimited supply of universal geniuses could not save the one-man chief-executive concept unless they could also bid the sun stand still in the heavens. And even Joshua could accomplish this only once, whereas the one-man chief executive would have to perform the miracle seven days a week.

The activities that together make up the chief-executive job are also too diverse to be performed by one man. The list includes things that have primarily to do with planning, analyzing and policy formulation, like the determination of the company's business, the setting of objectives and so forth. It includes things that require fast decisive action: for instance, the handling of a major crisis. Some of these things deal with the long-range future. Others with immediate problems. Yet, it is a rule that tomorrow's business will not get done if you mix it with today's—let alone with yesterday's. Some activities require the skill of the negotiator: the arbitration of internal clashes or the floating of a capital issue. Others require the skill of the educator. Others still are "relations" skills (and for some activities such as attending company social functions, a cast-iron stomach is probably the first requirement).

The least that would seem to be required is three distinctive characters: the "thought man," the "man of action" and the "front man," as one of my friends in a top management calls them. Two of these characters may be found combined in one man ("But do you really want a schizophrenic in the chief executive's job?" the same friend asks). All three are most unlikely to be found together. Yet, in all three major areas there are important activities that have to be discharged well if the enterprise is to prosper.

There is only one conclusion: the chief-executive job in every business (except perhaps the very smallest) cannot properly be organized as the job of one man. It must be the job of a team of several men acting together.

There are two additional arguments for this conclusion. The first is the isolation of the chief executive.

The president of a company, whether large or small, is insulated by his position. Everybody wants something from him. His managers want to "sell" him their ideas or want to advance their position. The supplier wants to sell him goods. The customer wants better service or lower prices. The president is forced to adopt an "arm's-length" attitude in his dealings with people in sheer self-defense. Also, as soon as the business attains even modest size, everything brought to him for information or decision is of necessity predigested, formalized and abstract. It is a distillation rather than the raw stuff of life. Otherwise, the president could not deal with it at all. His social life (if he has any at all, which is unlikely considering the pressures of the job) is usually spent with other people of similar rank and station so that he rarely as much as meets people whose point of view, experiences and opinions are not similar to his. He may be the most easygoing fellow in the world; but his plant visits or his executive luncheons will have, without any fault of his, all the informality of a Byzantine state visit. As a result, one of the shrewdest observers of management once said to me, "There is no lonelier guy anyplace than the fellow in the president's chair."

Organizing the chief executive's job properly will accentuate this isolation. For the things he should not do are precisely the things that break through the silken curtain that shuts him in. Everybody agrees that the chief executive should spend more time on thinking and planning. But this means that he should spend less time (or no time at all) talking to customers over the telephone, handling production or design details, seeing chance callers or charity canvassers, chatting with a newspaperman, or "being one of the boys" at a sales convention. Yet, these are all things that, however inadequately, break the chief executive's isolation.

Yet, proper organization of the job is imperative. To achieve it and with it a high degree of isolation, and still maintain the effectiveness (if not the sanity) of the human beings in the job, a team is needed. This alone can give the chief executive people to talk to who are on his level and who do not therefore want anything from him; people with whom he can "let down his hair" and speak freely, with whom he does not have to watch every one of his steps or words, with whom he can "think aloud" without committing himself. This alone would also enable us to bring into the job the variety of viewpoints, opinions and experiences which is needed for sound decisions but which not even the cleverest public-relations expert can bring to the one-man chief executive.

Similarly, the chief-executive team alone can adequately solve the problem of succession. If there is only one man in the job, his succession cannot really be planned; it will be fought over.[8] The retirement of the top man—and even more his death or disability—will produce a crisis. And once appointed, the one-man chief executive can, as a rule, be neither removed nor effectively neutralized, no matter how poor a choice he turns out to be. If the chief executive is a team, however—say, three men—there will seldom be a

[8] An entertaining and shrewd description of the typical process is given in Cameron Hawley's best-selling novel *Executive Suite*. It is realistic except that there are perhaps fewer happy endings in actual business life.

total turnover. To replace one man out of three is fairly easy; it produces no crisis; and a mistake is neither fatal nor normally irrevocable.

Ralph J. Cordiner, president of General Electric (itself a notable example of top management by chief-executive team) brought this point out strongly in a speech to the Harvard Business School on "Efficient Organizational Structure," given in 1953. He said: "The chief executive officer, if he is discharging his responsibility . . . should, within a period of not longer than three years after he has accepted his assignment, have at least three officers equal to or better than himself in performance who could succeed to his position. . . . We [therefore] think it is very important that there be a number of positions at top level that are virtually as important, are compensated almost on the same level, and carry the same dignity as the position of chief executive officer. Thus, we have created a number of executive vice-presidents who act as group executives. The idea is that these men, along with the president and the chairman of the board, should be a team, with each having his own specific responsibilities, yet able to carry the ball or run interference for the other fellow as occasion requires."

Finally the chief-executive job of tomorrow will include understanding of a host of new basic tools of mathematical and logical analysis, synthesis and measuring. It will require ability to see where these tools can be applied, the power to educate other members of management in their meaning and use, and some elementary skill in applying them. These tools will include the techniques of analyzing and anticipating the future that were discussed earlier. They will also include such new tools as "operations research," "information theory" and "symbolic logic." (How these tools apply to the decision-making process will be discussed in Part Five of this book, "What It Means To Be a Manager".)

Thus, twenty years hence, and possibly sooner, the chief-executive job will require not only a "front man," a "thought man" and a "man of action" but, in addition, a first-rate analyst and synthetizer. Certainly no one man can play these four parts well in one life, let alone crowd them all into one working day.

The Crisis of the One-Man Chief-Executive Concept

That the chief executive should be a team will be considered rank heresy—even by many who in their own companies have organized the job on a team basis (Mr. Cordiner of General Electric, for instance, stressed the need for a team of equals in the speech quoted earlier; but he still talked of the one "chief executive officer"). Most organization theorists seem to think that the one-man chief executive is a law of nature, requiring no proof and admitting of no doubt.

That there is no such law of nature is abundantly proven, however, by the fact that the most successful managements outside the United States always organize the chief executive as a team. The large company in Germany has always had a team management. One member customarily presides over the team but all are equal. (It is ironical that Hitler attacked this as "effete democracy" and "Americanism" and tried to impose the pattern of the one-man chief executive.) Similarly those marvels of efficient management organization, the "Big Five" of British banking, have always been managed not by one but by two chief-executive teams: the chairman and the deputy chairmen concerned with basic objectives, and the joint general managers concerned with policies, practices and personnel.

That a great deal of doubt regarding the one-man chief executive is appropriate is indicated by the severe crisis in which the concept finds itself today, especially in the large business. The one-man executive is no longer capable of making the decisions he is supposed to make. He approves the most fundamental decisions affecting the survival of the company on the basis of a one-page recommendation—that is, on a basis which does not allow him to judge the decision at all, let alone to change it. He cannot even know whether all the important facts are presented to him. Worse still, he makes his decisions increasingly on the basis of highly stylized "presentations" which aim at getting a "yes" from the boss with a minimum of discussion—and that means with a minimum of understanding on the part of the boss of what it is he actually approves.

Even worse is the growth of "kitchen cabinets." Being unable to do his job, the chief surrounds himself with a motley staff of personal confidantes, miscellaneous assistants, analysts, a "control section" and so forth. None of them have any clearly defined duties. None have clear responsibility. But all have direct access to the boss and are credited throughout the organization with mysterious powers. They undercut the authority of operating managers, duplicate their work, and cut them off from easy communication with the chief executive. They are the worst causes of malorganization—"government by crony." Yet the one-man chief executive needs his kitchen cabinet. Not being allowed to organize a proper team, he has to make do with errand boys, private secretaries, chief clerks and favorites into whose hands critical control of the basic decisions increasingly drifts.

The worst example of this I have seen was in a fairly large steel company where the president had twice as many assistants as there were vice-presidents. Not one of these assistants had clearly defined responsibilities; they did whatever the president assigned them to do. The same man, for instance, did the president's Christmas shopping and the company's financial planning. Not one of them was supposed to have any authority, but they made the final decisions in effect. Yet, when the president was asked by a new board chairman to get rid of this monstrosity, he answered: "I know I ought to. But how else can I get through my work load?" The solution was quite simple. The vice-presidents were organized in a "Planning Committee." They were asked to set aside two days each week for the work of the committee (to make this possible some functions were split and four new vice-presidents were appointed). The committee has full responsibility for the formulation of objectives, the preparation of all recommendations on policy, organization and senior management personnel, and for the preparation of financial plans and budgets. The company, in other words, is run by a team composed of the president as "man of action" and "front man," and the Planning Committee as "thought man." There has been no trouble since, and no tendency to restore the kitchen cabinet.

Another sign of the disintegration of the one-man chief-executive concept is the tendency toward a form of executive dropsy in the large company. More and more levels of top management intervene between the actual business and the chief executive. At General Motors—one of several examples—there are now two such levels of top management between the president and the chief operating officers, the heads of the autonomous product businesses or divisions. Even the general manager of as enormous a business as Chevrolet (employing 200,000 people and selling almost $4,000,000,000 worth of automobiles a year) does not work directly with the chief executive of General Motors. He reports to a group executive who in turn reports to an executive vice-president. And only then does anything go to the president himself. But this is no longer management—at least not if the word management is considered to have any kinship to "manageable." Surely, the head of a business as large as Chevrolet—a business that is many times larger than a great many independent companies that are considered "big business"—must have direct access to the man who makes the final decisions. The reason for this dangerous and disturbing executive superstructure is simply that the president of General Motors could not handle the chief-executive job himself.

The final proof that the one-man chief-executive concept is a theoretical phantom is the speed with which it is being abandoned in practice by company after company. There is usually still someone called a "chief executive officer" in these companies—as there is at General Electric. But actually the job is discharged by a group working as a team.

This trend has gone furthest at the Standard Oil Company of New Jersey where the chief executive consists of a fourteen-man Board of Directors, composed entirely of full-time officers of the company. More common is the General Electric pattern of an Executive Office composed of the president, a number of group executives who are, so to speak, deputy presidents, and a number of vice-presidents charged with responsibility for objectives and policy-formulation in major areas, such as Research, Marketing or Management Organization. The New Haven Railroad, the American Can Company, Union Carbide and Carbon, and duPont are among the companies with such an Executive Office.

Actually there is serious doubt whether the successful business ever used the one-man concept. Practically every case of business growth is the achievement of at least two, and often three, men working together. At its inception a company is often the "lengthened shadow of one man." But it will not grow and survive unless the one-man top is converted into a team. General Motors, in the period of its great growth, was managed by a team consisting always of two and usually of three men: Alfred P. Sloan, Jr. (president and later chairman of the Board) working with Donaldson

Brown (vice-president, later vice-chairman of the Board) and usually with a third man, the company's actual president. At Sears, Roebuck, under the aegis of Julius Rosenwald, the chief executive consisted of three men, Mr. Rosenwald himself, his legal advisor, Mr. Loeb, and Mr. Doering in charge of mail-order operations. Under General Wood, Sears, too, was run by a three-man team, General Wood himself, his merchandising vice-president, Mr. Houser, and the company's president. The same is true of both Standard Oil of New Jersey and its traditional closest competitor, Socony-Vacuum, which were built in the twenties by two-man teams.

The list could be extended indefinitely. It would include American Telephone and Telegraph, General Foods, the duPont Company—indeed, most of America's large companies. Even the Ford Motor Company, in the period of its greatest growth and prosperity, was run by a team consisting of the elder Ford and James Couzens.

That the team organization of the chief-executive job is the rule in successful large companies, and one of the main reasons for their success, it is indicated in the following report that appeared in a recent (April 1954) issue of *Harper's Magazine*.

One of the country's smartest and most venerable banks recently sent a question to the chief of its research department.

"Are there any earmarks," it asked, in effect, "which will tell us whether the management of a corporation is good or bad?"

The research people quickly found that this question is tougher than it looks. Profits alone are not a reliable guide. It is fairly easy for short-sighted executives to show good profits—for a few years—by letting their companies' plant run down, or by gutting reserves of raw material. On the other hand, a firm which has never earned a penny may be just on the doorsill of spectacular success, because years of developmental work and long-visioned management are finally ready to pay off.

In the end—after studying hundreds of corporations—the researchers discovered just one clue. It was totally unexpected; it apparently is still unknown to the business colleges or professional market analysts; and it has enabled the bank to place its financial bets with remarkably consistent results. (This, incidentally, is the first time it has ever been made public.)

Here, in effect, is what the research chief reported:

"If the top executive in a company gets a salary several times as large as the salaries paid to the Number Two, Three and Four men, you can be pretty sure that firm is badly managed. But if the salary levels of the four or five men at the head of the ladder are all close together, then the performance and morale of the entire management group is likely to be high.

"The *size* of the salaries doesn't seem to make much difference," the report continued. "Whether the president of the corporation gets $20,000 a year or $100,000 isn't important—so long as his vice presidents get something like 75 to 90 per cent as much. But when the president pulls down $100,000, and his main subordinates get only $50,000 to $25,000, it is time to look for trouble."

The same is true of successful small companies. Commonly they are run by a two-man or three-man team (typically the company's president and sales manager, and the treasurer) who together discharge the functions of "chief executive officer." Again the one-man chief does not work beyond the business babyhood.

And exactly the same is true of the federally decentralized unit within a company, such as a General Motors division or a General Electric product business. Whenever we analyze such a unit we find that its top management is a team. The team may consist of the unit's general manager and one of his senior men—frequently the comptroller (if only because he, being responsible for financial reports, has a direct pipe line into company headquarters). Or it may consist of the unit's general manager and the manager to whom he reports—the group vice-president at General Motors, the division general manager at General Electric. In the most successful examples I have seen, all three of these men work together as a team in which all are actually (though not officially) co-equals.

There is, in fact, only one argument for the one-man chief executive—and it is not very cogent. There must be, the argument runs, one man responsible to the Board of Directors; and he must be the final boss. But work with the Board, though tremendously important, is only one of the functions of the chief executive. Also most large-company Boards today have several of the company's officers among their members and therefore clearly expect to work with more than one of the executives (General Electric even has the chairman of the Board report to the president as one of the group executives).

In fine, the concept of the one-man chief executive officer is contrary to all experience and to the demands of the job. In successful companies it is not being applied. And where it is being applied it leads to trouble.

How to Organize the Chief-Executive Team?

How then should the chief-executive team be organized?

The first requirement is that it be a "team" rather than a "committee." There should be no collective responsibility. Each member should have assigned to him the areas in which he makes final decisions and for which he is responsible. Deliberation should be joint; decision single.

However it should not be forgotten that there are two ways of organizing a "team," exemplified perhaps best by the baseball team and the tennis doubles team respectively. In the baseball team each player has a fixed position which he does not leave. In playing doubles tennis each player too has an area of responsibility; but he is also expected to cover his partner. Under the first organization the lines are drawn for the team members. Under the second one the partners in collaboration work out the lines of demarcation themselves. The baseball-team way has the advantage that total strangers can play well together; but a good opponent can direct his plays into the gaps between positions which no one really covers. To play a winning doubles game at tennis a team has to have played together quite a bit; but once the partners have come to know and to trust each other there will be no gaps on their side of the net. The one team, in other words, depends entirely on proper organization; the other one adds to organization an element of personal adjustment and flexibility. Both ways are effective ways to organize a winning chief executive team; but the team and each member—as also the other managers throughout the business—must know which of the two ways of team-organization has been chosen.

In particular, there has to be clearly assigned responsibility for the determination of objectives in the eight key areas of business performance and for the careful consideration of the impact of all business actions and decisions on performance and results in these areas. This responsibility can be part of the job of every member of the team: it can be assigned to a Planning Committee of vice-presidents. It can be assigned to one man: in General Motors Mr. Donaldson Brown carried it in effect when he was vice-chairman. Or each key area can be assigned to a separate man as a full-time job—though that is for the very large business only. It is the approach of General Electric, where the executive office—in addition to president and group executives—contains a fair number of services vice-presidents, each charged with company-wide responsibility in one key area. Size of the company and character of the business are the determining factors here. What matters, above all, is that the responsibility for long-range planning and thinking, for clear objectives, for the development of adequate yardsticks to measure their attainment, and for the education of managers in the vision and the skills needed to reach the objectives, be clearly spelled out and unambiguously assigned.

The second requirement is that there be no appeal from one member of the chief executive to another. Whatever any one of them decides is the decision of all of top management.

This does not mean that there should be no one on the team who acts as its captain. On the contrary, a captain is needed. And one man is almost certain to stand out as the senior member by virtue of his intellectual or moral authority. There was, for instance, never any doubt in General Motors that the head of the table was wherever Mr. Sloan sat, nor at Sears, Roebuck that General Wood was a good deal more than the "first among equals." But whenever one man thus stands out, he has to be doubly careful not to countermand or overrule the others, not to interfere in the areas assigned to them, not to let his superiority turn into their inferiority. His strength, in other words, should strengthen his teammates—which is, after all, the definition of an effective and strong team captain. He is a playing captain not a manager calling signals from the bench.

How many members should the team have? The fewer the better—but more than two.

Indeed if two men can work together closely, they form an ideal team. But two people like this are rarely found. And two people in a team are always a highly unstable combination. "If there are only two men," a veteran member of a chief-executive team once told me, "even a slight disagreement may become dangerous. If there is a third member, the team can function even if two barely speak to each other." A two-man team can function only if the men are held together by strong emotional bonds, which is in itself undesirable. Finally a two-man chief-executive team aggravates the problem of succession. Precisely because the two members have to be so close to each other they usually retire together; for the survivor would find it almost impossible to adjust to a new partner. One example of this is Mr. Donaldson Brown's voluntary retirement from General Motors—many years before he reached retirement age—when Mr. Sloan retired because of age. Another is the joint retirement of Mr. Swope and Mr. Young from the top management of General Electric. Yet one of the important tasks of the chief-executive team is to give continuity to top management and to make succession easy instead of critical or stormy.

The Board of Directors

We talked earlier of the crisis of the chief-executive concept. One reason for this, however, has not been mentioned. It is the gradual erosion of the Board of Directors as a functioning organ of the enterprise.

To the law, the Board of Directors is the only organ of the enterprise. And in one form or another such a "Board" exists in every industrial country—even in Soviet Russian law. Legally it is considered the representative of the owners, having all the power and alone having power.

In reality the Board as conceived by the lawmaker is at best a tired fiction. It is perhaps not too much to say that it has become a shadow king. In most of the large companies, it has in effect been deposed and its place taken by executive management. This may have been achieved in the form of the "inside" Board, that is, one composed exclusively of executive management men who meet the first Monday in every month to supervise and to approve what they themselves have been doing the other twenty-nine days of the month. Or the Board may have become a mere showcase, a place to inject distinguished names, without information, influence or desire for power. Or—a typical pattern in the smaller company—the Board may be simply another name for the meeting of the family members, usually the ones actively engaged in the business, plus a few widows of former partners.

Since this has happened not only in this country but in every other—if our information is accurate, even in Russia—it suggests that the erosion of the Board of Directors is not an accident but rooted in profound causes. Some of these are: the much-publicized divorce of ownership from control which makes it absurd that the business enterprise be directed by the representatives of the shareholders; the complexity of modern business operations; and, perhaps most important, the difficulty of finding good men with the time to sit on Boards and to take their membership seriously.

But there are real functions which only a Board of Directors can discharge. Somebody has to approve the decision what the company's business is and what it should be. Somebody has to give final approval to the objectives the company has set for itself and the measurements it has developed to judge its progress toward these objectives. Somebody has to look critically at the profit planning of the company, its capital-investment policy and its managed-expenditures budget. Somebody has to discharge the final judicial function in respect to organization problems, has to be the "Supreme Court." Somebody has to watch the spirit of the organization, has to make sure that it succeeds in utilizing the strengths of people and in neutralizing their weaknesses, that it develops tomorrow's managers and that its rewards to managers, its management tools and management methods strengthen the organization and direct it toward its objectives.

The Board cannot and must not be the governing organ that the law considers it to be. It is an organ of review, of appraisal, of appeal. Only in a crisis does it become an organ of action—and then only to remove existing executives that have failed, or to replace executives who have resigned, retired or died. Once the replacement has been made, the Board again becomes an organ of review.

Those members of the chief-executive team who are charged with responsibility for company objectives must work directly with the Board. One way to achieve this in the large company (applied in several of our large businesses with good results) is the formation of Board committees in each major area of objectives, with the company officer charged with primary responsibility in that area, acting as the committee's secretary or chairman. But no matter how organized in concrete detail, the Board should have direct access to the top executives charged with objective-determination in all key areas.

The Board must also be detached from operations. It must view the company as a whole. This means that working executives of the company should not dominate the Board. In fact, the Board will be stronger and more effective if it is genuinely an "outside" Board, the bulk of whose members have never served as full-time officers of the company.

The complexity of the large company is often cited as a reason for an inside Board. But it is to the advantage of the Board in the large business that its members do not know the details. A dishonest chief executive can, of course, fool an outside Board (though not for long if its members demand the information they should be getting and ask the questions they should be asking). But while the inside Board cannot be fooled by anyone else, it can easily fool itself. Inside full-time executives tend to think too much in terms of immediate or technical problems. The very remoteness of the outside Board member counteracts this. It makes him look for the over-all pattern, see broad objectives and plans, and ask questions on concept and principle.

In the typical family-owned small company the outside Board member serves another but equally important function. Small-company managers often have no one to talk to, no one to test their decisions against. Management is isolated—and the management group is usually so small as not to provide the corrective of diversity of background and temperament which, in the large corporation, sometimes helps to offset management's isolation. In the small company, too, therefore there is need for a Board which contains outsiders.

However, to obtain real benefit from the Board its membership must be carefully selected. Both the large and the small business need Board members whose experience, outlook and interests are different from those of the management. This cannot be obtained by getting representatives of the company's bankers, suppliers or customers. It requires people whose entire background is different from management's. (In this respect, the British practice of inviting distinguished public servants to join a Board at the end of their public career is a major improvement over our practice of confining the Board to the small "business family.") What is needed on a Board is not people who agree with management anyhow, but people who are likely to see things differently, to disagree and to question—especially to question the assumptions on which the chief-executive team acts without, usually, knowing that it is making them.

And to get the kind of people the company needs; Board membership will have to be made financially attractive.

That the Board can be made into the vital, effective and constructive constitutional organ it should be has been demonstrated. The pharmaceutical house of Merck & Company, for instance, considers its work in building a strong and effective Board to have been a major factor in its rise to leadership in its industry. To make the Board of Directors a real organ of the enterprise rather than legal fiction; to define its functions clearly and to set it definite objectives; to attract outstanding people and make them able and willing to contribute to the company, are admittedly difficult. But it is one of the most important things the chief-executive team can do, and one of the major conditions for its own success in discharging its job.

CHAPTER 15

DEVELOPING MANAGERS

Manager development a threefold responsibility: to the enterprise, to society, to the individual—What manager development is not—It cannot be promotion planning or finding "back-up men"—The fallacy of the "promotable man"—The principles of manager development—Developing the entire management group—Development for tomorrow's demands—Job rotation is not enough—How to develop managers—The individual's development needs—Manager manpower planning—Manager development not a luxury but a necessity.

THE prosperity if not the survival of any business depends on the performance of its managers of tomorrow. This is particularly true today when basic business decisions require for their fruition an increasingly long time-span. Since no one can foresee the future, management cannot make rational and responsible decisions unless it selects, develops and tests the men who will have to follow them through—the managers of tomorrow.

Management itself is becoming increasingly complex. In addition to a rapidly changing technology which, at least in the United States, makes competition daily more important and more stringent, management today has to be able to handle many new "relations" problems—relations with the government, relations with suppliers and customers, relations with the employees or with labor unions—all of which require better managers.

The numerical demand for executives is steadily growing. For it is of the essence of an industrial society that it increasingly substitutes for manual skill theoretical knowledge, ability to organize and to lead—in short, managerial ability. In fact, ours is the first society in which the basic question is not: How many educated people can society spare from the task of providing subsistence? It is: How many uneducated people can we afford to have?

But manager development is also necessary to discharge the elementary responsibilities the business enterprise owes to society —and if the business does not discharge these obligations by its own actions, society will impose them. For continuity, especially of the big business enterprise, is vital. Our society will not tolerate— and cannot afford—to see such wealth-producing resources jeopardized through lack of competent successors to today's management.

Increasingly it is to business that our citizen looks for the fulfilment of the basic beliefs and promises of society, especially the promise of "equal opportunity." Manager development from this point of view is little but a technical name for the means through which we carry out a central and basic part of our social beliefs and political heritage.

Increasingly it is in his work that the citizen of a modern industrial society looks for the satisfaction of his creative drive and instinct, for those satisfactions which go beyond the economic, for his pride, his self-respect, his self-esteem. Manager development is therefore only another name for the way in which management discharges its obligation to make work and industry more than a way of making a living. By offering challenges and opportunities for the individual development of each manager to his fullest ability, the enterprise discharges, in part, the obligation to make a job in industry a "way of life."

Recognition of these needs underlies the sudden emergence of manager development as a major concern of American business during these last few years. Fifteen years ago when I first became interested in the subject, I could find only one company that even saw the problem: Sears, Roebuck. Today there are literally hundreds of manager development plans in operation. There is hardly a single large company without one. Even small companies are increasingly developing programs of their own.

What Manager Development Is Not

Manager development cannot be just "promotion planning," confined to "promotable people" and aimed at finding "back-up men" for top-management vacancies. The very term "back-up man" implies that the job of a manager as well as the organization structure of the company will remain unchanged so that one simply has to find people to step into the shoes of today's executives. Yet, if one thing is certain, it is that both job requirements and organization structure will change in the future as they have always done in the past. What is needed is the development of managers equal to the tasks of tomorrow, not the tasks of yesterday.

Ralph J. Cordiner, the President of General Electric, has made the point clearly:

> If we were forced to rely entirely on conventional methods of increasing productivity, I would be inclined to regard this goal [of increasing General Electric productivity by 50 per cent in less than ten years] as wishful thinking. Our laboratories and factories will continue to find ways to produce more and better goods with a lower expenditure of time, effort and cost. But we cannot expect the physical sciences to carry the whole load.
>
> There has been a growing realization in American industry that great untapped opportunities lie in finding ways to develop more fully our human resources—particularly the managers of our business enterprises. Technological advances and the increasing complexities of managing under today's and tomorrow's conditions have made manager development a necessity as well as an opportunity. Those who have been closest to this field believe that an opportunity exists in General Electric to increase productivity 50 per cent in the next ten years through better management alone.

The concept of the back-up man for top management jobs also overlooks the fact that the most important decisions regarding tomorrow's management are made long before a man is promoted to a senior position. Tomorrow's senior positions will be filled by men who today occupy junior positions. By the time we have to find a man to take over the managership of a big plant or sales organization, our choice will already be limited to three or four people. It is in appointing people to positions as general foreman or department superintendent, as district sales manager, as auditor, etc., that we make the decisions that are crucial. And in making these decisions the typical back-up planning helps us little, if at all.

Altogether the concept of a promotable man who shows high potential is a fallacy. I have yet to see any method that can predict

is not its intention to liquidate the business at the end of the term. In other words, it is not sufficient to find the men for the demands of the next five years. The main results of what will be done during these next five years will not show until ten or fifteen years later. But what is being done now and during the years immediately ahead may well determine whether the company survives or not.

It should no longer be necessary to debate whether manager development is a luxury which only big companies can indulge in in boom times. Most of our large—and many of our small—companies know today that it is no more of a luxury than is a research laboratory. It is not even necessary any longer to combat the old fear that a company may develop too many good people. Most managements have found out that the demand for good people is increasing faster than the capacity of even a successful manager-development program to supply them. (The smart businessman has, of course, always known that it has never done a company harm to be known as "the mother of presidents." On the contrary, the power of a company to attract good men is directly proportionate to its reputation as a developer of successful men for itself as well as for other companies.)

Manager development has become a necessity not because top managements have been allowed to become old as a result of depression and war, but because the modern business enterprise has become a basic institution of our society. In any major institution—the Church, for instance, or the Army—the finding, developing and proving out of the leaders of tomorrow is an essential job to which the best men must give fully of their time and attention.

It is also a necessity for the spirit, the vision and the performance of today's managers that they be expected to develop those who will manage tomorrow. Just as no one learns as much about a subject as the man who is forced to teach it, no one develops as much as the man who is trying to help others to develop themselves. Indeed, no one can develop himself unless he works on the development of others. It is in and through efforts to develop others that managers raise their demands on themselves. The best performers in any profession always look upon the men they have trained and developed as the proudest monument they can leave behind.

PART THREE

THE STRUCTURE OF MANAGEMENT

CHAPTER 16

WHAT KIND OF STRUCTURE?

Organization theory and the "practical" manager—Activities analysis—Decision analysis—Relations analysis.

UNTIL well into the seventeenth century, surgery was performed not by doctors but by barbers who, untaught and unlettered, applied whatever tortures they had picked up during their apprenticeship. Doctors, observing a literal interpretation of their oath not to inflict bodily harm, were too "ethical" to cut and were not even supposed to watch. But the operation, if performed according to the rules, was presided over by a learned doctor who sat on a dais well above the struggle and read what the barber was supposed to be doing aloud from a Latin classic (which the barber, of course, did not understand). Needless to say, it was always the barber's fault if the patient died, and always the doctor's achievement if he survived. And the doctor got the bigger fee in either event.

There is some resemblance between the state of surgery four centuries ago and the state of organization theory until recently. There is no dearth of books in the field; indeed, organization theory is the main subject taught under the heading of "management" in many of our business schools. There is a great deal of importance and value in these books—just as there was a great deal of genuine value in the classical texts on surgery. But the practicing manager has only too often felt the way the barber must have felt. It is not that he, as a "practical man," resisted theory. Most managers, especially in the larger companies, have learned the hard way that performance depends upon proper organization. But the practicing manager did not as a rule understand the organization theorist, and vice versa.

We know today what has been amiss. Indeed, we are speedily closing the gap by creating a unified discipline of organization that is both practical and theoretically sound.

We know today that when the practical manager says "organization," he does not mean the same thing the organization theorist means when he says "organization." The manager wants to know what kind of a structure he needs. The organization theorist, however, talks about how the structure should be built. The manager, so to speak, wants to find out whether he should build a highway and from where to where. The organization theorist discusses the relative advantages and limitations of cantilever and suspension bridges. Both subjects can properly be called "road building." Indeed, both have to be studied to build a road. But only confusion can result if the question what kind of a road should be built is answered with a discussion of the structural stresses and strains in various types of bridge.

In discussing organization structure, we have to ask both what kind of a structure is needed and how it should be built. Each question is important; and only if we can answer both systematically can we hope to arrive at a sound, effective and durable structure.

First, we must find out what kind of structure the enterprise needs.

Organization is not an end in itself but a means to the end of business performance and business results. Organization structure is an indispensable means; and the wrong structure will seriously impair business performance and may even destroy it. Still, the starting point of any analysis of organization cannot be a discussion of structure. It must be the analysis of the business. The first question in discussing organization structure must be: What is our business and what should it be? Organization structure must be designed so as to make possible the attainment of the objectives of the business for five, ten, fifteen years hence.

There are three specific ways to find out what kind of a structure is needed to attain the objectives of a specific business: activities analysis; decision analysis; relations analysis.

The Activities Analysis

To find out what activities are needed to attain the objectives of the business is such an obvious thing to do that it would hardly seem to deserve special mention. But analyzing the activities is as good as unknown to traditional theory. Most traditional authorities assume that a business has a set of "typical" functions which can be applied everywhere and to everything without prior analysis. Manufacturing, marketing, engineering, accounting, purchasing and personnel—these would, for instance, be the typical functions of a manufacturing business.

Of course, we can expect to find activities labeled "manufacturing," "engineering" or "selling" in a business that manufactures and sells goods. But these typical functions are empty bottles. What goes into each? And do we need a pint bottle or a quart bottle for the functions labeled "manufacturing," for instance? These are the really important questions. And to these the concept of typical functions has no answers. The average manufacturing business will indeed use these functions; but an individual manufacturing business may not need all of them or may need other functional containers as well. We also have to find out therefore whether these classifications are indeed appropriate for the activities of the specific business. To ignore these questions and operate in terms of a pre-established set of typical functions is like first giving a patient medicine and then diagnosing what ails him. And the results are just as dubious.

These questions can only be answered by analyzing the activities that are needed to attain objectives.

In the woman's dress industry engineering as such is unknown; and manufacturing is so simple by and large, as not to deserve ranking as a major function. But design is all-important.

At Crown-Zellerbach, the big West Coast pulp and paper manufacturer, long-range forest management is so important and so difficult that it had to be organized as a separate major function.

The American Telephone and Telegraph Company has organized the raising of capital in the financial markets as a separate major function, distinct alike from accounting and from long-range capital-investment planning.

One of the big manufacturers of electric bulbs considers the education of the public in the use of lighting and the creation of habits of good lighting to be a major need of the business, which can be satisfied only if the task is organized as a separate function. Since practically all American homes, shops and plants have electricity, the expansion of the market and the growth of the business depend indeed on increase in electric-bulb use per customer rather than on finding new customers.

To have organized any of these activities: forest management at Crown Zellerbach, raising capital at Bell Telephone, customer education at the lamp company, as part of another function would have resulted in their neglect. Indeed, they were organized as separate functions because an activities analysis revealed that as part of another function they were not being given the attention their importance warranted, and did not yield the performance the company required.

To substitute typical functions for an analysis of the activities actually needed is dangerous mental laziness, and in the end causes double work. For only a thorough and careful activities analysis can bring out what work has to be performed, what kinds of work belong together, and what emphasis each activity is to be given in the organization structure.

An analysis of the activities is needed most in the business that has been going for some time, and especially in the business that has been going well. In such a business the analysis will invariably reveal that important activities are either not provided for or are left hanging in mid-air to be performed in a haphazard fashion. It will almost invariably bring out activities that, once important, have lost most of their meaning, but continue to be organized as major activities. It will demonstrate that historically meaningful groupings no longer make sense but have, instead, become obstacles to proper performance. And it will certainly lead to the discovery of unnecessary activities that should be eliminated.

The new business also needs such thinking. But the worst mistakes in the organization of activities are invariably the results of growth—and especially of success. They occur most often where an enterprise that started out, so to speak, in a lowly but functional two-room cottage, put in, as it grew, a new wing here, an attic there, a partition elsewhere, until it is now housed in a twenty-six-room monstrosity in which all but the oldest inhabitants need a St. Bernard to bring them back from the water cooler.

Decision Analysis

The second major tool to find out what structure is needed is an analysis of decisions. What decisions are needed to obtain the performance necessary to attain objectives? What kind of decisions are they? On what level of the organization should they be made? What activities are involved in or affected by them. Which managers must therefore participate in the decisions—at least to the extent of being consulted beforehand? Which managers must be informed after they have been made?

It may be argued that it is impossible to anticipate what kinds of decisions will arise in the future. But while their content cannot be predicted—nor the way they ought to be made—their kind and subject matter have a high degree of predictability. In one large company I found that well over 90 per cent of the decisions that managers had to take over a five-year period, were what might be called "typical," and fell within a small number of categories. In only a few cases would it have been necessary to ask: Where does this decision belong? had the problem been thought through in advance. Yet, because there was no decision analysis, almost three quarters of the decisions had to "go looking for a home," as the graphic phrase within the company put it, and most of them went to a much higher level of management than they should have.

It has also been argued that a breakdown of decisions must be an arbitrary measure. "One president likes to make one kind of decision himself, another president another kind," the argument runs. Of course, personalities and their preferences play a part in any organization. But the area of personal preference is small and marginal, and adjustment to it is fairly easy (after all, how often do presidents change?). Furthermore what matters is not what the president likes to do but what he—and every other member of management—should do in the interests of the enterprise. Indeed, if personal preference rather than the objective needs of the business are allowed to control where decisions are being made, effective organization and good performance become impossible. It is no accident that the greatest single cause for the failure of businesses to consolidate their growth, and for their relapse into smallness if not into bankruptcy, is the failure of the boss to give up making decisions when they are no longer his to make.

To place authority and responsibility for various kinds of decisions requires first that they be classified according to kind and character. Such standard classifications as "policy decisions" and "operating decisions" are practically meaningless, however, and give rise to endless debates of a highly abstruse nature. There are four basic characteristics which determine the nature of any business decision.

First, there is the degree of futurity in the decision. For how long into the future does it commit the company? And how fast can it be reversed?

The decision whether the raw material requirements of a speculative commodity such as copper should be bought according to production schedules or according to a forecast of price fluctuations may involve a good deal of money, and a complex analysis of many factors. It may, in other words, be both a difficult and an important decision. But it is almost immediately reversible; all it commits the company to is the duration of a futures contract (which can be sold every business day). Such a decision, despite its importance and difficulty, should therefore always be pushed down to the lowest level of management on which it can be made: perhaps the plant manager or the purchasing agent.

The second criterion is the impact a decision has on other functions, on other areas or on the business as a whole. If it affects only one function, it is of the lowest order. Otherwise it will have to be made on a higher level where the impact on all affected functions can be considered; or it must be made in close consultation with the managers of the other affected functions. To use technical language: "optimization" of process and performance of one function or area must not be at the expense of other functions or areas; it must not be "sub-optimization."

One example of a decision which looks like a purely "technical" one affecting one area only, but which actually has a major impact on many areas, is a change in the methods of keeping the parts-inventory in a mass-production plant. This not only affects all manufacturing operations, but makes necessary major changes in assembly. It affects delivery to customers—it might even lead to radical changes in marketing and pricing, such as the abandonment of certain designs and models and of certain premium prices. And it may require substantial changes in engineering design. The technical problems in inventory keeping—though quite considerable—almost pale into insignificance compared to the problems in other areas which any change in inventory keeping will produce. To "optimize" inventory-keeping at the expense of these other areas cannot be allowed. It can be avoided only if the decision is recognized as belonging to a fairly high order and handled as one affecting the entire process: Either it has to be reserved for management higher than the plant; or it requires close consultation between all functional managers.

Third, the character of a decision is determined by the number of qualitative factors that enter into it: basic principles of conduct, ethical values, social and political beliefs, etc. The moment value considerations have to be taken into account, the decision moves into a higher order and requires either determination or review at a higher level. And the most important as well as the most common of all qualitative factors are human beings.

Finally, decisions can be classified according to whether they are periodically recurrent or rare, if not unique, decisions. Both kinds have to be made on the level in the organization that corresponds to the futurity, impact and qualitative characteristics of the decision. Suspending an employee for a breach of discipline would belong in the former category; changing the nature of the product or of the business, in the latter. The recurrent decision requires the establishment of a general rule, that is, of a decision in principle. Since suspending an employee deals with a human being, the rule has to be decided at a high level in the organization. But the application of the rule to the specific case, while also a decision, then becomes a routine matter and can be placed on a much lower level. The rare decision, however, has to be treated as a distinct event. Whenever it occurs, it has to be thought through from beginning to end.

A decision should always be made at the lowest possible level and as close to the scene of action as possible. Moreover, a decision should always be made at a level insuring that all activities and objectives affected are fully considered. The first rule tells us how far down a decision *should* be made. The second how far down it *can* be made, as well as which managers must share in the decision and which must be informed of it.

Analyzing the foreseeable decisions therefore shows both what structure of top management the enterprise needs and what authority and responsibility different levels of operating management should have.

Relations Analysis

The final step in the analysis of the kind of structure needed is an analysis of relations. With whom will a manager in charge of an activity have to work, what contribution does he have to make to managers in charge of other activities, and what contribution do these managers, in turn, have to make to him?

Traditionally we tend to define the job of a manager only in terms of the activity he heads, that is, only downward. We have already seen (in Chapter 11) that this is inadequate. Indeed, the first thing to consider in defining a manager's job is the contribution his activity has to make to the larger unit of which it is a part. In other words, the upward relationship must be analyzed first and must be established first.

One example of relations analysis and of its results is that of a large railroad. Traditionally railroads place the two engineering functions concerned respectively with the design of new, and the maintenance of existing, equipment and facilities under the transportation function which is concerned with the physical movements of goods and passengers. If the engineering functions are defined in terms of the downward relationships of their respective managers, this tradition makes sense. For seen in this way, these functions are adjuncts to transportation. But the moment the question is asked: What is the upward relationship of the two engineering managers, the traditional organization structure is seen as fallacious and as a serious impediment to good railroad management. For perhaps the most important job of either engineering manager is to advise top management and to participate in the long-range decision on what the railroad's business should be. They are directly charged, by virtue of their job and technical knowledge with making the decision on one of the most important objectives: the supply of physical resources. They have major responsibility both for setting innovation objectives and for attaining them. Their jobs should therefore be organized so as to bring them directly into the counsels of top management, if not to make them members of the chief executive team. Otherwise basic decisions affecting the long-range future of the business, if not its very survival, will be taken without the necessary knowledge. Even if the decisions themselves are the right decisions, they will not be understood by the people who have to carry them out—the two engineering managers—and are likely to be sabotaged by them. Upward relations, in other words require that these functions be by themselves, outside the transportation function and directly reporting to top management.

But the sideways relations must also be analyzed. The contribution which a manager makes to the managers of other activities is always an important part of his job and may be the most important one.

A good example is the job of the marketing manager. In his downward relationship he is a "sales manager" in charge of a sales force engaged in obtaining orders. But if this relationship determines the organizational structure of the job (as it has traditionally done) the most important contributions the enterprise requires from its marketing activity may not be made at all. To do its job properly, engineering must obtain from the marketing activity information on new products needed and on modification of old products. It must obtain guidance on product development and design. It must obtain pricing information. Similarly, only from the marketing activity can manufacturing obtain such vital information as the anticipated volume of sales and the delivery schedules. Purchasing similarly depends on information which only the marketing manager can supply. And in turn the marketing manager requires information and guidance from all these functions to discharge adequately his downward relationship, that is, his responsibility for running the sales department. Indeed, the sideways relations have become so important that more and more companies either subordinate the sales manager to a manager of marketing charged primarily with the sideways relations, or split the marketing activity in two, a marketing and a selling function, the managers of which have equal status and operate independently though in close co-operation.

Analyzing relations is not only indispensable to the decision of what kind of a structure is needed. It is also necessary to make the vital decision how the structure should be manned. Indeed, only an analysis of the relations in a job makes possible intelligent and successful staffing.

These three analyses—of activities, of decisions, of relations—should always be kept as simple and as brief as possible. In a small enterprise they can often be done in a matter of hours and on a few pieces of paper. (In a very large and complex enterprise, though, such as General Electric or General Motors, the job may well require months of study and the application of highly advanced tools of logical analysis and synthesis.) But these analyses should not be slighted or skimped no matter how small or simple the business. They should be considered a necessary task and one that has to be done well in every business. For only these analyses can show what structure the enterprise needs. Only on their foundation can a functioning organization be built.

CHAPTER 17

BUILDING THE STRUCTURE

The three structural requirements of the enterprise—Organization for performance—The least possible number of management levels—Training and testing tomorrow's top managers—The two structural principles—Federal decentralization—Its advantages—Its requirements—Its limitations—The rules for its application—Functional decentralization—Its requirements and rules—Common citizenship under decentralization—The decisions reserved to top management—Company-wide promotions—Common principles—The symptoms of malorganization—A lopsided age structure of the management group.

THE first concern in building a management structure is the requirements it has to satisfy. What are its typical stresses and strains? What performance does it have to be capable of?

There are three major answers to these questions.

1. *It must be organization for business performance.* This is the end which all activities in the enterprise serve. Indeed, organization can be likened to a transmission that converts all activities into the one "drive," that is, business performance. Organization is the more efficient the more "direct" and simple it is, that is, the less it has to change the speed and direction of individual activities to make them result in business performance. The largest possible number of managers should perform as businessmen rather than as bureaucrats, should be tested against business performance and results rather than primarily by standards of administrative skill or professional competence.

Organization structure must not direct efforts toward the wrong

in the large enterprise there should be several such jobs in succession for a man so that future top managers can be selected by the only rational principle of selection and tested by the only adequate test: that of actual business performance on their own.

The job must also be junior enough so that a man who fails can easily be removed. To remove a president or an executive vice-president is difficult. In the publicly owned corporation with its completely dispersed ownership it is well-nigh impossible. "Once you have a president you are stuck with him and can only hope for the intervention of providence through coronary thrombosis," a cynical company director once phrased it.

The Two Structural Principles

To satisfy these requirements organization structure must apply one or both of two principles:

It must whenever possible integrate activities on the principle of *federal decentralization,* which organizes activities into autonomous product businesses each with its own market and product and with its own profit and loss responsibility. Where this is not possible it must use *functional decentralization,* which sets up integrated units with maximum responsibility for a major and distinct stage in the business process.

Federal decentralization and functional decentralization are complementary rather than competitive. Both have to be used in almost all businesses. Federal decentralization is the more effective and more productive of the two. But the genuinely small business does not need it, since it is in its entirety an "autonomous product business." Nor can federalism be applied to the internal organization of management in every large business; in a railroad, for example, the nature of the business and its process rule it out. And in practically every business there is a point below which federal decentralization is no longer possible, below which there is no "autonomous product" around which management can be organized. Federal decentralization while superior is thus limited.

Functional decentralization is universally applicable to the organization of management. But it is a second choice for any but the small enterprise. It has to be used in all enterprises sooner or later, but the later it can be resorted to the stronger the organization.

Decentralization whether federal or functional has become so prevalent in American industry these last few years as to be a household word. Its practice goes back at least thirty years. DuPont, General Motors, Sears and General Electric all started to develop their decentralized organization before 1929.

Yet organization theory has paid little attention to it. To my knowledge my study of General Motors which appeared in 1946[1] was the first that considered decentralization as a distinct principle of organization.

The reason for this lag is that conventional organization theory starts with the functions inside a business rather than with the goals of a business and their requirements. It takes the functions for granted—if not for God-given; and it sees in the business nothing but a congeries of functions.

Moreover, conventional theory still defines a function as a group of related skills. And it considers this similarity of skills to be both the essence of functionalism and its major virtue. If we look at well-organized functional units, however, we shall find no such "bundle of skills." The typical sales department, for instance, includes selling activities, market research, pricing, market development, customer service, advertising and promotion, product development, often even responsibility for relationships with governmental bodies and trade associations. And the typical manufacturing department covers an equally wide range. No greater diversity of skills, abilities or temperaments could be imagined than that needed in these "functional" organizations. Indeed, no greater variety exists in the business as a whole. If functionalism were really, as the books say, organization by skill-relationship, the typical sales or manufacturing department would be absurd if not totally unable to function. But they work—indeed, they work much better than units organized on similarity of skills—because they bring together all the specialized activities needed in one fairly sharply delimited stage of the work. That they require different skills and different temperaments is irrelevant; what matters is that they bring together what is objectively needed for performance.

Actually what the textbook considers an a priori axiom of functionalism reflects nothing but the production management of fifty or sixty years

[1] Under the title *Concept of the Corporation* (New York: John Day, 1946).

ago—now hopelessly outdated. Then a plant was usually organized so as to have all machines of the same kind together: screw machines in one corner of the plant, reamers in another, planers in a third and so on. We have learned since that the first principle of good production organization is to bring the machines to the work, rather than the work to the machines. It is cheaper to have the work flow according to its own inner logic, even if it requires a few more machines, than to cart materials around. Similarly, we must always bring the special activity to the work, never the work to the special activity. For ideas and information cost even more to cart around than materials, and stand being handled even less well.

The stress on functional organization by related skills is thus a misunderstanding of what functional organization properly should be: organization by stage of process. This is illustrated by the unsatisfactory experience with those functions that are typically organized as bundles of skills: accounting and engineering. The typical accounting department is in constant friction with the rest of the organization. The typical engineering department has constant difficulty working out its objectives or measuring its performance. Neither condition is an accident.

The typical accounting department contains at least three different functions, put together because they all use the same basic data and require the ability to add and to subtract. There is the function of furnishing information to managers so as to enable each to control himself. There is a financial and tax function; there is finally a record-keeping and custodial function. To this is normally added a fourth, the function of doing the government's bookkeeping in payroll deduction for income tax, in social security, in countless reports and forms, etc. Even the theory and the concepts underlying these various functions are dissimilar. And the attempt to apply concepts pertaining to one function (for instance, financial accounting) to another (for instance, management information) causes both the perennial controversies within the accounting fraternity, and the constant friction between the accountant and his associates in management.

Similarly, the typical engineering department usually contains long-range basic research, product design, application engineering, service engineering, tool design, plant engineering and housekeeping jobs such as maintenance engineering, building engineering and so forth. Some of these specialties have to do with innovation, others with marketing, other with manufacturing, others with maintenance of fixed assets, that is, really with financial matters, etc. The only thing these tasks have in common are elementary tools—not even much in the way of skill. To put them together because they all have the word "engineering" somewhere in their title makes an unmanageable hodgepodge. No one can have proper performance standards, or can know what is expected of him or even whose expectations he has to fulfill.

Some of the large companies are today engaged in thinking through engineering organization and in putting the engineering jobs where they belong according to the logic of the work to be done rather than according to the tools needed. Some have also begun to divide the traditional accounting function according to the logic of work rather than according to the logic of personal skills and personal limitations. The faster we do these jobs, the better business organization we shall have.

The Weaknesses of Functional Organization

But even proper functional organization by stage of process does not adequately serve the structural requirements of the business. It makes it difficult to focus on business performance. Every functional manager considers his function the most important one, tries to build it up and is prone to subordinate the welfare of the other functions, if not of the entire business, to the interests of his unit. There is no real remedy against this tendency in the functional organization. The lust for aggrandizement on the part of each function is a result of the laudable desire of each manager to do a good job.

Functional organization of necessity puts the major emphasis on a specialty, and on a man's acquiring the knowledge and competence that pertains to it. Yet the functional specialist may become so narrow in his vision, his skills and his loyalties as to be totally unfit for general management.

A further weakness is the difficulty of setting objectives in the functional pattern and of measuring the results of functional work. For the function as such is concerned with a part of the business, not with its whole. Its objectives will therefore tend to be set in terms of "professional standards" rather than in terms of the success of the business. They will tend to direct the attention and efforts of managers away from business success rather than toward it, will tend too often to emphasize and to reward the wrong things.

Because of this, functional organization leads to levels upon levels of management. It can rarely train or test a man in business performance, and almost never in a position where he has full responsibility for results. And, largely because it needs many levels, it tends to erode the meaning of each job and to make it appear nothing but a steppingstone to a promotion.

Federal Decentralization

This is the reason why federal decentralization—that is, organization by autonomous product business—is fast becoming the norm for the larger company. In the last ten years it has been adopted or fully developed by Ford and Chrysler (General Motors has had it since 1923 or so), General Electric and Westinghouse, all the major chemical companies (except duPont who had developed it by 1920), most of the large oil companies, the largest insurance companies and so forth. And the principle is being expounded in articles and speeches, in management magazines and management meetings so that by now the phrase at least must be familiar to every American manager.

These are the main reasons for its emergence as the dominant structural principle of modern large business enterprise:

1. It focuses the vision and efforts of managers directly on business performance and business results.

2. Because of this the danger of self-deception, of concentrating on the old and easy rather than on the new and coming, or of allowing unprofitable lines to be carried on the backs of the profitable ones, is much lessened. The facts do not stay hidden under the rug of "overhead" or of "total sales figures."

3. The advantages are fully as great in respect to management organization. Management by objectives becomes fully effective. The manager of the unit knows better than any one else how he is doing, and needs no one to tell him. Hence the number of people or units under one manager no longer is limited by the span of control; it is limited only by the much wider span of managerial responsibility.

A Sears Roebuck vice-president may have a hundred stores under him—each an autonomous unit, responsible for marketing and for profits. And each store manager may have thirty section managers under him, each running his own autonomous unit and also responsible for marketing and profitability goals. As a result, there are only two levels in Sears between the lowest management job, section manager in a store, and the president: the store manager and the regional vice-president.

4. A Sears experiment showed dramatically the impact of federal decentralization on the development of tomorrow's managers.

Right after the war Sears hired a large number of young men. They were divided arbitrarily. About one third were put into the large stores, one third into the small stores, one third into the mail-order business. Five years later the best of the young men in the large stores were getting to be section managers; and the best of the young men in the small stores were getting ready to be managers of small stores themselves. In the mail-order houses there were actually more openings during these years. But mail order has always been organized by functional specialization. The best of the young men placed there had left the company; the others were, five years later, still clerks punching a time clock.

Similar is the experience of a large truck and tractor manufacturer.

The company's largest division has its own foundry run as part of its manufacturing department. All the other divisions—three in number—are supplied by the company's second and smaller foundry which is organized as an autonomous product business and which also sells to outside customers. The capital invested per ton of capacity in both foundries is about the same, the products closely akin. Yet, all the new processes developed during the last twenty years have come out of the foundry that operates as a product business. Its profits have been consistently one fifth higher even though it faces a more competitive and more widely fluctuating market. And while the second foundry has given the company three vice-presidents in the last twenty years, the first is still run by the man who was put in as manager when the plant was built in 1930.

5. Finally, federal decentralization tests men in independent command early and at a reasonably low level.

Two men in a large container-making company were generally considered the "heirs apparent"—one an extremely competent production man, one the president's chief assistant. When the company organized itself into autonomous product businesses, the two men were appointed general managers of the two largest of the new product divisions. Within three years it had become clear that neither was fit for a top executive job.

The former manufacturing man could not run a balanced business. He neglected marketing and engineering, could not plan or budget. The former chief assistant could not make decisions. He always came back "upstairs" for the answers rather than assume responsibility himself. In fact, both had to be moved back into positions as lieutenants. But three other men who had never been considered top management material rapidly emerged as leaders when entrusted with the general management of smaller divisions. "We put in decentralization more because it was the fashion than because we really believed in it or understood it," the company's president said recently. "It has developed our business almost twice as fast as we had dared hope; and the greatest growth of sales and profits has been in lines that had always been problem children before. Above all, it has saved us in the nick of time from making the fatal mistake of putting the wrong people in at the top. I'll never again make that decision on the basis of my judgment instead of by performance test in an independent responsibility. We put in eight division managers; only three performed as we had expected them to perform. Two—our winning entries—never got away from the post. And the three whom we thought the least of turned out to be world beaters."

Both the Sears store managers and the container-division managers know what is expected of them; for that is determined by the objectives of the autonomous units they manage. As long as they attain these objectives, they do not have to worry about what the boss wants; nor do they have any trouble getting across to him what they want and need.

The Requirements of Federal Decentralization

When federal decentralization is defined as the structural principle under which as many managerial units as possible are organized as if they were businesses in themselves, what does this mean concretely? What are the requirements? What are the limitations?

The autonomous product businesses under federal decentralization vary tremendously in size. On the lower end of the scale there are the small Sears, Roebuck stores with fewer than fifty employees and with annual sales well below half a million dollars. At the upper end of the scale there is the Chevrolet division of General Motors with annual sales of four billions or so and with 200,000 employees or more.

They also vary tremendously in scope.

A General Motors appliance division—AC Spark Plug, for instance—is all but a complete business in itself. It may sell the larger part of its products outside of General Motors: direct to the customer for replacement, and to other automobile companies that are competitors of General Motors. It purchases its own raw materials, does its own engineering and design, its own manufacturing and so forth. Because of the special nature of its products, it may not even make much use of the company's central research facilities. What it uses are services like product-testing, consumer research and legal advice which many entirely independent businesses buy on the outside anyhow. It does not conduct its own contract negotiations with the labor union. But many independent businesses also have industry-wide contracts negotiated for them by their trade association. And AC Spark Plug handles its own union grievances. The only important function which an independent business would have to discharge, and which AC Spark Plug does not, is the raising of capital. Its funds are provided by General Motors.

But federally decentralized units may also have a much narrower scope.

A Sears store, for instance—even a large one doing ten million dollars' worth of business a year—does not do its own buying, its own merchandise development, its own selection of goods. That is done for all stores by the company. The company rather than the store manager decides which kinds of goods the store will carry, and, roughly, in what proportion. Whether he likes it or not, the manager must give space in his store to a "catalogue order desk" accepting orders for the Sears mail-order business which is in direct competition with the store. Even the arrangement of the store counters and the display are largely controlled from Chicago headquarters. Finally the manager has no pricing authority. His concern and responsibility are for pushing the sales of merchandise designed, developed, bought and priced for him.

Between these extremes there is every conceivable variation.

At General Electric, there are product businesses that are as truly autonomous as AC Spark Plug. There are others that, though eventually responsible for their marketing, entrust the actual selling and servicing job to a separate sales division which handles the products of several GE businesses pretty much the way an independent manufacturer's representative handles a number of complementary lines produced by different manufacturers. Some General Electric product businesses do all their own research; some do research co-operatively with neighboring businesses; some depend heavily on the company's central research facilities.

The same variety can be found in some chemical companies. Indeed, it is one advantage of federal decentralization that it permits great diversity without undermining essential unity.

There is, however, one requirement that must be satisfied if federal decentralization is to result. The managerial unit must contribute a profit to the company rather than merely contribute to the profit of the company. Its profit or loss should directly become company profit or loss. In fact, the company's total profit must be the sum total of the profits of the individual businesses. And it must be a genuine profit—not arrived at by manipulating accounting figures, but determined by the objective and final judgment of the market place.

To be able to contribute a profit to the company the unit must have a market of its own. This may be purely a geographic entity.

A West Coast branch plant of a Pennsylvania manufacturer of pots and pans has a market of its own even though it makes the same products as the mother plant in Pittsburgh. For freight charges for pots and pans are too high to allow transcontinental shipments. The Atlanta region of a life-insurance company has a market distinct from that of the Boston region. So has the Sears store in Keene, New Hampshire, even though there is another Sears store offering the same goods at the same prices in Fitchburg, Massachusetts, less than thirty miles away.

But a market may also be defined by the product.

This is the basis on which the autonomous divisions in Ford and General Motors and the product-business departments in General Electric are organized. One of the large rubber companies has organized itself on the federal basis by dividing its products into four major lines; passenger tires, commercial-truck tires, specialty-truck tires and non-tire rubber goods. Each of these lines is distinct and separate—in its customers, in the competition it has to meet, in its distributive channels. And non-tire rubber goods has been further subdivided into six autonomous units—galoshes are one—each with a separate product line and its own management.

In some industries there may be more than one distinct market for the same product lines in the same geographic area.

Institutional buyers of chairs—hospitals, schools, restaurants, hotels. large offices—are a market quite different from retail customers, using different distributive channels, paying different prices, buying in different ways. I know a fair-sized furniture company that attributes its rapid growth largely to having set up retail furniture and institutional furniture as separate product businesses—to the point where each division gets its chairs from its own factory even though the design and the production of the chairs are identical.

The Rules for its Application

Federal decentralization, no matter how large or how small, how autonomous or how restricted the unit may be, should always observe five rules that are essential to its successful application.

1. Any federal organization requires both strong parts and a strong center. The term "decentralization" is actually misleading—though far too common by now to be discarded. It implies that the center is being weakened; but nothing could be more of a mistake. Federal decentralization requires strong guidance from the center through the setting of clear, meaningful and high objectives for the whole. The objectives must demand both a high degree of business performance and a high standard of conduct throughout the enterprise.

Federal decentralization also requires control by measurements. Indeed, wherever we see a federal organization in trouble (wherever, for instance, layers of top management are being heaped on top of a federal structure), the reason is always that the measurements at the disposal of the center are not good enough so that personal supervision of the managers has had to be substituted. The measurements available must be so precise and so pertinent that a manager and his performance can really be judged reliably by them.

2. The federally decentralized unit must be large enough to support the management it needs. The aim should be to have as many autonomous units as possible and to have them as small as possible; but this becomes absurdity when the unit gets too small to support management of the necessary number and quality.

How small is too small depends, of course, on the business. A Sears store can be very small and yet support adequate management. All a small store needs is one manager and a few department heads who are actully first-line supervisors and paid accordingly.

In the mass-production metalworking industry a truly autonomous product business with its own engineering, manufacturing and marketing organization is not, I believe, capable of supporting adequate management unless it sells ten or twelve million dollars' worth of merchandise a year. Product businesses with a significantly lower sales volume are in danger of being understaffed, staffed with inadequate people, or actually managed by the central office.

One solution that combines the benefits of smallness in federal decentralization with adequate management is that of Johnson and Johnson in New Brunswick, New Jersey. The autonomous businesses are kept as small as possible; some, having only two hundred employees or so, represent probably a degree of "smallness" comparable to the Sears, Roebuck store of fifty employees. These small units are responsible for all functions, even for their own financing. Unlike the Sears store they are really complete businesses. Each has its own president. But several units together share the expenses of a number of "Board members"—top officers of the mother company who themselves were once managers of autonomous units, and who act as advisors and experts. In this way the unit can afford top-flight management despite its small size and volume.

3. Each federally decentralized unit should have potential for growth. It is poor organization to put all the stable lines into one autonomous unit and all the promising and expanding ones into another.

4. There should be enough scope and challenge to the job of the managers. I can best explain what I mean by an illustration.

In the otherwise radical decentralization of a large rubber company, the design of manufacturing processes was deliberately made a concern of the company rather than of the product businesses, even though there would have been enough income in each product business to support the necessary staff. That the various businesses had fairly similar problems in manufacturing processes was not the reason for centralizing the activity. On the contrary, it was the major argument for decentralizing this function along with the rest, so as to obtain the benefits of competition between the new divisions. But "designing manufacturing processes" demands bold imagination, new thinking and elbow room for experimentation. And that, the company felt, required more scope and challenge than the autonomous-product divisions could provide.

Yet, the decentralized unit and its managers also need scope and challenge. They should, for instance, have considerable responsibility for innovations—otherwise they may become set in a routine. There is thus a balance to be found between the need of certain activities to have more scope than a federally decentralized unit can offer, especially if it is small, and the need for enough challenge for decentralized managers.

5. Federal units should exist side by side, each with its own job, its own market or product. Where they touch it should be in competition with each other—as are the automobile divisions of General Motors or of Ford. But they should not normally be required to do anything jointly. Their relation should be close and friendly—but based strictly on business dealings rather than on the inability of individual units to stand alone.

Where federal units cannot be organized on the basis of an arm's-length relationship, where the one feeds the other and the other depends on the first for its operations, they must be given what, following the terminology of federalist political theory in America, I would call a "right of nullification." What I mean by this is illustrated by the General Motors rule regarding the relationship between automobile divisions and accessory divisions producing parts.

The automobile divisions have the right to buy from the outside rather than from their own accessory divisions if they can get the part at a lower price or in better quality from an outside supplier. In turn, the accessory divisions are entitled to sell on the outside—even to a direct competitor of their automobile divisions—if they can get a better deal. This right, though used sparingly, is by no means a dead letter. Its existence strengthens both parties and makes them more autonomous, more efficient, more responsible and better performers.

It is often argued that such a right of nullification denies the very values of integration; also it is said that it does not really matter which unit makes the profit since it all goes into the same corporate pocket. But this assumes that a surface appearance of harmony is preferable to efficiency and low costs. It assumes further that a company benefits by integration regardless of the performance of its constituent parts. Both are untenable assumptions. Above all, the argument overlooks the impact of such a right of nullification on the performance of both units and on their responsibility.

Cases in point are the two large oil companies which both run their own fully owned tanker fleets. In the one the transportation division which runs the tankers has the right to hire them out to refineries other than those of its own company if it can thereby get a higher tankerage rate. The refineries in turn can hire outside tankers if they can get them cheaper. In the other company the tanker fleet is run by a separate, though wholly owned, company. But the tankers can only be used for the company's own refineries which in turn cannot use outside tankers. And the frequent disputes over the rate charged for tankerage are decided by top management.

Both companies consider their tanker service to be autonomous and to have responsibility for profit and loss. The "right to nullification" has not been used in the first company in many years. But its very existence makes tanker management feel that it indeed runs its own business. Tanker-management in the second company feels that it runs a plant facility rather than a business. Indeed, the people in the transportation unit resent as hypocritical top management's talk about their autonomy. And there is little doubt that it is the company with the truly "federal" tanker unit that gets the better and cheaper transportation service.

That there must be a distinct market sets the limits for the application of federal decentralization. It seems to rule it out for a railroad, for instance. Three quarters of the business handled on every division of the line normally originate on another division or are destined for another division. There is, in other words, no distinct market and no distinct product for any managerial unit within a railroad.

But the need for a genuine market also prevents federal decentralization from being applied on all levels of a business and to all managerial units.

There are Sears stores that contain only federally decentralized units. The manager in charge of the hardware department runs a little store of his own; there is no management under him and only the store manager above him. This is, of course, possible only because the store and its management have the minimum of business responsibility compatible with genuine autonomy. In all other businesses, however, there is a point below which there must be managerial units that only contribute to the profit rather than contribute a profit themselves. There has to be someone responsible for manufacturing, for instance, if the company wants to have a product to sell. Manufacturing only contributes to the profit; from the point of view of accountant and economist alike, it is, indeed, purely a charge against profit. We speak of "cost of manufacturing," but rightly never of "profit of manufacturing." There is, in other words, in practically every business a point below which organization must be by functional decentralization.

It is important to stress the limitations of federal decentralization and the rules which it must observe so as to prevent abuse of our best concept of organization. But it needs to be said, too, that federal decentralization could be applied a great deal more than it has been so far. It applies to many more industries than have yet adopted it. It applies much further down than most of the decentralized companies have yet pushed it. And the more thoroughly it is being applied, the better are the structural requirements of business performance being satisfied.

Functional Decentralization

Organization by function is the more effective and the less problematical the more it approaches federal decentralization.

The best illustration of this is the Lamp Division of General Electric. Its organization was first developed more than forty years ago when the division was formed by the merger of several independent businesses. It survived an almost twenty-fold growth of business and the emergence of a host of new products.

At first sight the Lamp Division organization chart looks like that of the typical manufacturing company, with its centralized functions of manufacturing, marketing and so forth. Actually the division is in the hands of more than a hundred managers each of whom runs an integrated unit. Some of these units manufacture glass and parts such as the metal base of the bulb. They supply the Lamp Division but also sell a sizable part of their output on the market, mainly to competitors of the division. They therefore have a market of their own and are genuine product businesses. Some components sell finished bulbs to the consumer. They buy the bulbs from the division's own manufacturing plants at a set price—the way a Sears store buys from the Chicago buying office. But they sell in their own territory, New York or Texas or California. Their marketing is directly under their control. Their profitability is partly under their control—in respect to volume of sales, product mix and sales expenses—though both purchase and sales price are set for them. The least decentralized units are the manufacturing plants. They buy glass and parts at a genuine market price from the parts plants. But they sell finished bulbs at an administered price to the sales units. Even so the manufacturing unit can be given innovation and productivity objectives of its own. It can have objectives derived directly from market standing—in respect to quantity and quality of output, for instance. And it has a profitability objective which, while not a completely valid test of performance in a competitive market, is at least impersonal enough to permit comparison between the performance of different manufacturing plants.

The division has both a manufacturing manager and a marketing manager. But their job is not to supervise the unit managers but to serve them. The unit manager himself is appointed by the division's top man, the General Manager, can only be removed by him and reports to him.

Functional work should thus always be organized so as to give the manager the maximum of responsibility and authority, and should always turn out as nearly finished or complete a product or service as possible. Otherwise functional managers will not have objectives of performance and measurements of results that are really derived from business objectives and really focus on business results. They would have to set their goals in terms of "professional personnel management" or "good professional engineering." They would have to measure their results by technical skill rather than by the contribution to the success of the business. Instead of saying: "We succeeded in increasing the productivity of the company's employees by 5 per cent last year," they will say: "We succeeded in selling eighteen new personnel programs to the line managers."

Decentralization is always the best way to organize functional activities. But if the system of production contains any elements of Automation, it becomes absolutely essential. For the production organization of any company using either automatic materials handling or feed-back controls—two main elements of Automation—must be set up as a series of centers of information and decision at very low levels and with a high degree of integration.

This shows clearly in the engine plant of the Ford Motor Company in Cleveland—a mass-production plant "old style" producing uniform products rather than uniform parts, but recently organized with completely automatic materials handling and materials flow. That fairly minor technological change required a thoroughgoing shift of the organization within the plant from the orthodox functional "chain of command" to something that might be called a "task force pattern"—many small centers of information and decision way down the "chain of command" but cutting across functional lines.

Similar centers of information and decision-making must also be established outside the production organization in any business using modern technology for the mass manufacture of parts with assembly into diversified products, or using process production. To design a product is no longer a job which starts in the engineering department, after which the plant tools up, after which the sales department goes to work pushing the product. It is a team effort in which marketeers, production people and engineers work together right from the start—again a "task force" concept. This requires that instead of organizing the work along lines of functional centralization, it must be organized in decentralized, though still functional, units which have the maximum of information and decision, and the broadest possible scope.

The compromise between broad scope and small size that has to be found for the decentralized functional unit should in practice be largely determined by the number of levels of management required. Ideally every functional manager should himself report to the general manager of a federal unit or product business. At the most there should be one level between—no more.

The reason for this is that every manager will, in a well-run enterprise, participate responsibly in the determination of the objectives of the unit that is headed by his immediate superior. He will derive the objectives of the unit he manages directly from those of the next-bigger unit. Thus, a functional manager who reports to the manager of a federal unit will himself take active part in developing the objectives of a business and will therefore focus the functional objectives of his own unit on business ends. The manager one level below will also be actively engaged in the setting of objectives that directly reflect genuine business goals. But one level further down—where there are two levels between functional manager and federal unit or product business—all the objectives the manager deals with are functional. They can hardly bear much closer relationship to the business objectives which they must help attain than a literal prose translation of a lyric poem will bear to the original. The biggest decline in the performance of functional managers, in their contribution to the business and in their awareness of business needs, is to be found, in my experience, when we go from the two-tiered to the three-tiered functional unit.

I realize that in manufacturing plants a limitation to the two levels of functional management is impossible; there are just too many people to manage. In all other functional activities, however, the rule should be observed. That Automation promises to make possible a "flat" organization structure in the manufacturing plant may well be one of its major attractions. It means that Automation will facilitate decentralization rather than undermine it.

An enterprise is too big or too complex for functional organization whenever the organization requires more than two levels of functional managers. Then the principle of federal decentralization should be introduced if it is at all feasible; for by then functional organization has ceased to be able to serve adequately the structural requirements of the business, even at its most functionally decentralized.

Whereas federal units should be connected "in parallel," functional units should be connected "in series." Since by itself no functional unit produces anything, all have to work together. Their best arrangement is similar to that of tiles on a roof: with some overlap around the edges, to make sure that every necessary activity is actually covered, and to set out clearly the areas of necessary co-operation. For while in a federally decentralized unit the job to be done can be spelled out concretely, largely in dollars and cents, in a functional unit objectives are not "hard" enough—or rather their impact on final business results is not close enough. It is difficult to say with precision: This is what the unit must perform. There should therefore be some room for adjustment to the personality of the individual manager and to his competence. There is need for some allowance for an expansion of the role of the unit under a strong man, and for shrinkage under a weaker man. There is need, in other words, for the flexibility of the roof-tile arrangement between functional units.

Common Citizenship under Decentralization

Decentralization, whether federal or functional, requires a common citizenship throughout the enterprise. It is unity through diversity. The most autonomous product business is still not independent. On the contrary, its very autonomy is a means toward better performance for the entire company. And its managers should regard themselves all the more as members of the greater community, of the whole enterprise, for being given broad local autonomy.

Actually decentralization does not create the problem of achieving common citizenship. It is likely to exist in much worse form in a functionally centralized organization, where the local loyalties—to the engineering department or to the manufacturing department—are apt to degenerate into cliques and feuds and to come into head-on collision with the needs and demands of the business. Under federal decentralization these local loyalties are in harmony with the demands of business performance. A man is likely to be a "better General Motors man" for being stoutly devoted to Buick.

Management has three means at its disposal to build common citizenship and to contain centrifugal forces, whether resulting from functional clannishness or from product-business parochialism.

The first lies in the decisions which top management reserves to itself. At General Electric, for instance, only the president can make the decision to abandon a business or to go into a new one. At General Motors, top management at the central office sets the price ranges within which each automobile division's products have to fall, and thus controls the competition between the major units of the company. At Sears, Chicago headquarters decide what kinds of goods—hard goods, appliances, fashion goods and so forth—each store must carry.

In other words, there must be a kind of "general welfare clause" reserving to central management the decisions that affect the business as a whole and its long-range future welfare, and allowing central management to override local ambitions and pride in the common interest.

Secondly, there should be systematic promotion of managers across departmental and unit lines. It has been said that the United States will not have a unified defense service until there is only one ladder of promotion and one career for all the services. Until then, each service will tend to think of its own needs and interests, will see in the other services rivals rather than partners. The same holds true in a business enterprise. A man who knows that one unit—

let us say the AC Spark Plug Division of General Motors—is his career will become an "AC Spark Plug man" rather than a General Motors man. A man who knows that his promotion depends entirely on the powers that run the accounting department, will emphasize "professional accounting" rather than contribution to the company. He will have a greater stake in the expansion of the accounting department than in the growth of the company. Both men, knowing only a corner of the enterprise, will become parochial in their vision.

There is not too much point to shuttling very junior people around a great deal. But once a man has risen above the bottom positions in management, once he has shown exceptionally good performance, he should be considered a candidate for promotion out of his original unit. In General Motors, where this practice is followed fairly consistently, most of the men in the senior management of a division—manufacturing manager, sales manager, chief engineer and so on—have seen service in another division—though usually in the same function—sometime during their career in management. And the division general manager who has not earlier held a senior management job in another division is exceptional.

Common citizenship requires adherence to common principles, that is, common aims and beliefs. But practices should have no more uniformity than the concrete task requires.

Thus, for instance, it is a principle in several large and federally decentralized companies that the company be given the utmost benefit of the talents and abilities in its management group. It is also a principle that each manager be given the maximum of promotional opportunities that his performance has earned for him. To realize these principles requires some uniformity of practice. There must be some way to bring together the names of management people and their records. Managers making promotion decisions must be required to consider all eligible men within the company rather than just the men in their unit. But beyond that it is a manager's decision how he appraises the men, what procedures he uses, and whom he recommends for promotion.

Another example: a large and successful machine-tool maker adopted fifteen years ago the principle of accepting only business demanding the highest engineering standards. But the application of the rule is left to the division managers. And they vary quite a bit in their practices. One division has intentionally restricted itself to supplying highly specialized equipment at premium prices and has thereby converted the restriction of high-quality engineering into a sales-promotion asset. Another has stayed in a competitive field but has systematically worked on educating the customers to demand high engineering standards. Its slogan is: "Better engineering costs no more." A third considered the new principle a serious handicap in its low-priced small tool business, but one that could be overcome by better manufacturing and marketing methods. As the manager put it: "We start out with a handicap of higher engineering costs compared with the competitors. Our customers don't pay for better engineering; they buy by price. Hence we must be able to sell below competitor's price to get the volume our engineering costs require."

In other words, the unity of purpose and beliefs that makes a community with common citizenship is strengthened by diversity of practice. Practices should be uniform only where performance directly affects other units of the business. But principles should be common, clearly spelled out and strictly observed.

Symptoms of Malorganization

Anyone with experience in management knows a healthy organization structure when he sees it (which is seldom enough). But he is like the doctor who knows a healthy person when he sees one but can only define "health" negatively, that is, as the absence of disease, deformity and pathological degeneration.

Similarly, a healthy organization is hard to describe. But the symptoms of malorganization can be identified. Whenever they are present there is need for thorough examination of the organization structure. Whenever they are present the right structural principles are not being observed.

One telling symptom of malorganization is the growth of levels of management—bespeaking poor or confused objectives, failure to remove poor performers, overcentralization or lack of proper activities analysis. Malorganization shows itself also in pressure for "frictional overhead"—for co-ordinators, expediters, or "assistants" who have no clear job responsibility of their own but are supposed to help their superior do his job. Similarly it shows in the need for special measures to co-ordinate activities and to establish communications between managers: co-ordinating committees, incessant meetings, full-time liaison men and so forth.

Equally telling is the tendency to "go through channels" rather than directly to the man who has the information or the ideas needed or who should be informed of what is going on. This is particularly serious under functionalism, for it greatly aggravates the tendency of functional organization to make people think more of their function than of the business. It tends to insulate people —and functional organization, even at its most decentralized, is a heavy insulator. "Going through channels" is not just a symptom of malorganization; it is a cause.

Finally, whatever the organization pattern and structure, management must watch out for a serious and crippling constitutional disorder: a lopsided management age structure.

We have heard lately a good deal of the dangers of having a preponderantly old management. But a preponderantly young management is at least as dangerous. For overage in management liquidates itself fairly fast; and if the enterprise survives till then, its recurrence can be prevented. A preponderantly young management means, however, that for years to come there will be no promotional opportunities for young people. All the good jobs are filled by men with twenty or more years of service-life ahead of them. Good men either will not join such a company or will quit. If they stay, they will soon cease to be good men as they turn into frustrated time servers. Twenty years hence the preponderantly young management of today will be a preponderantly old management—with no one in sight to succeed them. In fact, every company that suffers from an old management today does so because, twenty years ago, under the impact of the Depression, it brought in a young management.

To insure a balanced age structure should be one of the main concerns of manager manpower planning. There must be enough older men to insure opportunities for younger men, enough younger men to insure continuity; enough older men to provide experience and enough younger men to provide drive. Age structure of management is like the metabolism of the human body; unless it is balanced all constitutional processes are diseased.

Good organization structure does not by itself produce good performance—just as a good constitution does not guarantee great presidents, or good laws a moral society. But a poor organization structure makes good performance impossible, no matter how good the individual managers may be.

To improve organization structure—through the maximum of federal decentralization, and through application of the principle of decentralization to functionally organized activities—will therefore always improve performance. It will make it possible for good men, hitherto stifled, to do a good job effectively. It will make better performers out of many mediocre men by raising their sights and the demands on them. It will identify the poor performers and make possible their replacement by better men.

A good organization structure is not a panacea. It is not, as some organization theorists seem to think, the only thing that matters in managing management. Anatomy, after all, is not the whole of biology either. But the right organization structure is the necessary foundation; without it the best performance in all other areas of management will be ineffectual and frustrated.

CHAPTER 18

THE SMALL, THE LARGE, THE GROWING BUSINESS

The myth of the idyllic small business—How big is big?—Number of employees no criterion—Hudson and Chrysler—The other factors: industry position; capitalization needs; time cycle of decisions, technology; geography—A company is as large as the management structure it requires—The four stages of business size—How big is too big?—The unmanageable business—The problems of smallness—The lack of management scope and vision—The family business—What can the small business do?—The problem of bigness—The chief executive and its job—The danger of inbreeding—The service staffs and their empires—How to organize service work—The biggest problem: growth—Diagnosing the growth stage—Changing basic attitudes—Growth: the problem of success.

It is almost an article of the American creed that in the small business there are no problems of spirit and morale, of organization structure or of communication. Unfortunately this belief is pure myth, a figment of the Jeffersonian nostalgia that is so marked in our national sentiment. The worst examples of poor spirit are usually found in a small business run by a one-man dictator who brooks no opposition and insists on making all decisions himself. I know no poorer communications than those of the all too typical small business where the boss "plays it close to the chest." And the greatest disorganization can be found in small business where everybody has four jobs and no one quite knows what anyone is supposed to be doing. In fact, if the Ford Motor Company in the thirties was a model of poor spirit, poor organization and poor communications, it was because the elder Ford tried to run it the way the typical small business tends to be run. It was only the size of his operations that made appear extraordinary what in a small business might well have passed for commonplace.

It is not even true that the small business offers greater opportunities for the development of managers—let alone that it develops them "automatically." The large business has definite advantages. It can much more easily do a systematic job of manager development. It can afford to keep promising people even if it does not have immediate use for them. Above all, it can offer many more management opportunities, especially to the beginner. For it has opportunities to move sideways which allow a beginner to find the place for which he is most fitted. And it is rare luck for a beginner to start out in the work or place for which he is best fitted. That so many of our young college graduates look for jobs in the big business may reflect their search for security, as is so often said. It certainly expresses a sound appraisal of the realities and of their own best interests.

Size, then, does not change the nature of business enterprise nor the principles of managing a business. It does not affect the basic problems of managing managers. It in no way affects the management of work and worker.

But size vitally affects the structure of management. Different size demands different behavior and attitudes from the organs of management. And even more influential than size is change in size, that is, growth.

How Big Is Big?

How big is big has been a perennial question in economic and business literature. The most common measurement used is the number of employees. When a business grows from thirty to three hundred employees, it does indeed undergo a change in structure and behavior; and another qualitative change usually occurs when a business grows from three thousand to thirty thousand employees. But while relevant, number of employees is not by itself decisive.

There are businesses with a handful of employees that have all the characteristics of a very large company.

One example would be a large management consulting firm. "Large" here means about two hundred employees (which in an insurance company would be tiny and in the automobile industry impossibly small). Yet the business has all the "feel" of a large company, requires the organization structure and the attitudes and behavior of large-company management. The reason is, of course, that everybody in a management consulting firm (excepting only secretaries, messengers and file clerks) is top management or at least upper middle management. A management consulting firm, like the Romanian Army, has only generals and colonels. And a senior management group of two hundred men is large business indeed.

Conversely, companies with a large force of employees may well be fairly small business in every other respect, and especially in the demands on management structure and behavior.

The best example I know is a water company supplying a large metropolitan area. The company has 7,500 employees. But as the company's president puts it: "We don't need more management than a toy store does." Being a franchised monopoly, there is no competition. The danger of water's becoming obsolescent is remote. A good deal of technical skill is needed in the building of reservoirs, filter stations and pumping stations, but the contractors supply that; all the engineering the company has to do can be done by the president himself with two engineering draftsmen. Cost control in meter-reading and billing is important; but again there are no business decisions here, only careful procedures work. The only area that requires management of any sort are the relations with the state Public Utility Commission, the City Council and the public. But, as the president points out, they would be the same whether the company had 75 or 7,500 employees.

Another example was the Hudson Motor Car Company which was managed successfully as a medium-sized company until its recent merger with Nash-Kelvinator. It had well over 20,000 employees. But it was only a marginal producer in the automobile market, supplying less than 3 per cent of all cars sold. It was actually too small to exist in an industry that must have national distribution and service; and in the end it had to merge with another company, precisely because it was too small.

During the thirties, however, it prospered because it understood what it means to be a small company. It understood, for instance, that a marginal supplier cannot get anywhere by undercutting price except into bankruptcy. But it shrewdly competed by putting a higher price tag on its cars, which enabled it to offer a larger trade-in price for its used cars.

In this way, the customer was offered a "medium-priced" car which cost him only the same differential between new-car and used-car price that he would have had to pay for the low-priced cars. (This is the classic model for the right price policy of the marginally small business.) Hudson's entire organization—except in the sales area—was that of a small business. One top man made all business decisions. And there were only a small number of functional managers.

The most interesting example is another automobile company: Chrysler. By World War II, Chrysler had become the second largest automobile producer in the world. It had well over 100,000 employees, and its annual sales were well above one billion dollars. Yet, Chrysler in the thirties was (apparently deliberately) organized and run as a medium-sized business. This was done by removing all the complexities. Chrysler only manufactured engines. Everything else that goes into an automobile—frame and bodies, accessories and instruments—was bought on the outside. Production was a pure assembly job, and while requiring great technical skill assembly requires few business decisions. Capital investment in an assembly plant is low, as neither heavy buildings nor complicated machinery is needed. (Few people realize that automobile assembly is done by hand, with a wrench the most complicated tool in general use.) The difference between good and poor assembly-plant management is simple and obvious: the difference between fifteen and seventeen cars coming off the line. And whatever else was needed Chrysler tried to contract out; its union negotiations, for instance, were handled by a partner in a New York law firm. Marketing and design remained as areas of business policy and management decision. Otherwise Chrysler needed only first-rate assembly technicians by and large. As a result, one man could do most of the actual managing: Walter P. Chrysler himself with one or two close associates helping him. The management group was small, compact and easily organized—yet harmonious.

It is, of course, debatable whether this was the right thing to do. Post-war developments have already forced the company into a sharp reversal of its policy and into considerable integration. Whether Chrysler can produce the management it needs and can solve the problems of management organization, behavior and performance its new structure requires, only the next few years will show. Its earlier attempts to behave like a medium-sized company may well be the reason why Chrysler has been losing ground these last few years. But at least as long as Walter P. Chrysler was alive, the colossus was run as if it were a medium-sized business—and successfully at that. The company grew steadily and it earned constantly the highest return on invested capital of all automobile companies.

Sometimes even geography is decisive. I know a company that owns five small plants in five parts of the world—the total number of employees is just over a thousand. Yet, because the production and sales of all five plants are closely integrated, management faces most of the problems of a business employing ten thousand or twenty thousand men.

But all these factors come to a head in the structure of management, in the behavior required of the various organs of management and in the extent to which management has to manage by planning and thinking rather than by "operating." Management structure, especially the structure of top management, is therefore the only reliable criterion of size. A company is as large as the management structure it requires.

The Four Stages of Business Size

If we apply this criterion of management structure, we find that there are not only the "small" and the "big" business. There are at least four, sometimes five, different states of business size—each with its distinct characteristics and problems.

First we have the *small business*. A small business is distinguished from the one-man proprietorship by requiring a level of management between the man at the top and the workers. A business will still be a one-man entrepreneurship if two people run it in partnership, one, for instance, primarily concerned with selling, one with manufacturing. It will still be a one-man entrepreneurship if there are a few foremen in the shop who act only as gang leaders or as skilled workers. But if, for instance, a plant superintendent, a treasurer and a sales manager are needed, it is a small business.

In the small business neither the action part of the chief-executive job nor the objective-setting part of it are full-time preoccupations. The man at the top in a small business can even combine running the business with running a function such as sales or manufacturing. Still the business already needs a management organization.

The next stage of business size is probably the most common; it is also one of the most difficult. Inability to solve the problems of management organization at this stage is one of the most common and serious causes of trouble. Yet, this stage has no name of its own, it is not even usually recognized as a specific stage. For want of a better term I would call it the *fair-sized business*.

The fair-sized business is distinguished from the small business in two ways. In the first place the top operating job has become a full-time assignment. And the over-all business objectives can no longer be set by the man who holds the top operating job. Setting objectives may indeed still be carried on as a part-time job; the treasurer, for instance, may handle it in addition to his financial duties. But it is usually better in the fair-sized business to organize objective-setting as a separate function, to be discharged, for instance, by the functional managers meeting regularly as a planning committee.

The fair-sized business therefore always has to have a chief-executive team. It always has a problem of the relationship of functional managers to top management, though the problem is still small.

It is at this stage that a decision has to be made concerning which of the principles of organization structure apply. The small business is, as a rule, is organized functionally; and there is no difficulty in meeting the requirement that functional managers report directly to the manager of a genuine business. In the fair-sized business the federal principle of organization becomes both applicable and advantageous.

Finally, in the fair-sized business we encounter for the first time the problem of organizing technical specialists. "Staff services" by and large are still unknown (with the exception perhaps of a personnel department). But technical specialists are needed in many areas. Their relationship to functional and top management and to the objectives of the business therefore have to be thought through.

The next stage is the *large business*. Its characteristic is that either one or the other of the chief-executive jobs has to be organized on a team basis. Either the top action job or the job of setting over-all objectives is too big for one man and has to be split. Sometimes one job becomes a full-time job for one man and a part-time job for several other people.

There may, for instance, be a president who, full-time, is the chief action executive. But both the manufacturing vice-president and the sales vice-president may spend a considerable part of their time as top action officers in addition to their functional duties. Similarly, there may be an executive vice-president concerned full time with over-all objectives. Or (as is quite usual) the chairman of the Board, semi-retired from active executive office, may spend practically full time on objectives. At the same time the company's treasurer, its chief engineer and its personnel vice-president may all spend a large part of their time on setting objectives for the company.

In the large business the federal principle of management organization is always the better one. In most large businesses it is the only satisfactory one. This raises a problem of the relationship between top management and the autonomous managers of federal businesses.

The last stage of business size is the *very large business.* It is characterized first by the fact that both the action and the over-all objective-setting part of the chief-executive job must be organized on a team basis. And each job requires the full-time services of several people. Secondly, it can only be organized on the federal principle of management structure. The business is too big and too complex to be organized any other way. Finally, the organization of the chief executive and its relationship to operating management tend to become major problems which engage the attention and energy of top-management people before everything else. It is in the very large business that systematic organization of the chief-executive job is both most difficult and most needed.

How Big Is Too Big?

There may be yet another stage: the *unmanageably big business.* How big can a very large business grow? What is the upper limit of manageable business organization? Is there such a limit?

There is little reason to believe that mere size alone is against the public interest. It need not lead to monopoly. It need not curtail social or economic mobility (indeed, the fastest turnover in our economy is among the smallest and the hundred largest companies). The very large business, contrary to folklore, does not inhibit the growth of new or of small businesses. Entrance into an industry (unless monopolistic practices are permitted by law) depends on technological and market factors and on capital required rather than on the strategic situation within the industry. And the very large business tends to sponsor a host of small, independent businesses acting as suppliers or distributors. Similarly, mere size need not affect labor relations or social stability.

But mere size may make a business unmanageable. A business tends to become unmanageable when the chief executive of a product business can no longer work directly with the chief-executive team of the company but has to go through channels to get to the top. When, in addition to a number of deputy presidents, a layer of group vice-presidents is needed then the business approaches unmanageability. Similarly, when objective-setting officers no longer can work directly as part of the chief-executive team but need an executive vice-president or group vice-president of their own to coordinate them and to communicate their thinking to the top team, the business has grown too big to be manageable.

A very large business also becomes oversized when it needs so many levels of management that even a man of real ability cannot normally rise from the bottom to the top and yet spend enough time on each level to be thoroughly tested in performance. Such a business not only has to fall back on hothouse methods of executive growth. It inevitably suffers from executive anemia as it deprives itself of the full use of its own most precious resource. And it denies a basic premise of our society.

In practice this means that any business that needs more than six or seven levels between rank-and-file employee and top management is too big. Seven, incidentally, is also the number of levels in the military forces (for first and second lieutenant as well as lieutenant colonel and colonel are different pay grades rather than functionally differentiated levels); and the example of the military shows that seven levels is almost too many—for only under wartime conditions of expansion does the ablest officer reach the top ranks.

Finally, a business becomes unmanageable when it is spread out into so many different businesses that it no longer can establish a common citizenship for its managers, can no longer be managed as an entity, can no longer have common over-all objectives.

This danger is particularly great in the business that originated in a common technology, such as chemistry or electrical engineering. As the technology unfolds it creates more and more diversified products with different markets, different objectives for innovation—and ultimately even with different technologies. The point is finally reached where top management cannot know or understand what the diversified businesses require—or even what they are. The point may be reached where objectives and principles that fit one business (or group of businesses) endanger another.

This problem has been realized, it seems, by the big oil companies. The petroleum business is highly complex and closely integrated. But there are only a small number of main products—and they are closely interrelated in production and marketing. Hence even a giant oil company, operating on a world-wide scale, remains manageable. But when petroleum chemistry came along the big oil companies put their new chemical businesses into separate companies, retaining financial ownership but turning over the management job of chemical businesses to new companies. This deliberate break with their own tradition of close integration was their solution of the problem of unmanageability.

The new technology may make this danger of overdiversity the most serious problem of manageability. For Automation does not require larger businesses—it may well make smaller ones possible in many industries. But it requires that each process be conceived of and managed as a separate, integrated whole. Management policies and decisions taken for one process may not fit another; and management policies and decisions taken for one function or one area rather than for the entire process may not fit at all. This not only makes federal organization essential; it also may well set narrow limits to the diversity of product businesses any one top management can administer. It is, I think, no accident that the oil companies have chosen not to integrate their chemical businesses but to separate them out; after all, the oil companies had Automation long before the word was invented. And larger companies in the industries that are about to move into the new technology might well consider seriously the oil industry's example.

There is a great deal a business can do to counteract the forces making for unmanageability. Proper organization of the manager's job and of the business structure will go a long way toward preventing unmanageable size. The application of federal decentralization, for instance, and the proper organization of the chief-executive team should cure top-management dropsy. And I know of no case where the excess levels of management are really necessary.

But in most of the very large companies there is also no requirement of public policy or of public convenience compelling organization in one company. Top managements in the very large companies should therefore always ask themselves: How close are we to unmanageability? And if the answer is close, or very close, they owe an obligation to the stockholders, the managers and the public to find a way of dividing the business.

The Problems of Smallness

Each of the stages of business size not only requires a distinct management structure. It has its own problems and its typical weaknesses.

The main problem of small and fair-sized businesses is usually that they are too small to support the management they need. The top-management positions in the small and fair-sized business may require greater versatility than the corresponding positions in the large or very large company. They may well require as much competence. Top management is not, as in the larger business, supported by a host of highly trained technical and functional people. But the fair-sized business in particular is often too small to be able to offer its managers adequate inducements. Financially it may not be able to pay what a first-rate man can get in a large business even in lower-ranking positions. It cannot easily develop tomorrow's managers in adequate number or quality. Above all, it does not, as a rule, offer the challenge and scope in management positions which the large business offers. The perennial problem in the fair-sized business is the gap between the demands on management and the competence of management, a gap that, only too often, cannot be closed as long as the business remains fair-sized.

Another typical problem of the small or fair-sized business arises out of the fact that it is often family-owned. Senior management position are therefore frequently reserved to family members. This is all right as long as it does not lead to the vicious practice of giving jobs in management to members of the family not competent to hold them. The argument that "we have to support Cousin Paul and might therefore just as well put him to work" is common in the family business. It is also fallacious. The job Cousin Paul is appointed to is not done properly. What is worse, able, ambitious, competent men, who happen not to be members of the family, become discouraged. They either quit the company and go elsewhere, or they "quit on the job," cease to exert themselves and do just enough to get by.

Finally, top management of both the small and the fair-sized business is apt to suffer from narrowness of outlook and constriction of outside contacts. As a result it is in danger of becoming backward in knowledge and competence, technologically as well as economically, and ignorant of the social forces which, in the last analysis, determine the success if not the survival of the business. It may not even realize that it has problems of management organization. Above all, it may totally fail to see the need for thinking and planning, may try to manage intuitively and "by the seat of its pants" when the very survival of the business demands careful analysis.

In many fair-sized businesses these problems are so serious that there is only one solution: expand the business by merger with another small or fair-sized company, or by the acquisition of another such company. Even if it endangers family control, such a move may be preferable to the maintenance of an organization that is too small to be managed properly.

What can the small and the fair-sized business do? First, it has to take great pains to bring an outside viewpoint into its management councils to broaden its vision. (This is one of the main reasons why I stressed the need for an outside Board in the small company.)

Second, if the business is family-owned, it should adopt an ironclad rule that no member of the family should ever be given a job which he has not earned. That Cousin Paul must be supported is one thing. To support him, however, by making him sales manager or treasurer is something else again. As a charity case or as a pensioner, Cousin Paul costs only his annual stipend. As sales manager, he might well cost the company both its market and the services of the managers it needs most. Family members might be given preference if they are as qualified as non-family members, but they should never be appointed or promoted in preference to a better qualified non-family member of management.

The most important rule, however, is to make sure that planning, thinking, analyzing are not slighted under the pressure of action decisions. Top management in the small and in the fair-sized business should at least set aside one week each year for a planning and review conference. This conference should be held outside the office. It should be attended by every senior member of management. It should focus on the needs of the company five years ahead and lead to the setting of objectives in all key areas. It should appraise results in these areas achieved during the past year. And it should assign responsibility for performance in each area to individual members of the group.

The Problems of Bigness

The first problem in the large and very large businesses is the organization and scope of the chief-executive job. What is the job? How should it be organized? What decisions should be made at the top?

The means to tackle this problem have all been described. They consist partly of the proper structural principles, partly of proper organization of the chief-executive job as a team job, partly of proper use of the Board of Directors. An analysis of the activities, decisions and relations of the chief-executive job is also needed.

Still, there is an enormous amount of study to be done on the way top-management people should spend their time, before we know all the answers to the problem of the chief executive in the large and very large business. For the chief executive of the large business is a new thing. What it is, what it does and what it should do are all new questions that still are not fully explored.

The second problem of the large, and especially of the very large enterprise, is the tendency of its management group to become ingrown and inbred, smug and self-satisfied.

It is a biological law that the larger an organism grows the greater is the ratio between its mass and its surface, the less exposure to the outside there is for the cells on the inside. As living organisms grow they have therefore to develop special organs of breathing, perspiration and excretion. It is this law that sets a limit to the size of living organisms, that makes sure that the trees will not grow into the sky; and the business enterprise stands under this law as much as any other organism.

In the large and very large business, as a rule, managers grow up together. They know each other. They talk to each other on the telephone every day. They meet at company meetings, at training sessions, at lunch and at the country club. They have a topic of conversation of assured comon interest.

The resulting tendency of managers to cling together is just as natural as the tendency of Army officers to know only other Army officers, and of Navy officers to know only other Navy officers. And just as a good Navy wife knows only other Navy wives, so the wife of a General Motors, a Sears, Roebuck or a Telephone Company executive is likely to know primarily other General Motors, Sears or Telephone Company wives.

The large or very large company needs an *esprit de corps* among its managers just as does a military organization; it needs close comradeship; it needs pride in what the company is and what it stands for. But this *esprit de corps* must not degenerate into blind acceptance of company tradition as sacred and unchangeable just because "this is the way we have always done it." It must not become blindness to lack of performance or contempt for the "outside." It must not be allowed, in other words, to lead to internal dry rot.

This is so serious a problem that it requires not one but several remedies. One of them is a truly independent Board staffed with capable and hard-working outsiders. Another is the systematic attempt to move management people out of the business and into situations where they meet people from other businesses and other walks of life. One of the major benefits which company executives themselves believe they receive from attending advanced management courses, such as are offered now by a number of universities, is the opportunity to meet men from other businesses, to exchange ideas and information with them, and to learn that the way their own company does things is not the only possible, let alone the best, way. And while few executives enjoyed their wartime service with the government, a good many feel that they are better executives for having had to work with non-business people.

One of the easiest and most effective ways to provide outside exposure, challenge and stimulus is the systematic recruitment of a few people from the outside, even into major management positions. The large and very large enterprise, like the large animal, must systematically develop special organs of respiration and excretion. And the best and quickest way to bring a breath of fresh air right into the middle of the big mass that is the large business, is to bring into a senior management position an executive who has grown up in a different environment. The very thing that will make an outside executive unpopular at first—his tendency to be critical of the conventions, mores and axioms of his new associates—is what makes him useful and important.

But more important than any specific practice is a basic attitude. The large and very large business tends to expect of its managers today that they make the company the center of their universe. But a man who, as the phrase goes, "lives for his business," is far too narrow. Since the company is his life he clings to it with desperation; he is apt to stifle the development of the younger men so as to make himself indispensable and to postpone the horrible day of retirement into an empty world. In its own interest, management should encourage serious outside interests on the part of its executives. Nor should it limit these interests to community affairs that help the company's public relations, or to participation in trade associations and professional societies that are good for the company's standing in the industry. To be known as a minor poet (as was the late Field Marshal Lord Wavell) is an asset rather than a liability in that otherwise unpoetic institution, the British Army. To be known as an ardent and scholarly student of insects (or of Roman coins) is a definite recommendation in a Catholic priest. It is high time that the large businesses, too, realize that the man who "lives for the company" is a danger to himself and to the enterprise, and likely to remain a "perennial boy scout."

The Service Staffs and Their Empires

The large and the very large enterprise face another serious problem: the danger that central office service staffs will become "staff empires."

I am doubtful about the popular use of the terms "line" and "staff" to describe various kinds of activities within the business enterprise. The terms themselves derive from the military. They may have meaning in military organization. Applied to business, they can, however, only confuse.

There are two kinds of activities in any business enterprise: business-producing functions such as marketing and innovation, and supply functions. Some supply functions provide physical goods such as purchasing and production; some provide ideas such as engineering; some provide information such as accounting. But none of these is a staff function. None either advises another function or acts for it.

It would actually be undesirable to have any staff functions. As far as I have been able to grasp the concept, to be "staff" means to have authority without having responsibility. And that is destructive. Managers do indeed need the help of functional specialists. But these men primarily do their own job rather than advise the manager how to do his. They have full responsibility for their work. And they should always be members of the unit to whose manager they render functional service rather than part of a special staff.

In the small or fair-sized business, staff is usually confined to one area: the managing of worker and worker. Even there (as we shall see in Chapter 21) the confusion created by the staff concept has done serious damage. But in the large and in the very large business the staff concept has had the more serious result of creating a number of central office service staffs: groups of professional specialists attached to headquarters who are supposed to render service and advice to operating managers in a particular area. Typically we find in the large business a central-office marketing staff, a central-office manufacturing staff, a central-office engineering staff, a central-office personnel staff, a central-office accounting staff and so forth.

These central-office staffs seriously impede the performance of top management. Concern for each of the key areas of business performance should be the specific responsibility of someone on the chief-executive team. In the small business all eight key areas may well be assigned to one man, who is the "thought man" for the company. The very large company, on the other hand, may have to have a separate full-time executive for each key area: market standing, innovation, productivity, supply of resources, profitability, management organization and personnel, employee performance and attitudes and public responsibility.

But if these men are also supposed to run a service staff, they do not have time or thought for their real job: to consider the business as a whole and to think through the impact of every business decision on the area for whose results they are primarily responsible. They are much too busy running a big administrative machine, much too concerned with the perfecting of tools and techniques, much too interested in pushing their particular "program." General Electric has tried to counteract this; it expects of each of the services vice-presidents that he spend only 80 per cent of his time on administering his own staff and give 20 per cent to being a member of the chief-executive team concerned with the company as a whole. But the proportions should be reversed to insure proper performance of the job of thinking ahead. And no other company, to my knowledge, goes even as far as General Electric; everywhere else these men spend practically all their time on their service empires and little on their top-management job. Indeed, I know one very large company where the manufacturing services vice-president at central office does little except interview personally every man recommended by any one of the fifty-six plant managers for promotion to general foreman.

To be responsible for a service staff which does work for operating managers also means that the man at its head is unlikely to be equipped to discharge the top-management responsibility. He will be an "expert" rather than a "general manager," picked for his knowledge of personnel techniques or market research. But the job requires the vision and experience of a successful business manager. The expert, no matter how successful in building the staff empire, will rarely have either the vision of a general manager or his proven performance in managing a business.

Futhermore, the central-office staffs seriously impede the performance of operating managers.

In every large company I know, the biggest organization problem is the relationship between these service staffs and the managers whom they are supposed to serve. On paper, the concept makes sense, but in practice it does not seem to work out. Instead of serving the manager, the service staffs tend to become his master. Instead of deriving their objectives from the needs and objectives of his business, they tend to push their own specialty as if it were an end in itself. Increasingly the operating manager feels that his promotion depends on service staffs and their reports about him to top management. The service specialist, instead of gauging his own results by the performance of the manager he serves, tends to appraise the performance of a manager by the number of "packaged" special programs the manager allows the service man to install and to run. Loudly protesting their dedication to the ideal of decentralization, the service staffs in many large enterprises are actually the most potent force for centralization. They push toward uniformity of methods, tools and techniques throughout the company. Instead of saying: "There is one right goal but there are many ways of reaching it," they, being concerned with tools and techniques, tend to say: "There is one right tool, one right way, no matter what the goal." Instead of enabling the manager to do a better job himself, the service staff undermines the manager's authority and responsibility.

The proponents of the staff-and-line concept admit this indictment. But they explain it away as owing to the scarcity of good staff men with the right temperament for staff work. All the problems, we are told, will disappear once we have bred enough of the properly self-effacing staff men. I am always suspicious if function is based on temperament; and I have no use whatever for corporate eugenics. Above all, however, the specifications for this ideal staff man sound suspiciously like those for the most dangerous and most irresponsible of all corrupters, the behind-the-scenes wire-puller, intriguer and king-maker, the man who wants power but no responsibility.

How to Organize Service Work

The root of the trouble is the concept of staff-and-line. The root of the trouble is the belief that there is such a thing as staff functions. There are only management functions, either running a business, managing a business-producing function or managing a supply function.

Above all, service work does not belong in top management. It does not belong in the central office. For service work does not affect the business as a whole—it only deals with techniques and tools. Since service work is a help to operating managers, it should be organized as the tool of operating managers.

This means that service work should not, as a rule, be in the hands of professional specialists. There will be exceptions. Negotiations with the union, for example, have become highly centralized; and contracts have become so complicated as to require expensive and highly trained experts. Management should be trying to reverse this development by pushing union relations back to the local managers, which is where they belong. But there will still remain the need for a company-wide labor-relations activity staffed by specialists. This should, however, be considered a co-operative venture serving operating managers rather than a central-office staff. There may also be service activities which cut across the organization. An employment office, for instance, may do the selecting and hiring for the factory, for the office, the engineering department, the accounting department, the sales department, etc. There may be need for modern methods of office management in twenty places within the company—and yet no one may be big enough to justify having one man full time to work on the problem. This situation can be handled either by having the employment office part of the organization of the largest employer of labor—for instance, manufacturing—with the other areas using its services on a fee basis. Or it might be handled by setting up office management as a co-operative venture of all the interested areas, financed by them, and managed by appointees from all the interested areas in succession.

There remains a need for a headquarters organization in the large company. The members of the chief-executive team charged with objectives in the key areas need a small high-grade staff of their own. But this should not be a central office *services* staff. It should be as small as possible—and should never exceed a mere handful of people. It may not be practical to pay the top-management men responsible for these key areas more money the smaller their own staffs; it would not be a bad idea though, and it would be vastly preferable to the present system under which the importance of a service staff and its contribution tend to be measured by the size of the payroll it amasses.

This central-office group should preferably be staffed with men who have experience as operating managers rather than with specialists. It should have no authority—line, functional or advisory—over operating managers. It should never be allowed to hold power over promotions in operating management; for whoever controls a man's promotion controls the man.

The scope of the work of these groups should be rigidly limited, too. They should not, as a rule, work out policies, procedures or programs for operating managers. Such work should always be entrusted to people from operating management specially assigned to the job. The central-office group may indeed contain one man whose job it is to organize such task-force teams for specific policy-formulating assignments. But it should never do the work itself. These assignments are one of the major development opportunities within the business. To have them pre-empted by service professionals deprives a business of one of its most badly needed opportunities to develop managers. And since operating managers will have to apply the new policies, use the new tool, run the new program, it is only they that can decide what these should be.

Such a central-office group should have only three specific duties. It should have the responsibility (probably its most important contribution) to spell out what a manager can expect from the people whom he selects as his service specialists in the respective areas. It may have the responsibility for training these people after they have been appointed. It should always have the responsibility for research. But it should have no administrative duties. It should have no packaged program to sell. And its success should never be gauged by the number of programs it rams down the throats of operating managers. It should, in other words, not be a service staff for operating managers but an adjunct of the chief executive.

The Biggest Problem: Growth

The biggest problem of size—a problem of small, fair-sized, large and very large enterprise alike—is the fact that these four do not form a continuum. A business does not imperceptibly grow from fair-sized to large. Each of these stages is distinct. We deal, in respect to business size, not with the gradual matter of classical physics; we deal with a quantum phenomenon. It is this that makes size a problem of quality as well as of quantity.

The biggest problem of size is the problem of growth, the problem of changing from one size to another; and the problem of growth is largely one of management attitude, the requirement for successful growth is primarily the ability of management drastically to change its basic attitudes and behavior.

Several years ago a large plant burned to the ground—four months after it had started production. Safety experts still debate the lessons of the fire. But the main cause of the fire was not unsafe construction; it was management's inability to adjust its attitude to the realities of a large enterprise.

The enterprise had been founded by the man who was still managing it at the time of the fire. He started as a mechanic in the back room of his father's small shop. At first he employed two or three men. Twenty-five years later, at the time of the fire, he employed nine thousand. But he was still running a small shop, even though he, by the time of the fire, supplied a vital part to most of the mechanical industries of this country.

When the company had first started the plans for the new plant, several of the Board members urged that four or five plants be built rather than one. They pointed out that to put all production into one plant might create trouble in case of accident, bombing, or fire. They also pointed out that the customers were distributed all over the country so that freight considerations alone would argue for a multi-plant pattern. The chief executive turned a deaf ear to these suggestions. His argument was that he had to guarantee quality to his suppliers and therefore had to be personally responsible for production. The real reason was simply that he was emotionally unable to let go of any part of the responsibility.

That the fire spread so rapidly was owing to the absence of any fire-retarding walls. The president had vetoed any such walls in the architect's drawing so as to be able to view the entire plant from a gallery behind his office. When the fire started the foreman tried to reach the president. He was out—to lunch. There was no other management; the president was still his own plant manager, indeed his own department superintendent. As a result nobody co-ordinated the fire-fighting efforts, nobody even tried to remove the most important machines, files or blueprints when it became clear that the plant could not be saved.

Not only did the plant burn to the ground, but the business was destroyed. For there was no one, except the president, who could negotiate with customers, suppliers and machine builders or could subcontract the production while the plant was being rebuilt. The company had to be liquidated.

And yet, as one Board member remarked, the company and its stockholders did better than if they had waited until the old man died. "For" as he said, "we at least had the insurance money to distribute; if we had waited until the old man's death, we would have had not even this but would have been just as unable to continue the business."

This is, of course, an extreme example. But the situation itself is common. Perhaps the only difference between the typical situation and that of the plant that burned down is that no attempt was made there to camouflage reality by an elaborate pretense of paper management organization. But the man who has started a business is often fully as unwilling and unable to accept the fact that he no longer runs the back room of a small shop.

The real problem of growth is not ignorance. It is first the lack of a clear tool to ascertain what state a company has reached. It is secondly a problem of attitude: managers, especially top managers, may know intellectually what is needed, but be incapable emotionally of making themselves take the necessary steps. Instead they cling to the old and familiar. Indeed, they often set up beautiful mechanics, "decentralize" their organization chart, preach a "new philosophy"—and go on acting just as before.

The need for a diagnostic tool to test the growth stage that a company has reached is illustrated by two examples.

Johnson & Johnson, the surgical and pharmaceutical supply company in the Brunswick, New Jersey, area, has carried federal decentralization very far. It is by way of being a model of large company organization. But the realization that its original highly centralized, one-man organization would no longer do came about through accident. As the people in the company tell the story, one of their products was in trouble. The president asked his secretary to call a meeting in his office of all the people directly responsible for the product. Twenty-seven men showed up. The president decided there and then that there was something basically wrong with the way management was organized and began to look for the right structure.

In another case, the company's president realized that he had to decentralize when he found himself unable to answer questions raised in a Board meeting about a proposed forty-million-dollar capital project. "I suddenly realized," he told me, "that I was so busy putting out fires on the foreman level that I had slighted the basic problems of the company. I knew I had to get rid of operating and get some time for thinking."

There are exceptions—companies that have systematically thought through the problem. Henry Ford II, for instance, knew that a drastic change in management organization was needed when he took over the Ford Motor Company in 1945. But in most cases, the realization that the company has outgrown its management structure comes about by accident. And that is not good enough.

How difficult it is to change basic attitudes—even if the need to do so is understood—is illustrated by the following typical case.

The president of a very large company is well known throughout American industry for constantly preaching good management and for his emphasis on letting operating managers run their own businesses. The company consists today of fourteen large divisions each of which is an autonomous federal unit, each with its own general manager. The smallest of these divisions is about three times as large as the entire business was when the present president took over shortly after World War I. The way decentralization works in this company is, however, that the president spends all his time in the offices of the division general managers. As he himself sees it, he spends all his time helping these general managers. "I am only the servant of my division general managers" is his phrase.

The general managers, however, see things differently. What they see is that the president is trying to run their divisions—at least during the time he spends with them. What to the president appears as helping appears to his operating managers as straight interference, a denial of their authority and an undermining of their responsibilities. And there is no doubt that the president himself appraises division general managers not primarily by their performance results but by their willingness to let him run their divisions as he sees fit.

At the same time the top-management job is not being performed. Or rather it is being performed without any clear understanding, responsibility or objectives, by service vice-presidents each of whom is more interested in pushing his own specialty than in the company as a whole.

The problem is not one of top management alone. Operating and middle management in the growing company have to change as much; and they find it hard to do.

There are, I believe, few companies that have experienced major growth in which some key operating positions are not held by people unfit to accept the demands of the bigger business. These men were put into their present positions when the company was still small and when both their competence and their vision was adequate to the job. As the company grew, the job grew. It was lifted up as if by geological pressure. But the man did not grow with the job.

There is the bookkeeper who became comptroller of a large company because the accounting department grew under him and pushed him up. There is the plant superintendent who finds himself in charge of twenty plants because he was the senior foreman when the company started. These men often do not know how to manage. Indeed, they often do not even realize that these things are now required of them. They still behave as if their job were to keep the cash ledger or to supervise four production foremen. As a result, they stifle, frustrate and crush the men under them. And because managements—with commendable sentiment—do not like to hurt these old-timers by promoting people around them, they become a bottleneck depriving the entire company of management talent.

Growth always requires new and different competence in top management. It requires that top management realize that its own function is no longer to know what goes on in the plant or in the regional sales offices. It is important indeed for top management to learn that the problem of size cannot be met by trying to keep in communication with managers and employees as far down as possible—that this is neither required nor even desirable.

As the business gets larger, the job of top management acquires a different time dimension; the larger the business the further ahead in the future top management operates. It requires a different ratio between objective-setting and doing; the larger the business, the more will top management concern itself with setting objectives, the less will it be concerned with the steps to their attainment. It requires different relations inside management. The emphasis in communication shifts: the larger the enterprise the less will top management be concerned with communications down, the more it will have to work on establishing communications upwards, from lower management to itself.

Growth demands of management the understanding and application of principles, rigorous emphasis on organization structure, clear setting of objectives and unambiguous assignment of responsibilities on all levels. The change in attitude, vision and competence that is needed cannot be avoided through good intentions, through native intuition, through the warm heart or the glad hand. That the top man of a large company knows all his foremen by their first name is not something to boast of; it is rather something to be ashamed of. For who does the work of top management while he memorizes names? The personal touch is no substitute for performance.

Indeed, the good intentions that are all too common make impossible the solution of the problem of growth. They make it difficult for the managers themselves to see that a problem exists. Every one of the top executives in a company that has undergone great growth sees that his associates have not changed but are still behaving as if they managed the repair shop in which they started. He sees that the problem exists in other companies. Indeed, he usually sees that the attempt of these other people to tackle the situation with good intentions is a mistake. But (just as every girl at one stage of her growth seems to be convinced that she, and she alone, can reform a drunkard) every one of these men is convinced that he, and he alone, can continue to manage in the old way because "he knows how to keep in touch with his people," has the human touch, has "his communications." And the fine glow of righteousness that these phrases emit, blinds him to the fact that he has failed to face a problem that demands of him a change in attitude and in behavior.

I know only one way in which management can diagnose the state of growth of the enterprise. This is by analyzing the activities needed to attain objectives, analyzing the decisions needed and analyzing the relations between mangement jobs. These analyses would have shown at Johnson & Johnson that twenty-seven people had to be consulted in a decision on any one product. They would have shown in the other company cited both that the president had to give time to basic capital-expenditure decisions and that he had no business "fighting fires."

These three analyses are also the only means to bring about changes in attitudes and behavior. In the first place, they identify the priorities in a man's job. A decision analysis would have forced the president in the seemingly decentralized company to realize that he had too many basic long-range problems to worry about to spend all his time in the division general manager's office. At the least, it would have forced him to choose between the two things. A relations analysis would have forced him to realize that "keeping in touch with the employees" was no longer his job. The two might also have made it possible for the division general managers to get across to the president that he was actually running their job (at least they might have found some Board member willing and able to break this to the president).

These analyses of the kind of structure the enterprise needs also show operating managers what they are supposed to be doing They make clear to them what decisions they should take. They curb their tendency to "pass the buck upstairs." And they protect them against the boss's wrath if they really make the decision they are supposed to be making. Finally, they lead to the establishment of clear performance standards without which the problem of the incompetent old-timer cannot be tackled.

Growth (provided it is not the mere addition of fat) is the result of success. A company grows because it is doing a good job. Its products meet with increasing demand. It can only service its customers by becoming bigger; a company making tin cans, for instance, has no choice but to become a national distributor for the simple reason that its customers demand delivery of tin cans for crops that grow in Oregon as well as for those that grow in New York State. A company may grow because it has mastered a particular technology. It may grow, as most of the chemical companies did, because research produced new products for which a market had to be found. It is true that some big companies are the result of financial manipulation and of merger rather than of successful management. But, in an economy in which monopolies are outlawed, the normal reason for business growth is success. The normal cause of business growth is able and competent management.

That the problems of growth are problems of success is the reason why they are so difficult. Problems of success are always the hardest—if only because the human mind tends to believe that everything is easy once success has been attained. It is also for this reason that so few managers realize that growth requires a change in their attitudes. They tend to argue that the attitudes and behavior that have led to original success will also lead to further success.

There is therefore nothing more important in discussing the management of managers than to emphasize the problems created by growth and, above all, to emphasize that the first requirement of successful growth is willingness and ability to change the structure of management and the attitude and behavior of top-management people.

PART FOUR

THE MANAGEMENT OF WORKER AND WORK

CHAPTER 19

THE IBM STORY

The human resource the one least efficiently used—The one holding greatest promise for improved economic performance—Its increased importance under Automation—IBM's innovations—Making the job a challenge—The worker's participation in planning—"Salaries" for the workers—Keeping workers employed is management's job.

IT HAS become almost a truism in American management that the human resource is of all economic resources the one least efficiently used, and that the greatest opportunity for improved economic performance lies in the improvement of the effectiveness of people in their work. Whether the business enterprise performs depends in the final analysis on its ability to get people to perform, that is, to work. The management of worker and work is therefore one of the basic functions of management.

The way the worker works may change. The unskilled laborer of yesterday who contributed only animal strength has become the semi-skilled machine operator of today who has to exercise judgment—though of a routine nature—when he tends the machine, feeds in material and inspects the product. The skilled worker has moved from the workshop into the plant—remaining a skilled worker or becoming a supervisor or a technician. And three new groups, clerical workers, professional specialists and managers, have come into being.

Today we face another major change. The new technology promises once again to upgrade the entire working group. The semi-skilled machine operator of today will tend to become a trained and skilled maintenance man, tool setter and machine setter. The semi-skilled clerk will become, in many cases, a technician possessing basic training on a par with the laboratory technician perhaps, though still less trained than the typical plant worker of tomorrow. And the ranks of highly trained technical, professional and management people will swell beyond all experience or expectation.

Still the work will always have to be done by people. There may be no people on the factory floor in the automatic plant. But there will always be large numbers behind the scenes, designing equipment product and process, programming and directing, maintaining and measuring. Indeed, it is certain that the decrease in the total number of people needed to obtain a certain quantity of work will not be the really important development. The new technology does make possible the output of more goods with the same number of people. But Automation derives its efficiency and productivity mainly from the substitution of highly trained, high-grade human work for poorly trained or semi-skilled human work. It is a qualitative change requiring people to move from work that is labor-intensive to work that is brain-intensive, rather than a quantitative change requiring fewer people. And the people, required in the new technology to produce a certain output, will be much more expensive people on whose work will depend a good deal more.

No matter what kind of work men do, whether they are skilled or unskilled, production workers or salaried clerks, professionals or rank-and-file, they are basically alike. There are, indeed, differences between workers according to kind of work, age, sex, education—but basically they are always human beings with human needs and motivations.

IBM's Innovations

Again, the description of one company's experience will be used to show both the basic problems in managing worker and work, and some of the principles for their solution. The best example I know is that of International Business Machines (IBM), one of the largest producers of calculating, computing and office machinery.[1]

[1] Part of the IBM story has been presented and analyzed by Charles R. Walker and F. L. W. Richardson in *Human Relations in an Expanding Company* (New

Most of the equipment produced by IBM is of a high order of complexity. Some of the "electronic brains" contain hundreds of thousands of parts; and even the simplest IBM products, such as the electric typewriter, are complicated pieces of machinery. All products are, of necessity, precision instruments made to extremely close tolerances. And they must be capable of operation by mechanically unskilled personnel, such as typists or accounting machine operators, must stand up under rough usage and must keep running with a minimum of maintenance and repairs.

Yet, this equipment is not produced by highly skilled individual craftsmen. Indeed, the equipment could be turned out neither in large quantities nor at a price the customer could afford to pay were its production dependent on craft skills. IBM uses semi-skilled machine operators. It is prime evidence that Scientific Management and mass-production principles can be applied to the production of the most complex precision instruments in great diversity and in small numbers. Of a particular model, an electronic computer, for instance, only one sample may ever be made. Yet, by dividing into homogeneous stages the job of building this unique product IBM is able to use semi-skilled labor for all but a small part of the work.

But each job is designed so as always to contain a challenge to judgment, and an opportunity to influence the speed and rhythm of his work.

The story goes that Mr. Thomas J. Watson, the company's president, once saw a woman operator sitting idly at her machine. Asked why she did not work, the woman replied: "I have to wait for the setup man to change the tool setting for a new run." "Couldn't you do it yourself?" Mr. Watson asked. "Of course," said the woman, "but I am not supposed to." Watson thereupon found out that each worker spent several hours each week waiting for the setup man. It would, however, only take a few additional days of training for the worker to learn how to set up his own machine. Thus machine setup was added to the worker's job. And shortly thereafter inspection of the finished part was included, too; again it was found that little additional training equipped the worker to do the inspecting.

Haven: Yale University Press, 1948). IBM executives themselves have freely discussed their work in the field at management meetings. For the interpretation of the data, however, I bear sole responsibility.

Enlarging the job in this way produced such unexpected improvements in output and quality of production that IBM decided systematically to make jobs big. The operations themselves are engineered to be as simple as possible. But each worker is trained to be able to do as many of these operations as possible. At least one of the tasks the worker is to perform—machine setting, for instance—is always designed so as to require some skill or some judgment, and the range of different operations permits variations in the rhythm with which he works. It gives the worker a real chance to influence the course of events.

This approach has not only resulted in a constant increase in productivity at IBM, but has also significantly affected the attitudes of workers. In fact, many observers both inside and outside the company think that the increase in the worker's pride in the job he is doing is the most important gain.

The policy of "maximizing jobs" has also enabled IBM to create significant opportunities for semi-skilled workers. In each foreman's department now there are one or more "job instructors." These are senior workers who do their own work but who also help the other, less experienced workers learn higher technical skills and solve problems requiring experience or judgment. These positions are greatly coveted and carry high prestige. They also have proven to be an excellent preparation for a manager. They both train and test men so well that IBM neither has much difficulty in finding candidates for promotion nor is it plagued by the failure of newly promoted foremen to perform or to command their subordinates' respect. Yet, in most other industrial plants these are real problems. In some companies less than half of all promotions to foreman turn out really well.

The second IBM innovation also seems to have developed half by accident. Several years ago one of the first of the new complicated electronic computers was being developed. Demand for it was so great (or maybe engineering design had taken so much longer than expected) that production had to be begun before the engineering work was fully completed. The final details were worked out on the production floor with the engineers collaborating with foremen and workers. The result was a superior design; the production engineering was significantly better, cheaper, faster; and each worker, as a result of participating in engineering the product and his work, did a significantly better and more productive job. The lesson of this experience is being applied today whenever IBM introduces a new product or a major change in existing products. Before design engineering is completed, the project is assigned to one of the foremen who becomes manager of the project. He works on the final details of design with the engineers and with the workers who will produce the machines. He and his workers—with whatever expert technical help is needed—plan the actual production layout and set up the individual jobs. The worker, in other words, gets in on the planning of the product, of the production process and of his own job. And wherever used this method has given the same benefits in design, production costs, speed and worker satisfaction as were obtained the first time.

IBM has been equally unorthodox in its rewards and incentives for workers. For many years it used the standard approach: output norms set by the industrial engineer for each operation, a base wage for production according to the norm, and incentive premium pay for production above the norm. Then, in 1936, it did away with the traditional norms and with pay incentives. Instead of wages per unit produced, IBM pays each worker a straight "salary" (plus, of course, overtime payments, vacation pay, etc.). Instead of output norms imposed from above, each worker develops with his own foreman his own rates of production. Of course, both know pretty well how much output can normally be expected. But even for new operations or for major changes in process or job the determination of output norms is left to the men themselves. Indeed, IBM maintains that there is no such thing as a norm, but that each man works out for himself, with his superior's help, the speed and flow of work that will give him the most production.

One important result of this has been increasing emphasis by foremen and workers alike on training and, especially, on placement. It is obvious to everybody at IBM that there are tremendous differences in the ability of men to do any kind of work, no matter how unskilled. Consequently, each foreman tries hard to put each man on the job for which he is best fitted. And the man himself tries to find the job he can do best—or to acquire the skills to do his own job better.

When worker output went up right after the new plan had been installed, many people critical of the whole idea (including a good many in IBM) explained this away as owing to the worker's fear of losing his job; 1936, after all, was a depression year. But worker output kept on climbing right through the war years when even large wage incentives could not prevent its slipping in most other industries. And it has continued to go up.

Worker output, however, would hardly have stayed up, let alone rise steadily, but for the company's policy of stable employment. This, the most radical of IBM's innovations, was adopted early in the depression.

IBM is a capital-goods producer. Its products are used almost exclusively by business. By definition, employment in such an enterprise is extremely sensitive to economic fluctuations. At IBM's main competitors', employment was cut back sharply during the depression years. IBM management decided, however, that it was its job to maintain employment. There was obviously only one way to do this: to develop new markets. And IBM was so successful in finding and developing these markets that employment was actually fully maintained right through the thirties.

As a result IBM workers are not afraid of "working themselves out of a job." They do not restrict their output. They do not resent it if one of their fellow-workers produces more; after all, this will neither result in a higher output norm for themselves nor endanger their job security. And they do not resist change.

It may be said that the IBM experience in maintaining employment by finding new markets proves nothing. For the office-machine industry the thirties were not a time of depression but of boom. The New Deal required so much office machinery that one Washington wag in the mid-thirties called it the "IBM Revolution." In addition to the vast number of office machines required by such new government agencies as Social Security and Wage and Hours Administration, business had to go in heavily for machinery to keep the records the government demanded. There was, besides, a strong long-term upward trend in the use of office machinery that would have cushioned the depression impact on IBM even without the New Deal.

The fact remains, however, that many of IBM's competitors suffered heavily during the depression despite New Deal and favorable long-term trend. There is something to be said for the argument used by one IBM executive: "It is not correct to say that we managed to maintain employment during the depression because we grew. We grew because we had committed ourselves to the maintenance of employment. This forced us to find new users and new uses for our existing products. It forced us to find unsatisfied wants in the market and to develop new products to satisfy them. It forced us to develop foreign markets and to push export sales. I am convinced that we would not today be one of the world's leading producers and exporters of office machinery but for our commitment to maintain employment during the depression years. Indeed," he added, "I sometimes wonder whether we wouldn't be well advised to commit ourselves to *increasing* employment constantly."

CHAPTER 20

EMPLOYING THE WHOLE MAN

The three elements in managing worker and work—The worker as a resource—*Human* resource and human *resource*—Productivity is an attitude—Wanted: a substitute for fear—The worker and the group—Only people develop—The demands of the enterprise on the worker—The fallacy of "a fair day's labor for a fair day's pay"—The worker's willingness to accept change—The worker's demands on the enterprise—The economic dimension—Wage as seen by enterprise and by worker—The twofold meaning of profit.

IN HIRING a worker one always hires the whole man. It is evident in the IBM story that one cannot "hire a hand"; its owner always comes with it. Indeed, there are few relations which so completely embrace a man's entire person as his relation to his work. Work was not, Genesis informs us, in man's original nature. But it was included soon after. "In the sweat of thy brow shalt thou eat thy bread" was both the Lord's punishment for Adam's fall and His gift and blessing to make bearable and meaningful man's life in his fallen state. Only the relationship to his Creator and that to his family antedate man's relationship to his work; only they are more fundamental. And together with them the relationship to his work underlies all of man's life and achievements, his civil society, his arts, his history.

That one can hire only a whole man rather than any part thereof explains why the improvement of human effectiveness in work is the greatest opportunity for improvement of performance and results. The human resource—the whole man—is, of all resources entrusted to man, the most productive, the most versatile, the most resourceful.

The IBM story also demonstrates that when we talk about the management of worker and work, we are talking about a complex subject. First, we are dealing with the worker as the human resource. We have to ask what the specific properties of this resource are. And we get entirely different answers according to whether we put stress on the word "resource" or on the word "human."

Second, we must ask what demands the enterprise makes on the worker in its capacity as the organ of society responsible for getting the work done, and what demands the worker makes on the enterprise in his capacity as a human being, an individual and a citizen?

Finally, there is an economic dimension grounded in the fact that the enterprise is both the wealth-producing organ of society and the source of the worker's livelihood. This means that in managing worker and work we must reconcile two different economic systems. There is a conflict between wage as cost and wage as income which must be harmonized. And there is the problem of the worker's relation to the enterprise's fundamental requirement of profitability.

The Worker as a Resource

If we look at the worker as a resource, comparable to all other resources but for the fact that it is human, we have to find out how best to utilize him in the same way in which we look at copper or at water power as specific resources. This is an engineering approach. It considers what the human being is best and least capable of. Its result will be the organization of work so as to fit best the qualities and the limitations of this specific resource, the human being at work. And the human being has one set of qualities possessed by no other resource: it has the ability to co-ordinate, to integrate, to judge and to imagine. In fact, this is its only specific superiority; in every other respect—whether it be physical strength, manual skill or sensory perception—machines can do a much better job.

But we must also consider man at work as a human being. We must, in other words, also put the emphasis on "human." This approach focuses on man as a moral and a social creature, and asks how work should be organized to fit his qualities as a person. As a resource, man can be "utilized." A person, however, can only utilize himself. This is the great and ultimate distinction.

The qualities of the person are specific and unique. The human being, unlike any other resource, has absolute control over whether he works at all. Dictatorships tend to forget this; but shooting people does not get the work done. The human resource must therefore always be motivated to work.

Nothing brought this out better than the reports of the teams of European technicians and managers who came to this country under the Marshall Plan to study the causes of American productivity. These teams (and there were several hundred) expected to find the causes in machines, tools or techniques, but soon found out that these elements have little to do with our productivity, are indeed in themselves a result of the real cause: the basic attitudes of managers and worker. "Productivity is an attitude" was their unanimous conclusion. (For details see my article "Productivity Is an Attitude" in the April, 1952, issue of *Nation's Business*). In other words, it is workers' motivation that controls workers' output.

This is particularly important in industry today. For fear, the traditional motivation of the industrial worker, has largely disappeared in the modern West. To eliminate it has been the main result of the increased wealth produced by industrialization. In a society rich enough to provide subsistence even to the unemployed, fear has lost its motivating power. And to deprive management of the weapon of fear has also been the main aim of unionism; indeed, the worker's rebellion against this weapon and its use is among the main driving forces behind the union movement.

That fear has gone as the major motivation is all to the good. It is far too potent to be relied upon except for emergencies. Above all, we used the wrong kind of fear. Fear of a threat to the community unites; there is no greater stimulus to effort than common peril, as Britain proved after Dunkirk. But fear of someone within the community divides and corrodes. It corrupts both him who uses fear and him who fears. That we have got rid of fear as motivation to work is therefore a major achievement. Otherwise managing the worker in industrial society would not be possible.

But, contrary to what some human-relations experts assert, to remove fear does not by itself motivate. All it creates is a vacuum.

We cannot sit back and expect worker motivation to arise spontaneously, now that fear is gone. We must create a positive motivation to take its place. This is one of the central, one of the most difficult, one of the most urgent tasks facing management.

The human being also has control over how well he works and how much he works, over the quality and quantity of production. He participates in the process actively—unlike all other resources which participate only passively by giving a preconditioned response to a predetermined impulse.

In the most completely machine-paced operation, the speed and quality of which appear to be completely determined by the machine, the worker still retains decisive control. It may be almost impossible to find out how he manages to beat the machine; but, as the old Latin proverb has it, human nature asserts itself even if thrown out with a pitchfork—or with a conveyor belt. And in any operation which is not the tending of semi-automatic machinery by semi-skilled operators, that is, in all work of a clerical, skilled, technical, professional or managerial nature, this control is practically absolute.

This will be increasingly true under the new technology. There nobody "tends" machines; the semi-skilled operations servicing the machine—handling and feeding in materials, starting and stopping—are performed by the machine itself. As a result the worker, instead of being paced by the machine, paces it. He determines what it does and how well it does—by setting it, directing it, maintaining it. His control is complete; and because the production process is integrated, the way each man controls his own job shapes the performance of the entire operation. The worker's participation in modern mass production and process production is of the essence—it may well be the critical and controlling factor.

The human being works in groups and he forms groups to work. And a group, no matter how formed or why, soon focuses on a task. Group relationships influence the task; the task in turn influences personal relationships within the group. At the same time the human being remains an individual. Group and individual must therefore be brought into harmony in the organization of work.

This means specifically that work must always be organized in such a manner that whatever strength, initiative, responsibility and competence there is in individuals becomes a source of strength and performance for the entire group. This is the first principle of organization; indeed, it is practically a definition of the purpose of organization. That this is not the case on the traditional automobile assembly line is in itself sufficient evidence that we do not as yet know how to manage worker and work. The worker who is able to put on more fenders does not thereby help his fellow-workers on the line. On the contrary, all he does is to put pressure on the man next to him (who may have to put on bumper guards), throw off his rhythm of work, cause him trouble either by overloading him or by giving him more to do than he has supplies for, and finally cause him to perform less well, to turn out less work. This is a violation of ethical law; for there is no worse sin than to turn man's capacity to grow into a threat to himself and his fellow-men. It is also poor engineering.

Finally, man is distinguished from all other resources in that his "development" is not something that is done to him; it is not another or better way of using existing properties. It is growth; and growth is always from within. The work therefore must encourage the growth of the individual and must direct it—otherwise it fails to take full advantage of the specific properties of the human resource.

This means that the job must always challenge the worker. Nothing is more contrary to the nature of the human resource than the common attempt to find the "average work load" for the "average worker." This whole idea is based on a disproven psychology which equated learning speed with learning ability. It is also based on the belief that the individual worker is the more productive the less control he has, the less he participates—and that is a complete misunderstanding of the human resource. Above all, the concept of the average work to be performed is inevitably one which considers average what any but a physically or mentally handicapped person could do. The man who is just barely normal but who has neither aptitude nor liking for the job becomes the measure of all things, his performance the norm. And human work becomes something that requires neither skill, effort, nor thought, presents no challenge, allows of no differentiation between the highly skilled and highly motivated and the near-moron.

This whole concept, as the IBM story shows, is poor engineering. It results in constantly lowering performance norms rather than in raising the performance levels of the entire work group. It destroys the productivity of the human resource. The nature of man demands that the performance of the best, not of the poorest worker should become the goal for all.

The Demands of the Enterprise on the Worker

If we turn to the demands of enterprise and worker on each other, the first question is: What must the enterprise demand in order to get the work done?

The standard answer to this is the catch phrase "a fair day's labor for a fair day's pay." Unfortunately no one has ever been able to figure out what is fair either in respect to labor or to pay. The real trouble with the phrase is, however, that it demands too little, and demands the wrong thing.

What the enterprise must demand of the worker is that he willingly direct his efforts toward the goals of the enterprise. If one could "hire a hand," one could indeed demand delivery of fair value for fair price. If one could buy labor, one could buy it by whatever unit applies to it; but "labor is not an article of commerce," as the law knows. Precisely because labor is human beings, a fair day's labor is unobtainable. For it is passive acquiescence—the one thing this peculiar being is not capable of giving.

The enterprise, if it wants to get anything at all, must demand something much bigger than a fair day's labor. It must demand, over and above fairness, willing dedication. It cannot aim at acquiescence. It must aim at building aggressive *esprit de corps.*

This will be particularly important under mass production of uniform parts and their assembly into diversified products, under process production, under Automation. For these systems of production require that almost every worker take responsibility for actions, for the simple reason that almost every worker controls and determines the output of the whole through the way in which he performs his job, runs his operation, maintains his equipment. A fair day's labor for a fair day's pay, consciously or unconsciously, assumes a system of production under which the worker does nothing but what he is being told to do. It really assumes the technology in which the ditchdigger with his shovel represents production at its most advanced stage. For the ditchdigger technology "a fair day's labor for a fair day's wage" may not be too bad a slogan; this, however, is a main reason for its being an unproductive technology. For anything more advanced the slogan is totally inadequate. And for the new technology ahead of us it is absurd—and complete misdirection.

The enterprise must expect of the worker not the passive acceptance of a physical chore, but the active assumption of responsibility for the enterprise's results. And precisely because this is so much bigger a demand, we are likely to be able to realize it—where we have never obtained the fair day's labor. For it is a peculiarity of man that he yields best to high demands, that, indeed, his capacity to produce is largely determined by the level of the demands made on it.

There is a second demand the enterprise must make on the worker: that he be willing to accept change. Innovation is a necessary function of business enterprise; it is one of its major social responsibilities. It requires, however, that people change—their work, their habits, their group relations.

The human being has a capacity to change beyond all other animals, but it is not unlimited. In the first place, while man can learn amazingly fast, his unlearning capacity is much lower (fortunately for the race). We know today that learning capacity does not disappear with age. But the more one has learned the more difficult is unlearning. Experience rather than age, in other words, is the bar to easy unlearning and with it to easy or fast learning of new things. The only way to get around this is by making ability to unlearn itself part of what a man learns. This requires that one learn by acquiring knowledge rather than simply by experience. It requires "teaching" rather than "training" programs—many of the typical programs of today make a man rigid, rather than flexible, teach tricks of the trade rather than understanding. And the need to train workers in the ability to unlearn and to learn will become greater as the skill and knowledge level of the worker increases.

Change is not only an intellectual process but a psychological one as well. It is not true, as a good many industrial psychologists assert, that human nature resists change. On the contrary, no being in heaven or earth is greedier for new things. But there are conditions for man's psychological readiness to change. The change must appear rational to him; man always presents to himself as rational even his most irrational, most erratic, changes. It must appear an improvement. And it must not be so rapid or so great as to obliterate the psychological landmarks which make a man feel at home: his understanding of his work, his relations to his fellow-workers, his concepts of skill, prestige and social standing in certain jobs and so forth. Change will meet resistance unless it clearly and visibly strengthens man's psychological security; and man being mortal, frail and limited, his security is always precarious. The enterprise's demand for the worker's ability to change therefore requires positive action to make it possible for him to change.

The Worker's Demands on the Enterprise

The demands of the worker on the enterprise are also misdefined in the phrase of the "fair day's pay." The worker in making his demands on the enterprise is a whole man not an economic sub-section thereof. He demands, over and above economic returns, returns as an individual, a person, a citizen. He demands the fulfilment of status and function in his job and through his work. He demands the realization of the promises to the individual on which our society rests; among them the promise of justice through equal opportunities for advancement. He demands that his work be meaningful and that it be serious. High standards of performance, a high degree of competence in the way the work is organized and managed, and visible signs of management's concern for good work are among the most important things demanded of an enterprise and of its mangement by the worker.

As a human being and citizen, the worker, especially in a free society, also imposes limitations on the business enterprise. The enterprise hires the whole man, but it has no right to take delivery of the whole man. Serving only partial needs of society, it must never control more than a part of society's members, its citizens. Business enterprise must not become the "welfare corporation" and attempt to embrace all phrases of the individual life. It must, both in its demands and in the satisfactions it offers, confine itself to its proper sphere as one, though a basic, organ of society. A claim for absolute allegiance of the worker is as impermissible as a promise of absolute responsibility for him.

The Economic Dimension

Finally there is a big group of problems that have their origin in the economic sphere.[1]

The enterprise lives in two economic systems, an external and an internal one. The total amount available for the internal economy (and that means, above all, for wages to the employee) is determined by what the business enterprise receives for its product in the external economy. It is externally and market-determined.

Internally, however, the enterprise is not a market economy. It is a "redistributive" one in which the product of the whole is distributed among the members of the enterprise according to a predetermined formula. Both market and redistributive economy are basic patterns; but the business enterprise is the only human institution known to us in which the two have ever become indissolubly linked. While the effort of management must be directed toward receiving more, that is, toward making the total product greater, the attention of the worker within the enterprise is directed toward receiving a larger share of whatever the total product may be. An extreme example of this is the purblind indifference of John L. Lewis and his coal miners' union to the steady shrinkage of the market for coal. All they are interested in is an ever-increasing share of an ever-shrinking pie. While extreme, their attitude is typical—indeed, it is almost inevitable. Outside the enterprise the considerations are economic. Inside the enterprise they are based on power balance and power relationships.

To the enterprise, wage—that is, the financial reward of labor—must necessarily be a cost. To the recipient, however—to the employee—wage is income, the source of his livelihood and that of his family. Wage to the enterprise must always be wage per unit of production. Wage to the recipient must always be the economic

[1] For a fuller discussion of some of these economic aspects see my book *The New Society* (New York: Harper & Brothers, 1950) and my article "The Employee Society" in *American Journal of Sociology*, January, 1953.

basis for his and his family's existence which is before and beyond the units of production turned out. There is thus a basic divergence. The enterprise needs flexibility of the wage burden. The individual values, above all, a steady, stable and predictable income based upon a man's willingness to work rather than upon economic conditions.

Finally, there is the twofold meaning of profit. To the enterprise profit is a necessity of survival. To the worker profit is somebody else's income. That profitability should determine his employment, his livelihood, his income, is to him subjection to an alien domination. It is arbitrary, if not "exploitation."

It is a common belief that opposition to profit is a phenomenon of modern industrial society, if not a product of modern left-wing doctrine and agitation. Nothing could be further from the truth. It goes back hundreds of years to the dawn of modern society. The roots of the European worker's bitterness against "capitalist exploiter" and "profiteer" lie, for instance, in the bitter hostility to profit of the Flemish or Florentine weaver of the fifteenth century. And modern industry, far from aggravating this hostility, has greatly eased it. It is no accident that the more industrialized an area the less radical its workers, the less bitterly hostile to management, enterprise and profits. It is no accident that revolutionary Marxism has succeeded only in countries that knew none but pre-industrial society.

But it is still true that the worker's hostility to profits is a serious threat in an industrial society. Such a society depends for its existence on the adequate profitability of its enterprises. In such a society, moreover, the bulk of the citizens and voters are employees. This makes hostility to profit such a serious threat that it would indeed be a powerful argument for nationalization of industry if it resulted in the disappearance of the hostility to profit. And it was, I believe, the real death blow to the socialist dream when the nationalization of industries in Britain and France after World War II proved that workers resist and resent the profits of nationalized enterprises fully as much as those of "capitalist" ones (perhaps more).

The enterprise must operate at an adequate profit—this is its first social responsibility as well as its first duty toward itself and its workers. Management must therefore find some way to get the worker to accept profit as necessary, if not as beneficial and in his own interest.

This is admittedly the merest sketch of an enormous subject. But it should be enough to show that the management of worker and work requires principles. To be "good at handling people" is obviously not enough; in fact, it is likely to be irrelevant. Techniques by themselves will not do the job either. What we need are basic concepts.

The basis for these concepts is clear: it must be the assumption that people want to work. We cannot make the assumption that they do not want to work. It is contrary to what we know about human nature. Most people disintegrate morally and physically if they do not work. And the few who do not disintegrate survive intact only because their inner resources enable them to generate their own work. To assume that people do not want to work would make the job of managing worker and work totally hopeless.

The task facing management therefore is to reach the worker's motivation and to enlist his participation, to mobilize the worker's desire to work. What basic concepts, what tools, and what experience do we have for this task?

CHAPTER 21

IS PERSONNEL MANAGEMENT BANKRUPT?

Personnel Administration and Human Relations—What has Personnel Administration achieved?—Its three basic misconceptions—The insight of Human Relations—And its limitations—"Scientific Management," our most widely practiced personnel-management concept—Its basic concepts—Its world-wide impact—Its stagnation since the early twenties—Its two blind spots—"Cee-Ay-Tee" or Cat"?—The "divorce of planning from doing"—Scientific Management and the new technology—Is Personnel Management bankrupt?

A FEW years ago I received the following letter from the president of a company:

> I employ 2,300 people mostly women doing unskilled assembly work. Please send me at your earliest convenience a suitable personnel policy and enclose a statement of your fee.

For a long time I thought this letter a good, though unintentional, joke. But lately it has dawned on me that the laugh was really on me. My correspondent, I have come to suspect, is much like the child in Andersen's story of "The Emperor's New Clothes" who had the innocence to say out loud that the emperor was naked when everybody else was trying to pretend that he could see the ruler's garments.

A good deal of what passes today for management of the human organization is mechanical in nature and might indeed be dispensed by mail. The two generally accepted concepts of managing the worker—Personnel Administration and Human Relations—see the task to be done as something one tacks onto a business. To manage worker and work does not seem to require any change in the way the business is being conducted. And the tools and concepts needed seem to apply equally to any business.

An indication that this may not be the right approach is the lack of progress, of new thinking and of new contributions in either Personnel Administration or Human Relations. There is no field in the entire area of management where so many people are so hard at work. Personnel departments are growing like Jack's beanstalk; and not one but contains some research men complete with calculating machines and Ph.D. degrees. In every university hundreds of people lecture, research and gather data in the field. Indeed, a raft of new disciplines has been created—industrial psychology, industrial sociology, industrial anthropology, industrial relations, personnel management and so forth. They all produce supposedly original dissertations. They produce books and hold meetings. There are dozens of magazines devoted to the field. And no self-respecting business organization, whether the Seedgrowers of America or the Sioux City Chamber of Commerce, would consider a convention complete without at least one talk on the management of people at work.

And what has been the result of all this activity, what has all this work by so many good, devoted, intelligent people produced?

Personnel Administration, as the term is commonly understood, began with World War I. It grew out of the recruiting, training and payment of vast masses of new workers in the war-production effort. World War I has been over for thirty-five years. Yet everything we know today about Personnel Administration was known by the early twenties, everything we practice was practiced then. There have been refinements, but little else. Everything to be found in one of the big textbooks of today (save only the chapter on union relations) can be found, for instance, in the articles and papers Thomas Spates (one of the founding fathers of Personnel Administration) published in the early twenties. We have only poured on a heavy dressing of humanitarian rhetoric—the way a poor cook pours a brown starchy sauce on overcooked brussels sprouts.

There has been the same intellectual aridity in the field of Human

Relations—though there is perhaps even more activity there. Human Relations, too, grew out of World War I; but it took a little longer to mature. It reached its bloom in the famous Hawthorne experiments conducted by Elton Mayo of Harvard and his associates around 1928—twenty-six years ago. And the reports of the Harvard group on the work at Hawthorne are still the best, the most advanced and the most complete works on the subject. Indeed, it is debatable whether the many refinements added since by the labor of countless people in industry, labor unions and academic life have clarified or obscured the original insight.

Novelty is, of course, no argument for soundness. Still, it is most unlikely for any new discipline to emerge fully formed and perfected at its birth like Venus from the waves. It takes decades to build the edifice on the foundations laid by the first thinkers in the field. That two new disciplines should have been blessed with full maturity at their birth is altogether improbable. We are, I submit, justified in wondering whether the reason that there has been so little building on the foundations of Personnel Administration and Human Relations is not that the foundations themselves were inadequate.

What Has Personnel Administration Achieved?

The limitations of Personnel Administration are not hard to perceive. They are indeed admitted by most of the people in the field—at least by implication. The constant worry of all personnel administrators is their inability to prove that they are making a contribution to the enterprise. Their preoccupation is with the search for a "gimmick" that will impress their management associates. Their persistent complaint is that they lack status. For personnel administration—using the term in its common usage—is largely a collection of incidental techniques without much internal cohesion. Some wit once said maliciously that it puts together and calls "personnel management" all those things that do not deal with the work of people and that are not management.

There is, unfortunately, some justice to the gibe. As personnel administration conceives the job of managing worker and work, it is partly a file clerk's job, partly a housekeeping job, partly a social worker's job and partly "fire-fighting" to head off union trouble or to settle it. The things the personnel administrator is typically responsible for—safety and pension plans, the suggestion system, the employment office and union grievances—are necessary chores. They are mostly unpleasant chores. I doubt, though, that they should be put together in one department; for they are a hodgepodge, as one look at the organization chart of the typical personnel department, or at the table of contents of the typical textbook on personnel management, will show. They are neither one function by kinship of skills required to carry the activities, nor are they one function by being linked together in the work process, by forming a distinct stage in the work of the manager or in the process of the business.

None of these activities is in itself of such a nature as to call for more than moderate capacity in its management. None by itself has a major impact upon the business. Putting a great many of these activities together in one function does not produce a major function entitled to representation in top management or requiring the services of a top executive. For it is quality (that is, the kind of work and its impact upon the business) that alone makes a major function or defines the orbit of a senior executive.

Even if these things were best assembled into one department, they would not add up to managing people. They have indeed little to do with the job to be done in this area. That the personnel department as a rule stays away from the management of the enterprise's most important human resource, managers, has already been mentioned. It also generally avoids the two most important areas in the management of workers: the organization of the work, and the organization of people to do the work. It accepts both as it finds them. (There are exceptions to be sure. A notable one is the Sears, Roebuck personnel department; but it is no accident that personnel work in Sears did not start with Personnel Administration at all, but with the management of managers.)

The reason for the sterility of Personnel Administration is its three basic misconceptions.[1] First it assumes that people do not

[1] They have recently been brilliantly analyzed by Douglas McGregor, president of Antioch College and himself one of our leading personnel experts. His paper *Line Management's Responsibility for Human Relations* (American Management Association, Manufacturing Series Number 213, New York, 1953), is "must" reading for any manager.

want to work. As Douglas McGregor points out, it views "work as a kind of punishment that people must undergo in order to get satisfaction elsewhere." It tends therefore to put emphasis on satisfactions outside and beyond the work. Secondly, Personnel Administration looks upon the management of worker and work as the job of a specialist rather than as part of the manager's job. It is the classical example of a staff department and of the confusion the staff concept causes. To be sure, there is constant talk in all personnel departments of the need to educate operating managers in managing people. But 90 per cent of the budget, manpower and effort is devoted to personnel programs, thought up, established and operated by the department. The best textbook of Personnel Administration,[2] for instance, starts out by saying that the two first jobs of the personnel administrator are to advise operating management and to diagnose the stability or morale of the organization as an effective team. But then it spends 301 of its 321 pages on the programs that the department itself organizes and manages.

This means, in effect, either that personnel administration has to usurp the functions and responsibility of the operating manager (since whoever manages the people under him is the "boss," whatever his title); or else it means that operating managers, in self-defense, have to confine personnel administration to the handling of incidental chores, that is, to those things that are not essential to the management of worker and work. It is not surprising that the latter has been the all but universal trend.

Finally, Personnel Administration tends to be "fire-fighting," to see "personnel" as concerned with "problems" and "headaches" that threaten the otherwise smooth and unruffled course of production. It was born with this tendency. But the unionization drives of the thirties have made it dominant. It is not too much to say that many personnel administrators, though mostly subconsciously, have a stake in trouble. Indeed, there was some truth in the joking remark made by a union leader about the personnel department of a big company: "Those fellows ought to kick back 10 per cent of their salaries into the union treasury; but for the union they'd still be fifty-dollar-a-week clerks." But worker and work simply cannot be managed if trouble is the focus. It is not even enough to make

[2] *Personnel Administration* by Paul Pigors and Charles A. Myers (New York: McGraw-Hill, 1947).

"fire prevention" rather than "fire-fighting" the focus; managing worker and work—the IBM story shows this clearly—must focus on the positive and must build on underlying strength and harmony.

The Insight of Human Relations—and Its Limitations

Human Relations, the second prevailing theory of the management of worker and work, starts out with the right basic concepts: people want to work; and managing people is the manager's job, not that of a specialist. It is therefore not just a collection of unrelated activities. It also rests on a profound insight—the insight summarized when we say that one cannot "hire a hand."

Human Relations recognizes that the human resource is a specific resource. It emphasizes this against mechanistic concepts of the human being, against the belief in the "slot-machine man" who responds only and automatically to monetary stimulus. It has made American management aware of the fact that the human resource requires definite attitudes and methods, which is a tremendous contribution. Human Relations, when first developed, was one of the great liberating forces, knocking off blinkers that management had been wearing for a century.

Yet, Human Relations is, at least in the form in which it exists thus far, primarily a negative contribution. It freed management from the domination of viciously wrong ideas; but it did not succeed in substituting new concepts.

One reason is the belief in "spontaneous motivation." "Remove fear," the Human Relations people seem to say, "and people will work." This was a tremendous contribution at a time when management still felt that people could be motivated only through fear. Even more important was the implied attack on the assumption that men do not want to work. Yet, absence of wrong motivation, we have learned, is not enough. And on positive motivations Human Relations offers little but generalities.

Human Relations also lacks an adequate focus on work. Positive motivations must have their center in work and job, yet, Human Relations puts all the stress on inter-personal relations and on the "informal group." Its starting point was in individual psychology rather than in an analysis of worker and work. As a result, it assumes that it is immaterial what kind of work a man does since

Work was taken for granted; and it is an axiom that one never sees what one takes for granted. Scientific Management was thus one of the great liberating, pioneering insights. Without it a real study of human beings at work would be impossible. Without it we could never, in managing worker and work, go beyond good intentions, exhortations or the "speed up." Although its conclusions have proved dubious, its basic insight is a necessary foundation for thought and work in the field.

It is one American concept that has penetrated the entire world. It is practiced in India and in the Soviet Union, in Argentina and in Sweden. The Germans have made a pseudo-metaphysics out of it; they call it "rationalization." The critics of America everywhere think that they are attacking the "real America" if they attack Scientific Management.

When we started, after World War II, to give assistance to western Europe's attempt to improve productivity, we thought that that meant primarily the exportation of Scientific Management techniques. We preached that "productivity is an attitude." We stressed the importance of mass distribution, of capital investment, of research. But what we actually did was to send over industrial engineers equipped with Scientific Management tools and imbued with its philosophy. And where the European industrialist on the whole turned a deaf ear to our recommendations of mass distribution, capital investment or research, he took to Scientific-Management techniques with alacrity. For, in common with the rest of the outside world, he had come to believe—though wrongly—that Scientific Management was the essence of America's industrial achievement.

Yet, Scientific Management, too, has been stagnant for a long time. It is the oldest of our three approaches to the management of worker and work; it rose together with the new profession of engineering in the last decades of the nineteenth century. It also ran dry first. From 1890 to 1920 Scientific Management produced one brilliant new insight after the other and one creative new thinker after the other—Taylor, Fayol, Gantt, the Gilbreths. During the last thirty years, it has given us little but pedestrian and wearisome tomes on the techniques, if not on the gadgets, of narrower and narrower specialties. There are, of course, exceptions—especially

Mrs. Lillian Gilbreth and the late Harry Hopf. But on the whole there have been oceans of paper but few, if any, new insights. There has been a great deal of refinement; yet the most mature and most cogent statement on Scientific Management is still the testimony Taylor gave before a Special Committee of the House of Representatives in 1912.[3]

The reason for this is that Scientific Management, despite all its worldly success, has not succeeded in solving the problem of managing worker and work. As so often happens in the history of ideas, its insight is only half an insight. It has two blind spots, one engineering and one philosophical. What it does not see is as important as what it sees; indeed, if we do not learn to see where Scientific Management has been blind, we may lose even the benefit of its genuine vision.

The first of these blind spots is the belief that because we must analyze work into its simplest constituent motions we must also organize it as a series of individual motions, each if possible carried out by an individual worker. It is possible that Taylor himself saw the need to integrate; Harry Hopf certainly did. But practically all other writers—and all practitioners—see in the individual motion the essence of good work organization.

This is false logic. It confuses a principle of analysis with a principle of action. To take apart and to put together are different things. To confuse the two is grossly unscientific. For the beginning of science is the realization that classification, while absolutely necessary, does not tell us any important fact about the nature of the thing classified.

The belief that work is best performed as it is analyzed is also wretched engineering.

The best proof of this is in the greatest achievement resulting from the application of the concepts that underlie Scientific Management: the alphabet. Its inventor, an anonymous clerk in a long-forgotten Semitic trading town, 3,500 years ago, will never be awarded the Gold Medal of the International Management Congress. But his analysis of the basic, simple and standardized elements that underlay the thousands of picto-

[3] Reprinted in *Scientific Management* by Frederick Winslow Taylor (a collection of Tayor's most important papers); New York: Harper & Brothers (latest edition 1947).

grams, ideograms, logograms, syllable signs and phonetic marks of the writing of his day, and their replacement by two dozen signs capable of expressing all sounds and of conveying all words and thoughts, was straight Scientific Management—of the highest order. Yet, the alphabet would not only be totally useless—it would be a complete barrier to communication—were we expected to say "Cee-Ay-Tee," when we wanted to say "cat," just because we spell the word with these three letters.

The job of integrating letters into words is not a simple one. Even an idiot child can usually learn the letters, but even a bright one has difficulty making the jump from Cee-Ay-Tee to cat. Indeed, practically all reading difficulties of children (the biggest problem of elementary education) are problems of integrating letters into words; many people, we know, never learn to do that but learn instead to recognize common words and syllables—they learn pictograms and ideograms rather than letters. And yet the alphabet not only triumphed despite the difficulty of integration. It is the integration that is its triumph and its real achievement.

Finally, the confusion between analysis of work and action in work is a misunderstanding of the properties of the human resource. Scientific Management purports to organize human work. But it assumes—without any attempt to test or to verify the assumption—that the human being is a machine tool (though a poorly designed one).

It is perfectly true that we have to analyze the work into its constitutent motions. It is true that we can best improve work by improving the way the individual operations are performed. But it is simply not true that the closer the work comes to confining itself to the individual motion or operation, the better the human being will perform it. This is not even true of a machine tool; to assert it of human beings is nonsense. The human being does individual motions poorly; viewed as a machine tool, he is badly designed. Let us leave aside all such considerations as man's will, his personality, emotions, appetites and soul. Let us look at man only as a productive resource and only from the point of view of engineers concerned with input and output. We have no choice but to accept the fact that man's specific contribution is always to perform many motions, to integrate, to balance, to control, to measure, to judge. The individual operations must indeed be analyzed, studied and improved. But the human resource will be utilized productively only if *a job* is being formed out of the operations, a job that puts to work man's specific qualities.

The second blind spot of Scientific Management is the "divorce of planning from doing"—one of its cardinal tenets. Again a sound analytical principle is being mistaken for a principle of action. But in addition the divorce of planning from doing reflects a dubious and dangerous philosophical concept of an elite which has a monopoly on esoteric knowledge entitling it to manipulate the unwashed peasantry.

To have discovered that planning is different from doing was one of Taylor's most valuable insights. To emphasize that the work will become the easier, more effective, more productive, the more we plan before we do, was a greater contribution to America's industrial rise than stopwatch or time-and-motion study. On it rests the entire structure of modern management. That we are able today to speak seriously and with meaning of management by objectives is a direct result of Taylor's discovery of planning as a separate part of the job, and of his emphasis on its importance.

But it does not follow from the separation of planning and doing in the analysis of work that the planner and the doer should be two different people. It does not follow that the industrial world should be divided into two classes of people; a few who decide what is to be done, design the job, set the pace, rhythm and motions, and order others about; and the many who do what and as they are being told.

Planning and doing are separate parts of the same job; they are not separate jobs. There is no work that can be performed effectively unless it contains elements of both. One cannot plan exclusively all the time. There must be at least a trace of doing in one's job. Otherwise one dreams rather than performs. One cannot, above all, do only; without a trace of planning his job, the worker does not have the control he needs even for the most mechanical and repetitive routine chore. Advocating the divorce of the two is like demanding that swallowing food and digesting it be carried on in separate bodies. To be understood, the two processes have to be studied separately. They require different organs, are subject to different ailments and are carried out in different parts of the body.

But to be nourished at all, the same body needs both, just as a job must contain planning as well as doing.

Taylor's divorce of planning from doing was both specifically American and specifically late nineteenth century. It is a descendant of our oldest tradition: the New England theocracy of the early Puritans. It puts the priestly-elite concept of Increase and Cotton Mather into modern dress, but leaves it otherwise almost unchanged; and like the Puritan divines Taylor deduced a God-given right of the planning elite to rule. It is no accident that we hear this right to rule described today as the "prerogative of management"—the term has always been applied to right by divine or priestly anointment.

But the divorce of planning and doing was also part of the elite philosophy that swept the Western World in the generation between Nietzsche and World War I—the philosophy that has produced such monster offspring in our time. Taylor belongs with Sorel, Lenin and Pareto. This movement is usually considered to have been anti-democratic. It was—in intent and direction—fully as much anti-aristocratic. For the assertion that power is grounded in technical competence—be it for revolutionary conspiracy or for management—is as hostile to aristocracy as to democracy. Both oppose to it the same absolute principle: power must be grounded in moral responsibility; anything else is tyranny and usurpation.

The divorce of planning from doing deprives us of the full benefit of the insights of Scientific Management. It sharply cuts down the yield to be obtained from the analysis of work, and especially the yield to be obtained from planning. We saw in the IBM story that productivity greatly increased when the workers were given responsibility for planning their work. The same increase in productivity (not to mention the improvement in worker attitude and pride) has been obtained wherever we have combined the divorce of planning from doing with the marriage of planner to doer.

The two blind spots of traditional Scientific Management explain why its application always increases the worker's resistance to change. Because he is being taught individual motions rather than given a job, his ability to unlearn is stifled rather than developed. He acquires experience and habit rather than knowledge and understanding. Because the worker is supposed to do rather than to know—let alone to plan—every change represents the challenge of the incomprehensible and therefore threatens his psychological security.

It is an old criticism of Scientific Management that it can set up a job so as to get the most output per hour but not so as to get the most output over five hundred hours. It may be a much more serious and better-founded criticism that it knows how to organize the present job for maximum output but only by seriously impairing output in the worker's next job. Of course, if the job were considered unchangeable, this would not matter. Henry Ford (one of the most thorough practitioners of Scientific Management, though he had never heard Taylor's name) believed that once the putting on of a fender had been properly engineered, the job would remain unchanged in all eternity.

But *we know* that change is inevitable; it is, indeed, a major function of the enterprise to bring it about. We also know that the next few decades will bring tremendous changes—and nowhere more than in the worker's job.

Scientific Management and the New Technology

The coming of the new technology converts what may have been considered limitations on the full effectiveness of Scientific Management into crippling diseases. Indeed the major problems of managing worker and work under the new technology will be to enable the worker to do a complete and integrated job and to do responsible planning.

The worker under Automation will no longer do the repetitive routine chores of machine feeding and materials handling. Instead, he will build, maintain and control machines that do the repetitive routine work. To do this he must be able to do many operations, must have the largest rather than the smallest content to his job, must be able to co-ordinate. This, as the IBM story shows, does not mean that he must be again a manually skilled worker as the worker of yore. On the contrary, every one of the operations should be analyzed by means of Scientific Management to the point where they can be done by unskilled people. But the operations must be integrated again into a job—otherwise the work needed under Automation cannot be done. In the new technology we have no choice, but to say "cat." We must learn how to put together—now that Scientific Management has taught us how to pull apart.

A telephone maintenance man in an automatic-dialling exchange shows what the work will be like. He is not a skilled mechanic. Every one of the things he has to do has been reduced to simple elements which can be learned in a short time. He "goes by the book" rather than by manual skill acquired in years of experience. But his job comprises a variety of operations. It requires a good deal of thought and judgment. It requires muscular as well as intellectual co-ordination.

Similarly, we will not be able to organize worker and work in the new technology on the basis of the divorce of planning from doing. On the contrary, the new technology demands that the least production worker be capable of a good deal of planning The more planning he can do, the more he can take responsibility for what he does, the more productive a worker he will be. If he just does what he is being told, he can do only harm. To maintain the equipment, to program it, to set it and to control it, all demand of the worker in the new technology knowledge, responsibility and decision-making—that is, planning. Our problem will not be that planning and doing are not divorced enough; the problem will be that many workers of tomorrow may have to be able to do more planning than a good many people who call themselves managers today are capable of.

We must preserve the fundamental insights of Scientific Management—just as we must preserve those of Human Relations. But we must go beyond the traditional application of Scientific Management, must learn to see where it has been blind. And the coming of the new technology makes this task doubly urgent.

Is Personnel Management Bankrupt?

Is Personnel Management bankrupt? asks the title of this chapter. We can now give the answer: "No, it is not bankrupt. Its liabilities do not exceed its assets. But it is certainly insolvent, certainly unable to honor, with the ready cash of performance, the promises of managing worker and work it so liberally makes. Its assets are great—the fundamental insights of Human Relations, the equally fundamental insights of Scientific Management. But these assets are frozen. There is also a lot of small stuff lying around in the form of Personnel Administration techniques and gadgets. But it does not help us too much in the big job of unfreezing the frozen assets, though it may produce enough saleable merchandise to pay the petty bills. Perhaps the biggest working capital is the things we have learned not to do; but what banker ever lent on such collateral?"

The facts permit, however, of a more optimistic interpretation. The last twenty years were years of minor refinements rather than of vigorous growth, of intellectual stagnation rather than of basic thinking. But everything points to a different picture for the next twenty-five years. Technological changes will force new thinking, new experimentation, new methods. And there are signs that the process has already begun. The relationship between a man and the kind of work he does, which traditional Human-Relations thinking pushed aside as almost irrelevant, is now being studied by men close to the Human-Relations school.[4] The problem of the organization of the job according to the properties of the human resource, rather than on the assumption of man as a badly designed machine tool, is being given serious attention by men of standing in Scientific Management.[5] And, as the IBM story shows, the practitioners are well ahead of the writers and theoreticians, and are already moving across the frontiers of the traditional concepts.

These are only beginnings, to be sure. But they give grounds for the hope that, twenty years from now, we shall be able to spell out basic principles, proven policies and tested techniques for the management of worker and work. The right basic approaches, however, we already know.

[4] One significant example is *The Man on the Assembly Line* by Charles R. Walker and Robert H. Guest (Cambridge, Mass.: Harvard University Press, 1952).

[5] See, for example, the various papers and articles of Professor Joseph M. Juran.

CHAPTER 22

HUMAN ORGANIZATION FOR PEAK PERFORMANCE

Engineering the job—The lesson of the automobile assembly line —Its real meaning: the assembly line as inefficient engineering—Mechanize machine work and integrate human work—The rules of "integration"—The application of Scientific Management—The worker's need to see the result—The worker's need to control speed and rhythm of the work—Some challenge in every job—Organizing people for work—Working as an individual—Working as a team—Placement—"When do ninety days equal thirty years?"

THE title of this chapter is a manifesto. By proclaiming peak performance to be the goal—rather than happiness or satisfaction—it asserts that we have to go beyond Human Relations. By stressing human organization, it asserts that we have to go beyond traditional Scientific Management.

Though a statement of what we have to do rather than a summary of what we are doing, it is not an expression of pious intentions. We are on the whole not doing the job today. But we know what it takes to do it.

Engineering the Job

This is particularly true of the first requirement of human organization for peak performance: the engineering of the individual job for maximum efficiency. It can be argued convincingly that our difficulties and failures here are not the result of ignorance but of refusal to accept our own knowledge.

We are, I think, pretty much in the position in which the bacteriologists were for fifty years. In their search for effective germ killers they concentrated on producing the absolutely pure bacterial culture. Again and again they found themselves frustrated by fungus infestations that killed the bacteria. These fungi became well known; the penicillium mold was isolated and its properties were described almost fifty years ago. But their conviction that a pure culture was the starting point of all research totally blinded the bacteriologists to the fact that the pesky fungus was what they were really hunting for: the potent germ killer. For decades they regarded the fungus as a nuisance, threw away the infested cultures and sterilized the equipment anew. It took genius to see that the infested culture rather than the pure one offered the clue to bacteria control. But once Alexander Fleming had had this true "flash of genius," it took but a few years to develop all of today's antibiotic medicines.

Similarly, in engineering the job, we have been blinded for a half century by the search for the elementary motion and by the belief that the job should correspond as much as possible to one such motion. We have had abundant evidence to the contrary: the IBM example is only one of a great many similar experiences. But we have brushed aside this evidence as a nuisance, have rationalized it away as nothing more than emotionalism, have apologized for it as poor engineering. We have, so to speak, thrown out the penicillin because it killed bacteria and thus hampered our search for what kills bacteria.

One reason for this self-imposed blindness has been the tremendous impact of the automobile industry on our thinking. I have mentioned earlier how Henry Ford's insistence on the uniform final product obscured our realization of the essence of mass production. Similarly, the tremendous success of his assembly line with its attempt to confine each worker to one operation, if not to one motion, has blinded us to the real meaning of the scientific and systematic analysis of human work and has deprived us of its full value.

Little work could actually be organized on the Ford principle of one motion to the worker. The specific conditions that made this an effective principle on the automobile assembly line, the production of one basically uniform *product*, exist in few other industries. In fact, they are to be found most often outside of manufacturing: in processing orders in a mail-order house, or in clearing checks. But for decades we have tried to apply the one-operation principle despite the difficulties. We have refused to accept reality, have indeed refused to see it, because it did not fit the pattern of the automobile assembly line.

In the automobile industry itself there has been plenty of evidence that the one-motion one-job concept does not automatically lead to peak performance. One example out of many will suffice.

During World War II unskilled, indeed almost illiterate, Negro women produced one of the most complicated aircraft-engine parts. The job required more than eighty different operations. But instead of each operation being done by one worker, the whole job, for metallurgical reasons, had to be done by the same operator. Normally this would have meant entrusting the work to skilled machinists. But there were no machinists available. And the quantities required were much too large, the urgency much too great, to permit organization on a skill basis. These unskilled women—the only labor still available—therefore had to do the work. Each job was analyzed into its eighty component operations. The operations were all laid out in logical sequence. And each woman was given a detailed instruction chart, showing step by step what to do, what to do before doing it and what to make sure of in doing it. Much to everybody's surprise, this resulted in more, faster and better work than could possibly have been turned out either by highly skilled machinists or on the orthodox assembly line.

In other industries the same results were always obtained whenever circumstances led to an abandonment of orthodox assembly line methods.

A mail-order plant recently reorganized the handling of customer letters. Till then this work was organized by individual motions. One clerk answered complaint letters, another one inquiries, a third correspondence on installment credit, and so forth. Each only handled what could be answered by printed form letter; the few letters that required individual handling or judgment she passed on to the supervisor. Now each clerk handles all correspondence with a customer—all customers whose names begin with the letter "A," for instance. Nine hundred and ninety-eight out of every thousand letters still are answered by form letter. And there the work itself is as fully engineered, as fully predetermined, as fully laid out—and as repetitive—as before. But instead of repeating one particular motion again and again, each clerk now handles the entire range of motions—thirty-nine to be precise—involved in routine relations with the mail-order customer. And while the rare letter that requires judgment is still not answered by the completely unskilled clerk, she is supposed to write on it her suggestion how to deal with it before handing it to her supervisor. As a result productivity has gone up almost 30 per cent; turnover of clerks has dropped by two thirds.

But IBM is, to my knowledge, the only company that has so far drawn the obvious conclusion from this experience.

One reason for our blindness is that we have only recently obtained the key to the understanding of our experiences. Till now the question has always been: How do we explain the undoubted efficiency and productivity of the automobile assembly line if it is true that people work more effectively when they do an integrated job rather than one motion? As long as the one-motion one-job concept produced the results so obvious in Detroit, experiences such as the ones cited here could always be dismissed as exceptions.

The Assembly Line—Inefficient Engineering

Now, however, we know that the automobile assembly line is not perfect engineering of *human work.* It is imperfect and inefficient engineering of *machine work.* This has been shown by the automobile industry itself, for instance, in the new Ford Motor Company plant in Cleveland. There a traditional assembly-line process has been completely mechanized—with significant increases in efficiency and output. All materials handling, machine tending and routine inspection is automatic. The total number of workers is not significantly lower than it would be in the traditional plant. But the workers are not on the production floor; they are designing, building, maintaining and controlling the automatic equipment.

We know today, in other words, that wherever the one-motion one-job concept can be used effectively, we have an operation that can and should be mechanized. In such an operation the assembly-line concept may indeed be the most effective principle for human work, but human work, in such an operation, is itself an imperfection. This is work that should properly be engineered as the work of machines rather than of men.

For all other work—and that means for most of the work done today in manufacturing industry and for all the work that will be created by Automation—the principle is the organization of the job so as to integrate a number of motions or operations into a whole

We have two principles therefore rather than one. The one for mechanical work is Mechanization. The one for human work is Integration. Both start out with the systematic analysis of the work into its constituent motions. Both lay out the work in a logical sequence of motions. In both attention has to focus on each motion, to make it easier, faster, more effortless; and improvement of the entire output depends on improvement of the constitutent motions. But the one organizes the motions *mechanically* so as to utilize the special properties of the machine, that is, its ability to do one thing fast and faultlessly. The other one *integrates* operations so as to utilize the special properties of the human being, that is, his ability to make a whole out of many things, to judge, to plan and to change.

The technological changes under way not only make possible the realization of the correct principles but force us to apply them. They give us the means to make fully mechanic those jobs in which the human being is used as an adjunct to a machine tool. But the work that is not capable of being mechanized—above all, the work that is needed to make the new technology possible and to support it—can under Automation only be organized on the principle of integration, can, in fact, not be done at all unless so organized. Productivity will therefore increasingly depend on understanding these two principles and applying them systematically.

How far to go with Automation and how fast, where to apply it and how, are engineering problems that have been considered elsewhere. Here we need only say that wherever work can effectively be organized on the one-motion, one-job concept, we have *prima facie* evidence of its being capable of being mechanized with a consequent increase in efficiency and productivity. Anything short of mechanization in such work should be considered a stopgap and evidence of incomplete or imperfect engineering rather than an example of human organization for work. The automobile assembly-line worker is not a model of human work, as we so long believed. He is an—already obsolescent—model of non-human, mechanic machine work.

The Rules of Integration

But do we know how to organize human work? Do we know what integration means, what its rules are? Can we tell effective from ineffective integration? Do we know, in other words, how human beings work to give peak performance?

We do not yet know the full answers to these questions. But we do know what the basic rules are. We even know what models to use in place of the automobile assembly-line worker. One, perhaps the best, is the surgeon.

The work of the surgeon is based on the most minute breakdown of the job into individual motions. Young surgeons practice for months on end how to tie this or that knot in a confined space, how to change their hold on an instrument, or how to make stitches. There is constant effort to improve each of these motions, to speed one up a fraction of a second, to make another one easier, to eliminate a third one. *And the improvement of these individual, constituent motions is the surgeon's main method for improving total performance.* The motions themselves are performed in a rigid, predetermined sequence. In fact, every member of the surgical team—the surgeon, his assistant, the anesthetist, the nurses—are drilled to the *n*th degree so that they know exactly what to do next. Whether the surgeon realizes it or not, he applies Scientific Management. But the surgeon's work is of necessity integrated. To take out tonsils, we do not have one surgeon put the clamps on the blood vessels, another make the first incision, another undercut the left tonsil—and so on until the last man takes the clamps out again. We have one man do the whole job.

The surgeon is the most elevated model we can see—but this makes him a good model. It shows us the basic rules. And it shows us the direction toward which the organization of human work should tend. Even if it never approaches the surgeon's work in respect to skill, speed, judgment or responsibility, work in industry and business will be more productive, more appropriate to human beings, the more it is governed by the principles that are realized in the surgeon's work.

The first of these rules is the application of Scientific Management to the analysis and organization of the work. Indeed, the scope of such analysis is much wider than generally realized. It applies not only to manual and clerical but equally to mental work. As the example of the surgeon shows, it applies to work requiring skill and judgment of the highest order as well as to the bricklayer—just as the zoologist's principles of classification apply to *homo sapiens* as well as to the amoeba. Even the job of top management demands such analysis.

The second rule is that improvement in performing the work comes fastest from improving performance of the individual motions or parts of the job. Systematic efforts to improve performance are indeed effective only as efforts to improve its parts.

Third, is the rule (still a part of Scientific Management) that the sequence in which these motions are to be performed must be laid out systematically and according to the logical flow of the work. To go back to one of our examples: the efficiency of the unskilled Negro women turning out highly skilled machinists' work depended, above all, on clear instructions concerning the right order of the motions. And no phase of the job was as difficult, took as much time and had to be modified as often as the sequence organization; even teaching the girls to read—and one third were completely illiterate when first hired—was easier.

When it comes to the job itself, however, the problem is not to dissect it into parts or motions but to *put together an integrated whole.* This is the new task.

Even here we know a good deal. We know first that the job should constitute a distinct stage in the work process. The man—or the men—doing one job should always be able to see a result. It does not have to be a complete part. But it should always be a complete step. Final heat treating of a metal part, for instance, is such a step. It contributes something visible, important and irreversible. The worker in charge of the heat-treating equipment will speak of it as "my equipment"—just as the girls in the mail-order plant handling all correspondence with a particular group of customers began to speak of them as "my customers."

Also the job should always depend for its speed and rhythm only on the performance of the man—or the men—performing it. It should not be entirely dependent on the speed with which the jobs before it are being done. The worker should be able to do it a little faster at times, or a little slower. And in turn the jobs following his should not entirely depend on his speed and rhythm, should not be put under pressure if he does the work a little faster, should not run out of work to do if for a short time he works a little more slowly.

Finally, as the IBM story shows, each job should embody some challenge, some element of skill or judgment. For the women in the aircraft plant this was the demand that the worker read the chart before doing anything. In the mail-order story the girls had to make three decisions—which of thirty-nine form letters to use, which letters not to answer by form letter, and what answer to suggest. Neither the reading of a chart nor the picking out of the right form letter requires great intelligence, higher education or a major skill (though they require literate people used to an industrial civilization). For the workers in question these were, however, real challenges. They kept saying: "On this job something new always keeps cropping up." Strictly speaking, this was not true at all. What they meant was: "On this job I have to think about what to do reasonably often." And that is an element each job should have.

The difference between jobs of a lower order and those of a higher order, between low-paid and high-paid jobs should lie in the ratio of routine, repetitive chores to work requiring skill or judgment. It should lie in the difference between the degree of skill and judgment required. It should express the difference in responsibility, that is, in the impact which lack of skill or error of judgment have upon the performance of the whole organization. But there should never be jobs for people, as distinct from machines, requiring no skill or judgment at all. And even the lowliest human job should have some planning; only it should be simple planning and there should be not too much of it.

There will be tremendous variations in practice. In one kind of work many more simple operations should be put together to comprise one job than in another kind of work. The level of skill and judgment needed will vary according to the kind of work, and so on. But in general we can say that the more manual skill is required in an operation, the fewer basic steps should be integrated into a job. The more judgment required, the more basic steps belong together.

Organizing People for Work

So far we have been talking about engineering the work so that it can be best performed by human beings. That is of course, only half the problem. We also have to organize people to do the work.

Scientific Management, as traditionally understood, assumes that people work best if organized like machines, that is, if linked in series. We know now that this is not correct. People work well in two ways: either alone, as individuals; or as a team.

Wherever an integrated job can be laid out as the job of one person, it is fairly easy to organize effectively.

The perfect example is the telephone installer. The job is a distinct, integrated whole. It does not require high skill or great judgment; the instruction book deals with practically all situations the installer will encounter. But there is enough skill and judgment to make "every telephone installation a challenge," as one veteran telephone installer once put it to me. And I have never had the telephone company call up to find out how satisfied I was with the work done for me, have never heard of any attempt to supervise installers, of any need for checking up on their work.

The technological changes ahead will greatly increase the number of individual jobs—maintenance jobs, for instance. But the vast majority of jobs will still require that two or more people work together. The team job will continue to be the rule.

Fortunately we know a good deal about the team and how it works. Here are some examples.

In packing chocolate candy, teams of two women, sitting across from each other, work together filling boxes. A candy company a few years back introduced incentive pay into this operation under which wages were to be paid at a steeply progressive premium for production above the norm. A production rate of thirty boxes an hour would bring double the base wage paid for twenty boxes, for instance. What happened was totally unexpected. Within a few weeks the workers had organized their own "Stakhanovite" system. On Monday, for instance, the first group of two were out to beat all production norms to get the benefit of the high premium. The four groups on either side of the day's "Stakhanovites" would keep their own production at the norm—which was easy to reach —and gave their spare time to the "shock-brigade" to enable them to get the maximum production and the maximum pay. On Tuesday the next team of two would be the "shock brigade" with the rest of the room organizing to help them and so forth. This gave the workers the highest possible income—a bigger income than they could get if each group had worked by itself to produce, say, 125 per cent of the norm all the time.

(Accidentally it also gave the company the maximum possible output and the lowest per unit cost.)

Another example that parallels some of IBM's experiences with teamwork is that of an aircraft engine plant during World War II. Because of the pressure of time, the engineers could not work out the full details of every man's job. Much to their surprise, each group of four or six men, engaged in the key job of setting cylinder heads and pistons into the cylinder blocks, worked out its own organization of the work, its own variations of pace and rhythm, its own group structure. Each of these groups began to compete against all the other groups to see who could do the job faster and with fewer rejects. And invariably the production standards that these groups developed for themselves were a good deal higher than the standards the industrial engineers had considered appropriate.

Wherever a job is too big, too complicated or too strenuous to be performed by an individual, it should be done by a community of individuals working as an organized team rather than by a series of individuals linked together mechanically. People who work together form a social group. They build personal relations over and above the work relationship. And when the organization of the work cuts across or runs counter to the group organization and its social demands, it is always the work that suffers.

The first requirement of effective work organization is, therefore, that it make the group and its social cohesion serve performance in the job. At the least, conflict between the two must be avoided.

To achieve this, there must be a job for the group to do, that is, a number of people working as a team must have a task that is an integrated whole of motions, constitutes a definite stage in the process, and contains some challenge to skill or judgment.

Moreover, the individuals must be organized as a true group organized for working together rather than against each other rewarded for their joint as well as their individual efforts, identified for themselves as well as for the people around them as a cohesive social unit, proud of themselves, of each other and of their performance. The work should be organized so that the ability and the performance of one man redound to the benefit of both himself and the whole group and result in greater individual and group performance. The individual motions and their sequence, while predetermined by analysis, should be group motions—with the individuals arranging them within the group as best fits the group needs—changing places, for instance, making a two-man operation out of one originally designed for one man, etc.

Even on the automobile assembly line—the antithesis of efficient group organization—ability to move from operation to operation has been found to increase both performance and contentment. Chrysler found this in experiments conducted during the thirties in which operators moved with the car from operation to operation. Ten years later Charles R. Walker[1] found in a new assembly plant in New England that "utility men" who take over temporarily whatever position on the line needs to be filled showed greater job satisfaction and less fatigue; and there was strong evidence that they also did a better job.

Placement

But organizing men for work also means putting the man on the job he will do best.

We have put a great deal of time and money into the selection of workers. Selection is, however, a negative process. It eliminates those who are unlikely to fit. But the enterprise needs more than passable performance. It needs the best performance a man is capable of. And a man needs more than a job he can perform. He needs the job that will provide the greatest scope for his abilities and talents, the greatest opportunity for growth and for superior performance. That the IBM approach to output norms results in intensive efforts by foremen and workers to place each man where he best fits, is considered by IBM executives one of its most valuable achievements.

Where and how a man is placed at any given time decides largely whether he will be a productive employee or not, whether he will add to the economic and social strength of the enterprise or detract from it, whether he will find fulfilment in his work or not. It decides to a large extent how well he is being managed by the enterprise.

General Motors, a few years back, conducted a survey among its foremen under the title: "When do ninety days equal thirty years?" The employee, it was pointed out, who survives his ninety-day probationary period is likely to stay around for thirty years. In

[1] As reported in *The Man on the Assembly Line* (Cambridge, Mass., Harvard University Press, 1952).

deciding where to place the man during the first ninety days, the supervisor thus actually makes a decision for a lifetime.

General Motors rightly emphasized the importance of the decision. But in doing so it only brought out the shortsightedness of our present approach to placement. For one cannot place a man in ninety days.

Many people have a knack of placing themselves. My experience indicates that the great majority of men on an assembly line eventually place themselves where they belong. But it takes years of drifting around and is at best a haphazard, frustrating and time-consuming process. When Charles R. Walker (in the study mentioned above) investigated an automobile assembly plant that had only been in existence for four or five years he found that few of the men on the line really belonged where they were.

Placement as a systematic and continual effort is therefore one of the most important tasks in the management of worker and work. It cannot be done when a man comes to work but must be done after he has had time to get to know the work and to be known. It cannot be done once and for all. Placement decisions must be reviewed continually.

We have a staggering amount of evidence that even on the lowest level, in totally unskilled repetitive work, even in work that appears to be entirely machine-paced, differences in temperament, ability, attitude and skill make a difference to output and performance. We also know that the old assumption that people do not want to work is not true. Man not only lives under the spiritual and psychological necessity of working. He also wants to work at something—usually at quite a few things. Our experience indicates that what a man is good at is usually the thing he wants to work at; ability to perform is the foundation of willingness to work.

Placement should therefore rank high in all businesses. But wherever an enterprise uses any advanced technology, placement becomes absolutely essential. The idea that work could be organized so as to be performed independently of the individual's contribution, skill or judgment becomes untenable under an advanced technology—such work is done by machines rather than by men. Where more and more men work by themselves and without close supervision, either as individuals or in small groups as maintenance men, repairmen, controllers and so forth, output and performance depend on their desire not only to work but to do a good job—and that means on their placement.

It costs, I understand, about sixty-seven dollars per worker per year to maintain the personnel department activities to be found in the typical medium-sized enterprise in this country. Many personnel administrators consider this far too small an amount; it is less than 2 per cent of the total wage bill, or considerably less than it costs to handle any material resource. If we spent only one quarter of this figure on a real effort at placing workers, we would, I am convinced, be well ahead in worker performance and motivation.

CHAPTER 23

MOTIVATING TO PEAK PERFORMANCE

What motivation is needed—"Employee satisfaction" will not do—The enterprise's need is for responsibility—The responsible worker—High standards of performance—Can workers be managed by objectives?—The performance of management—Keeping the worker informed—The managerial vision—The need for participation—The C.&O. example—The plant-community activities.

WHAT motivation is needed to obtain peak performance from the worker? The answer that is usually given today in American industry is "employee satisfaction." But this is an almost meaningless concept. Even if it meant something, "employee satisfaction" would still not be sufficient motivation to fulfill the needs of the enterprise.

A man may be satisfied with his job because he really finds fulfilment in it. He may also be satisfied because the job permits him to "get by." A man may be dissatisfied because he is genuinely discontented. But he may also be dissatisfied because he wants to do a better job, wants to improve his own work and that of his group, wants to do bigger and better things. And this dissatisfaction is the most valuable attitude any company can possess in its employees, and the most real expression of pride in job and work, and of responsibility. Yet we have no way of telling satisfaction that is fulfilment from satisfaction that is just apathy, dissatisfaction that is discontent from dissatisfaction that is the desire to do a better job.

We also have no standards to measure what degree of satisfaction is satisfactory. If 70 per cent of the employees answer "yes" to the question: "Do you think the company is a good place to work in?"

—is that "high satisfaction," "low satisfaction" or what? and what does the question mean? Could any manager answer it with "Yes" or "No"? We can measure the effectiveness of concrete company policies. It makes sense to ask: "Is the scheduling system good enough to enable you to work or do you often have to wait for parts?" It is meaningful to ask: "Is the parking lot adequate?" But "satisfaction" as such is a measureless and meaningless word.

And nobody knows which of the things that we are trying to measure in terms of satisfaction have any impact on behavior and performance, or how much impact they have. Is satisfaction with one's fellow-workers more important in motivating people to work than satisfaction with physical working conditions? Is either of them important? We do not know.

But satisfaction is, above all, inadequate as motivation. It is passive acquiescence. A man who is deeply dissatisfied may quit; or if he stays, he is likely to become bitter and move into opposition to company and management. But what does the man *do* who is satisfied? After all, the enterprise must demand of the worker that he do something, willingly, and with personal involvement. It must have performance—not just acquiescence.

The present concern with satisfaction arose out of the realization that fear no longer supplies the motivation for the worker in industrial society. But instead of facing the problem created by the disappearance of fear as the motive, the concern with satisfaction sidesteps it. What we need is to replace the externally imposed spur of fear with an internal self-motivation for performance. *Responsibility—not satisfaction—is the only thing that will serve.*

One can be satisfied with what somebody else is doing; but to perform one has to take responsibility for one's own actions and their impact. To perform, one has, in fact, to be dissatisfied, to want to do better.

Responsibility cannot be bought for money. Financial rewards and incentives are, of course, important, but they work largely negatively. Discontent with financial rewards is a powerful disincentive, undermining and corroding responsibility for performance. But satisfaction with monetary rewards is not, the evidence indicates, a sufficient positive motivation. It motivates only where other things have made the worker ready to assume responsibility

One can see this quite clearly when studying incentive pay for increased work. The incentive pay produces better output where there is already a willingness to perform better; otherwise it is ineffectual, is indeed, sabotaged.

The question whether people want to assume responsibility has been mooted for thousands of years. It is being discussed again today in industry. On one side, we are being told by the Human Relations group that people want responsibility; indeed, that they need it. On the other, we are told by management after management that people fear responsibility and shun it like the plague.

The evidence produced by neither side is particularly convincing. But the whole discussion is none too relevant. It does not matter whether the worker wants responsibility or not. The enterprise must demand it of him. The enterprise needs performance; and now that it can no longer use fear, it can get it only by encouraging, by inducing, if need be by pushing, the worker into assuming responsibility.

The Responsible Worker

There are four ways by which we can attempt to reach the goal of the responsible worker. They are careful placement, high standards of performance, providing the worker with the information needed to control himself, and with opportunities for participation that will give him a managerial vision. All four are necessary.

A systematic, serious and continual effort to place people right has already been described as a prerequisite to high motivation. Nothing challenges men as effectively to improved performance as a job that makes high demands on them. Nothing gives them more pride of workmanship and accomplishment. To focus on the minimum required is always to destroy people's motivation. To focus on the best that can just be reached by constant effort and ability always builds motivation. This does not mean that one should drive people. On the contrary, one must let them drive themselves. But the only way to do this is to focus their vision on a high goal.

Output standards for the *average* worker are always, of necessity, minimum standards. They therefore inevitably misdirect. They should not even be used as declared minimums with extra compensation for output above the standard, for the worker will still consider the standard as normal. Indeed, the good worker who can easily "beat the standard" is likely to be affected adversely. He will either feel that he has to keep his output down so as not to "put on the spot" his less competent fellow-workers; or he will lose respect for a management that does not know better than to set so absurdly low a standard. And whenever management attempts to raise the standard, he will be the first to complain that he is being driven.

The IBM decision to abolish general standards and to let the individual worker work out his own norm was sound—as its results showed. Its success suggests that industry might go further and set genuine objectives for the worker's job rather than output standards. Instead of starting out with what a worker can do physically, we might start out with what he needs to contribute. We ought to be able to spell out for each job what it has to contrib[illegible]ment of the objectives of the department, of the plant, or [illegible] company. For the jobs in the new technology an objective in place of a minimum norm will be required; they could not be done otherwise. But even for the machine-paced work in today's assembly plants, objectives can be set meaningfully if some challenge to skill and judgment is built into the job.

To motivate the worker to peak performance, it is equally important that management set and enforce on itself high standards for its own performance of those functions that determine the worker's ability to perform.

Few things demoralize employees as much as to sit around waiting for work while management fumbles—no matter how much they pretend to themselves that they enjoy their paid rest. Few things constitute such conclusive proof of management's incompetence in their eyes. To schedule so that there is always work to do for the men is not a minor matter. Nor is having the equipment in first-class condition or maintaining it before it breaks down or repairing it immediately when it breaks down. And one of the most important spurs to worker performance is spotless housekeeping. These activities directly reflect management's competence and its standards, by making manifest to the worker how good his management is and how seriously it takes his work.

This applies fully as much to salesmen as it does to machine operators, to office workers as it does to engineers. The first test of management's competence is its ability to keep people working with the minimum of disruption and the maximum of effectiveness. There are few worse cost leaks than the office manager who keeps his staff waiting in the morning until he has read and sorted the mail—only to put pressure on them in the afternoon to make up for lost time. No union speaker can curtail output as effectively as the foreman who keeps workers standing around while he hunts in the tool-room for a replacement part he should have procured a week ago. Nothing damages morale as much as the chief engineer who hoards a few men "just in case" and keeps them employed on "made work." Any such lack of sound planning lowers the men's respect for management. It convinces employees that the company does not really want them to perform, and destroys their willingness to exert themselves. Only one common saying is more damning to a company than the proverbial "They let you get away with murder around here." It is: "It's just like the Army; hurry up and wait."

A wise plant manager once told me that he didn't want his foremen to do anything except to keep their department and the machines in it spotlessly clean, always to schedule work three days ahead, to insist on the newest equipment available and to replace tools before they gave out. His successor has brought in a whole array of Personnel Management techniques and gadgets, spends time and money on selecting his foremen and even more on training them, and pelts them with Human-Relations talks—and yet he has never been able to equal his predecessor's production record.

Keeping the Worker Informed

To measure work against objectives requires information. The question is not: How much information does the worker want? It is: How much must the enterprise get him to absorb in its own interest? How much must he have to allow the enterprise to demand responsible performance of him, and when should he get it?

The worker should be enabled to control, measure and guide his own performance. He should know how he is doing without being told. The rules for procedures and information that apply to managers apply to workers as well.

But the enterprise must also attempt to have the worker take responsibility for the consequences of his actions. He should know how his work relates to the work of the whole. He should know what he contributes to the enterprise and, through the enterprise, to society.

I realize that it is not easy to provide the worker with the necessary information to do his own job. It requires new techniques. The figures themselves are usually on record, but new tools are needed to get them speedily to the worker whose work they measure. He alone can do anything about them. And if he lacks information, he will lack both incentive and means to improve his performance.

To provide the worker with information on the enterprise and his contribution to it is even harder. For most of the conventional data mean nothing to him, especially if presented in conventional form and with the conventional time lag. Still, management must try to convey this information—not because the worker wants it but because the best interest of the enterprise demands that he have it. The great mass of employees may never be reached even with the best of efforts. But only by trying to get information to every worker can management hope to reach the small group that in every plant, office, or store leads public opinion and molds common attitudes.

The Managerial Vision

Placement, performance standards and information are conditions for the motivation of responsibility. But by themselves they do not supply this motivation. The worker will assume responsibility for peak performance only if he has a managerial vision, that is, if he sees the enterprise as if he were a manager responsible, through his performance, for its success and survival. This vision he can only attain through the experience of participation.

We hear a great deal today about "giving" people pride in their work and a sense of importance or accomplishment. Pride and accomplishment cannot be given. People cannot be made to "feel" important. The president who writes letters to the workers as "dear fellow employees" will not make them feel more important; he will only make himself look foolish. Pride and accomplishment, further, cannot be created outside of the job and work, but must grow out of them. A "service pin" for twenty-five years' faithful work may be highly treasured by the recipient. But it will be appreciated only if it is an outward symbol of a reality of accomplishment in the job; otherwise it will be resented as hypocrisy.

People are proud if they have done something to be proud of—otherwise it is false pride and destructive. People have a sense of accomplishment only if they have accomplished something. They feel important if their work is important. The only basis for genuine pride, accomplishment and importance is the active and responsible participation of people in the determination of their own work and in the government of their own plant community.

An impressive example was recently provided by the employes of the Chesapeake & Ohio Railroad. Here is the story as reported in *Business Week* (November 14, 1953).

This week, a batch of Chesapeake & Ohio Ry. employees traipsed into the plush meeting room of the road's board to demonstrate their pride and joy: a big-scale model of how they think the Huntington (W.Va.) shops should be remodeled.

The model was a labor of love run up during six weeks' intensive work —a lot of it on their own time—by some 60 blacksmiths, electricians, carpenters, metalsmiths, engine hostlers, and apprentices. One measure of the scope of their effort: C&O brass had figured that a similar planning job would take from 30 months to three years.

The idea sprouted when C&O realized it would have to re-do the 60-acre facility at Huntingdon to take care of diesel locomotives. Men in the 11-acre shop building—it houses the wheel, electric, coach, blacksmith, battery, and related shops—began talking over the project at their lunch hour.

They were fed up with the existing setup, built in 1928 and poorly laid out in the first place, according to E. E. Slack, the supervisor. One example: The wheel shop was half a mile from the optimum site, wheels had to be trundled that distance.

That noon talks soon got down to cases; everyone told how he would cure the bugs in his own setup. Slack, the boss, listened and took notes. He had a draftsman get the ideas down on paper, then invited all hands to get in on the mass planning. The end product was the scale model that was shown to the directors this week.

There are some pretty persuasive arguments in favor of the plan, quite apart from the fact that it would make the workers happy. For one thing, estimated costs of the whole conversion job are around $2.5-million. That's a more heartening prospect than the $10-million to $15-million that management had expected to have to spend.

Of course, one rarely has to rebuild the entire shop. But management always has the problem of designing the individual job, the work of one man or that of a group.

The job should always be broken down into its constituent elements, always be laid out in logical sequence of elements. But there is no reason why this analysis has to be made for the worker by the engineer—other than the superstition of the divorce of planning from doing. We have overhelming evidence that there is actually better planning if the man who does the work first responsibly participates in the planning. This is the essence of the technique known as "work simplification" which has been used with conspicuous success for thirty years. Wherever it is applied the results are the same: better engineering of the work, better performance and disappearance of the resistance to change. It is no accident that the Chesapeake & Ohio shops had adopted a work simplification program several years before their workers took the initiative in redesigning the entire plant.

The Plant Community Activities

But participation in setting one's own job is not the only way of acquiring managerial vision. The worker must also have opportunities for leadership in the plant community as the best means of acquiring actual managerial experience.

The qualities that make a man a leader and respected in his plant community are often not the qualities that fit a man for promotion to a management job. Yet, promotion is the only way in which the enterprise can normally recognize and reward. No matter how abundant the promotional opportunities, no matter how fair the promotional system, some of the most generally respected leaders are likely to go unpromoted, will be disappointed and driven into opposition in order to exercise their leadership. It is no accident that so many of our union leaders chose the union career because the enterprise did not reward their leadership abilities through promotion.

Walter Reuther is, of course, the outstanding example. There is little doubt—perhaps not even in his own mind—that his conviction that the free-enterprise system is not much good rests on the premise that a good system would have found and used such leadership abilities as his. But I also know a number of railroad union officials

—ultra-conservative men in temperament and outlook—who trace their interest in union work to their failure to get the recognition of a promotion into management.

In every business there are opportunities for workers—while remaining workers—to acquire managerial vision. In every business there are dozens of activities that are not business activities but plant-community activities. These must be run by somebody. But they have often only the most incidental relationship to the business, and the most peripheral impact on its success. They need not, therefore, be run by management. Some such activities are the Red Cross Blood Bank or the Christmas Party, shift schedules or safety programs, the cafeteria or the employee publications. Each of these activities by itself appears to be of minor importance, but in the aggregate they present a large area of responsibility. To the employee these activities are important, if only because they affect his social life directly.

There is also a whole area of information services which employees could perform for themselves. An annual report for employees is issued; an employee handbook is written for new employees. There are training courses to be given on new techniques or new skills, on serving customers or answering telephone calls.

To have management run these things instead of forcing the responsibility onto the employees deprives the enterprise of its best opportunity to imbue its employees with managerial vision. But it is also poor business. Management has enough to do without adding non-business activities to its business responsibilities. To run community activities well requires time and a large staff. Control of these activities by management, instead of making employees eager and able to perform better, invariably creates additional targets for criticism and discontent. Has any management ever gotten anything but complaints about the way it runs the cafeteria?

Let me make one point clear: I am convinced that in managing the business employees as such cannot participate. They have no responsibility—and therefore no authority. Nor do I want to see more community activities in the typical business—in fact, I think that in many businesses we could well do with fewer than there are today. I do not advocate more staff people, constant meetings or any of the other symptoms of organizational dropsy. I advocate only that those things which are desirable anyhow, be done sensibly—with less staff and by the plant community itself.

Standards for these activities ought to be high. Indeed, they offer an excellent opportunity to drive home the meaning of genuine standards of performance. But the actual responsibility for their discharge ought to be imposed on the plant community and its members. They ought to become the means by which the worker acquires the motivation to peak performance that can only result from his attaining the managerial vision.

To develop the effective alternative to fear as motivation of the worker will not be easy. But it has to be done. We have today the engineering knowledge to design individual and team jobs for peak performance. We have the social knowledge to organize men for effective work. In the new technology we have a system of production and distribution that will again give scope to the worker's ability, drive and desire for accomplishment. Without the worker's desire for performance these opportunities will not, however, become fruitful. That fear is gone is all to the good. But the absence of fear is not enough. We need positive motivations—placement, high standards of performance, information adequate for self-control, and the participation of the worker as a responsible citizen in the plant community.

I called the preceding chapter a "manifesto"; and the same could be said of this one. Both chapters are indeed programmatic; for though there exist many partial examples of the successful management of the worker and his work, the whole job has not, to my knowledge, been tried in any one place.

We know a good deal already. We know what we ought to do—at least we know that much more can be done than we are doing today. Certainly we have reason to expect—if not to demand—that, twenty years hence, what is now goal will have become accomplishment, what is now manifesto will have become history.

CHAPTER 24

THE ECONOMIC DIMENSION

Financial rewards not a source of positive motivation—The most serious decisions imminent in this area—An insured expectation of income and employment—The resistance to profit—Profit-sharing and share ownership—"No sale, no job."

I HAVE intentionally postponed any discussion of the economic relationship between enterprise and worker. Not that it is of minor importance. But financial rewards, as already indicated, are not major sources of positive motivation in the modern industrial society, even though discontent with them inhibits performance. The best economic rewards are not substitutes for responsibility or for the proper organization of the job. Yet, conversely, non-financial incentives cannot compensate for discontent with economic rewards.

It is in this area that we may face the most serious immediate decisions. If only because of the union demand for the "guaranteed annual wage," the next few years may well determine whether we can resolve economic conflicts to the lasting benefit of enterprise, worker and society, or will instead aggravate them for years to come.

The main problem is not one of high or low wage rates. It is not even primarily one of wage differentials, powerful though resentment against "wrong" differentials may be. The real problems lie much deeper.

The first of these is the conflict between the enterprise's view of wage as cost and its demand for wage flexibility, and the employee's view of wage as income and his demand for wage stability. This conflict can be resolved only by a predictable wage and employment plan.[1]

To demand or to give a guarantee of absolute employment security—the "guaranteed annual wage" of current union propaganda—is as inane as to promise a man that he will never die. It is less than worthless; for it could not be honored when the worker needs security, that is, in a depression. And its spread, by making the whole economy rigid, would make a depression inevitable and twice as severe. The danger is clearly shown by the experience of Italy with such a promise of "guaranteed employment." In the bleakest days after the Italian collapse in World War II when Communist victory seemed all but inevitable, the Italian Government enacted a law which forbids employers to dismiss regular workers except when the business is in extreme economic distress. As a result nobody in Italy hires people; for once they have been hired they become right-away regular workers and are permanently on the pay roll. Companies prefer to forego expansion rather than hire more men. Even though there is an acute power shortage in the industrial areas of Northern Italy the power companies, for instance, are stretching out their building programs rather than hire additional men into construction gangs where there would be no work for them after five years or so. This law enacted to prevent unemployment—and perhaps necessary under the conditions of 1945 or 1946—has become one of the major causes of large-scale unemployment in Italy. Yet nobody dares say so in public, let alone suggest that the law be changed or repealed; since it is labeled "a guaranteed employment law," it has become the holy of holies of the labor unions and completely sacrosanct.

What is needed is not the promise of immortality that is the unions' traditional "guaranteed annual wage." What is needed is a life-insurance policy. And that can be given.[2]

Most companies can anticipate on the basis of their own past experience the worst drop in employment likely to occur within any twelve-month period. (For most American businesses the worst such

[1] For a detailed discussion see my *The New Society*, page 232 ff.

[2] One very simple but effective plan for a small company—the Resistoflex Corporation, Belleville, New Jersey—is described in the January, 1954 issue of *Personnel* Magazine.

drop came in 1937-38.) On the basis of this experience the probable worst for today's workers can be worked out. That alone would give an expectation of employment and income that goes far beyond workers' expectations. Only a small minority of enterprises has ever experienced a drop of one third in the hours worked within a twelve-month period; and even a one-third drop means that 80 per cent of the workers can expect to work 80 per cent of their present hours during the twelve months ahead. And 80 per cent of present income is enough of an expectation to allow them to budget.

Once we have such an expectation we can actually insure it and thus limit the risk for enterprise as well as for employee. Of course, there is always the danger of the unpredictable catastrophe. An insured expectation of employment and wages will not protect jobs if a business goes bankrupt or a whole industry collapses. But this is like saying that fire insurance is no good because it does not cover damage done by tornadoes.

We have enough experience by now to know that, properly done, stabilizing employment and wages directly benefits the enterprise and cuts costs of operations. It is not a philanthropic venture and should not be tackled as such. Indeed, the most successful predictable wage and employment plans have grown out of attempts to reduce costs by stabilizing operations.

One example is that of maintenance operations on a railroad. Maintenance work used to be conducted according to current income. This meant, however, that most work was done when traffic was high—that is, when maintenance workers often spend more time standing by for passing trains than on their work. By putting maintenance work on a fixed budget and by scheduling the peaks for periods of slack traffic, costs were cut by well over a third. And employment could be stabilized with a maximum fluctuation of 10 per cent or less for any twelve-month period.

The new technology will force the enterprise into stabilizing employment. Not only will automatic equipment have to be run at a continuous rate as nearly as possible, but the highly trained and skilled employees will represent an almost irreplaceable investment. In its own interest the enterprise must do everything possible to keep them in its employ—regardless of economic fluctuations.

The modern economy offers for the first time in human history the opportunity to resolve the age-old conflict between economic flexibility and economic security. It can be resolved so as to greatly strengthen the enterprise and reduce its economic burden. The IBM example alone proves this.

But if management fails to realize this and to act accordingly, something like the "guaranteed annual wage" will be forced on it. We justly stress that in a modern industrial society the worker becomes "middle class." But the symbol of middle-class position has always been the weekly or monthly salary that is the regular, expected, stable income—the most visible symbol of the "proletarian," the hourly or piece wage.

We also know that security of continuing employment is the one really important security to most employees. Next to it all the other security gains, such as old-age pension or medical care, pale into insignificance. Whether our unions demand an employment guarantee this year or next, it is bound to come simply because it corresponds to social reality. Management has only the choice between an employment and wage prediction that benefits the enterprise and the worker and the "guaranteed annual wage" that hurts both; between a resolution of the old conflict that will strengthen the enterprise, and a phony promise of economic immortality that can only create new bitterness and further conflict.

The Resistance to Profit

A predictable income and employment plan may also be the key to overcoming the deep-rooted resistance to profit. There is no greater danger to a free economy than the hostility of employees toward profit. Most of the remedies we have used on the disease so far have turned out to be only palliatives.

Profit-sharing would appear to be the obvious solution. It has now been tried for well over a century, however, and the results, especially in the large enterprise, are not encouraging. As long as an enterprise makes big profits so that the workers get large shares, the plan is popular enough. But the real job is to convince workers that there is an ever-present danger of loss, that therefore profit is necessary to build their own future job and their livelihood. And this profit-sharing does not do. On the contrary, in its customary form (under which the worker gets an annual dividend), it tends to convince workers that making a profit—a big profit—is easy if not automatic. It may make them feel that the profitability of their company is a nice thing to have. It may even convince them that the way they perform themselves has something to do with the size of the check they get at the end of the year—though the evidence is not such as to impress any but the most convinced devotee of profit-sharing. It does not, however, make employees understand the function of profit. It does not make them accept profit as absolutely necessary—the only alternative to loss and economic decline. Profit-sharing may ease the problem; and anything that does that is welcome. But in its present form, at least, it is not the answer needed (and needed even more in the class-war ridden countries of Continental Europe than in this country).

Similarly, while widespread share-ownership is in the interest of enterprise and society alike, the belief that a worker will change his attitude toward profits because he now owns ten or twenty-five —or even a hundred—shares of stock in the company is a naive illusion. His opposition goes much deeper than his economic interest; it is grounded in his resistance to having his own individual purposes and objectives subordinated to the impersonal objectives and laws of the enterprise. Even total worker-ownership is no answer, as the experience of all worker-owned or nationalized enterprises shows. That in a decade or two the bulk of the shares of America's publicly owned companies will be in the hands, directly or indirectly, of the employees, their pension trusts, investment trusts and life-insurance funds, will not change the employees' resistance to the principle of profit.

The reason for the ineffectiveness of these well-meaning and serious attempts is probably that they focus away from the worker's job. Yet, the job is his stake in the enterprise. He must therefore be brought to realize that his job depends on profits, is made better, more secure, more enjoyable through them. The aim of all schemes to make the worker accept profits is to make him feel like an "owner." Yet, the job is the worker's real ownership in the enterprise—profit-sharing or stock-ownership are extras and as such very nice, but hardly central.

As long as the purpose of the enterprise is seen by the employee as making a profit, he will be convinced of a basic divergence between his interests and those of the enterprise. He will also be confirmed in the ancient superstition that production produces a profit, that, in other words, he produces it. And no argument in the world will make him see the fallacy of the hoary contrast between "production for use" and "production for profit." But if the purpose of the enterprise is to create a customer, then there is harmony instead of conflict. For there can be no job if there is no sale, any more than there can be a sale if there is no job.[3]

Perhaps when the IBM management decided in the thirties that it had to find new markets because it was responsible for maintaining employment, it provided a clue to the solution of this problem. For this decision converted profit from something that the worker supplies and the company takes from him, into something that the market supplies and both company and worker need equally. It made workers see that their real stake in the company was identical with the welfare of the company. And it made them see that both required profitability.

Profit-sharing may well be used to strengthen an effort to anticipate employment and income. Indeed, my experience leads me to believe that this, of all possible uses of profit shares, is the one employees want the most. But that is in all probability secondary—as is any attempt to give the employee a share in profits as such. What is probably central is management's commitment to the attempt to maintain jobs, and the direct and visible connection between the enterprise's success and the worker's job security which it creates. (This commitment should, I believe, be kept to what experience indicates can be delivered, that is, to the employment and income that past experience makes appear reasonable. And even this anticipation I would guaranteee only up to a specified amount of risk—against which it is then possible to take out insurance or to set aside contingency reserves in good times. I would, in other words, advise managements to be more conservative than IBM was twenty years ago.)

But the approach is basically sound and effective. It shows that the interest of enterprise and of employee are in harmony. It shows that management in serving the interest of the enterprise serves the

[3] Alexander R. Heron, vice-president of Crown Zellerbach and a pioneer in managing worker and work, has recently developed the same thesis in his lucid book *No Sale, No Job* (New York: Harper & Brothers, 1954).

employee as well; that indeed management considers itself hired to procure and safeguard the jobs of the employees. It shows, above all, that profitability is an absolute necessity for the employee and for his stake in the enterprise: his job.

Obviously we lack knowledge and experience in this area. So far we can only sketch out the approach; how to do the job we still have to learn. But, after all, it is only in the last few years that we have acquired the basic economic insights to make the worker himself see that his own interest requires not that he ask: "Are profits too high?", but always: "Are they high enough?" "Economic education" also will not give him this understanding—even if it is real education rather than propaganda. It requires clear actions on the part of management to establish visibly and simply the harmony of purpose between enterprise and worker, their mutuality and their common dependence on adequate profitability.

CHAITER 25

THE SUPERVISOR

Is the supervisor "management to the worker"?—Why the supervisor has to be a manager—The supervisor's upward responsibility—The supervisor's two jobs—Today's confusion—Cutting down the supervisor's department the wrong answer—What the supervisor needs—Objectives for his department—Promotional opportunities for the supervisor and the worker—His management status—What the job should be—Managers needed rather than supervisors.

THE first-line supervisor is not, as the overworked catch phrase has it, "management to the worker." The engineering of the job and the organization of people for work; the presence or lack of proper motivation; the employee's economic relations to the enterprise; the spirit, principles and practices of an organization, are not determined by the supervisor or even greatly influenced by him. They originate in top management—and the worker knows it. Even the best supervisor is no substitute for poor principles and practices in managing workers. To overemphasize his importance, as current management oratory tends to do, may cause harm; for it sometimes leads management to content itself with haranguing the supervisor to do a better job in the mistaken belief that it is thereby discharging its responsibility for managing workers.

Yet, the first-line supervisor (whether called "foreman," "chief clerk" or "section manager") alone can really bring to management what the worker needs for peak performance. On his ability to plan and schedule depends the worker's ability to work. His performance in training and placing makes the difference between superior and mediocre performance of the work.

The first-line supervisor has to schedule so that the work flows evenly and steadily. He has to see to it that the men have the equipment to do the work, that they have the proper surroundings to work in and that they have an organized team of fellow-workers. He is also responsible for their being willing and capable of doing the work. He has to set objectives for his group that are focused on those of the entire enterprise. From these objectives he has to develop, together with the men themselves, the objective for every single man's performance. He has the main responsibility in placement. He has at least the first responsibility for developing all of the leaders that can be found in the group.

Today's Confusion

These specifications are much more modest than those often given today for the supervisor's job—specifications that call for a universal genius. There is no mention here of counseling workers, none of being competent to impart economic education to them, none of representing and explaining management to the workers. Yet they are specifications for a big job requiring a capable man of real stature.

Few supervisors will be found whose job is so designed as to enable them to live up to these specifications. For the supervisor's job has not been designed, or even thought through. In American business at least it is a hodgepodge—the end product of decades of inconsistency. Everybody knows, or says he knows, what the supervisior should be doing. He is expected to be a clerk shuffling papers and filling out forms. He is to be the master technician or the master craftsman of his group. He is to be an expert on tools and equipment. He is to be a leader of people. Every one of these jobs he is expected to perform to perfection—at four thousand dollars a year.

Worse still, while management tends to preach that the supervisor's first duty is human relations, it tends to promote a supervisor for keeping good records. No wonder that the few attempts made so far to find out what the supervisor is actually doing have discovered that he rushes around doing forty to fifty different and largely unconnected things without knowing which to concentrate on. We may talk about the supervisor's being part of management;

we may paint in glowing colors the importance and dignity of the job. The reality is, alas, much closer to the picture drawn by that supreme realist, the local union leader, to whom the supervisor is management's errand boy who cannot make a decision, who is always in the wrong and who has to be by-passed to get anything done.

This confusion has its roots partly in the origin of the supervisory job. It is a hybrid. One parent is the "master" of old who was the real boss. As recently as 1880 there were plants in New England where the first-line supervisor was a genuine entrepreneur bidding on a job of production, hiring his own men, organizing them for work as he saw fit and making his living out of the difference between his bid and his actual costs. But the supervisor's job also grew out of the old "lead man" of a gang of ditchdiggers or tow-rope pullers who was the "fore man" because he had the forward position in the gang, and whose authority consisted mainly in chanting the "one, two, three, up" that set the speed for the group. (The German word "*Vorarbeiter*" or the British "charge hand" bespeak this origin even more clearly than our "foreman.") From the master craftsman the supervisor of today has largely inherited what is expected of him. From the lead man he has, however, largely inherited his actual position.

On top of this we have, over the years, systematically taken out of the job everything that was not nailed fast. The organization of the work of the men under him has largely become the responsibility of the industrial engineer. The management of people, their selection, their placement, their training, their payment has been taken over increasingly by the personnel specialist. Inspection, quality control, cost accounting have all made inroads on the foreman's job. Finally, the coming of the union has deprived him of his disciplinary control. What is left is a collection of rainbow-hued tatters that will never make a garment.

Finally, recognizing that there was trouble, we have, since the middle twenties, tried to make the job more manageable by cutting down on the number of people a supervisor manages. Thirty years ago the typical supervisor in manufacturing industry was responsible for the work of sixty or more people. Today the typical production supervisor has no more than twenty to twenty-five men under him.

There is no doubt that the job badly needs to be made manageable. But cutting down the size of the work group does not accomplish this. In the first place, the supervisor's problem is not that he has so many people under him; it is that he has so many things to do without knowing which are important. Secondly, cutting down the size of the group also cuts down the status of the job. It makes it practically impossible to provide the help to free the supervisor of non-essentials, for instance, record keeping and filling out reports. Above all, it diminishes the supervisor's ability to represent the worker to management.

In other words, the problem is not the supervisor's span of control. It is his span of managerial responsibility. He is responsible for far too many things (in a recent study made by the U.S. Army[1] forty-one different activities were found to be within the typical production supervisor's job.) At the same time he has neither the authority nor the status, let alone the time, to discharge his responsibility.

Making the supervisor's unit smaller does not solve the problem; indeed, it aggravates it. The only way to solve it is to set the job up properly.

What the Supervisor Needs

What the supervisor needs to discharge his job is first of all clear-cut objectives for his own activity. These objectives must be focused directly on the objectives of the business. Like all true objectives, they must contain goals both in terms of business results and in respect to the realization of basic beliefs and principles. They must balance the requirements of the immediate and the long-range future.

The supervisor needs the authority that goes with the responsibility for reaching these objectives. He needs knowledge about the company's operations, its structure, its goals and its performance without which his own objectives cannot be meaningful. He needs the means to reach these objectives and the measurements that focus on their attainment. In fact, everything that is necessary to

[1] "Activities and Behaviors of Production Supervisors" Report No. 946, Personnel Research Section, PR & P Branch, The Adjutant General's Office, Department of the Army, Washington, D.C., 1952.

achieve the objectives of his department should be under his control—otherwise he cannot be held responsible.

Secondly, the supervisor needs adequate promotional oportunities and a rational promotion system based on clear performance standards.

The lack of promotional opportunities is probably the most serious complaint of supervisors—and their most justified one. As many as 70 per cent of all supervisors in certain surveys say flatly that they see no opportunities for promotion no matter how well they do their job.

Depriving the supervisor of promotional opportunities is a criminal waste of human resources. Here are the people who have proven that they know how to do the things any enterprise needs, such as planning and scheduling or leading, training and placing people. Yet every company I know complains bitterly that it cannot find men with these qualities. To search constantly among the supervisors for men to become managers or technical specialists would seem to be obvious necessity.

Promotional opportunities for the supervisor are also important for his performance as a manager of workers. They largely determine whether he will be motivated to strive for peak performance, or whether he will just try to get by and stay out of trouble. It is not necessary that each supervisor be promoted; no matter what we do, the percentage of supervisors actually promoted will always be limited. But it is essential that supervisors know that there are opportunities for the man who performs well. It is important that they do not feel—as most of them, at least in manufacturing industry, seem to feel today—that it makes no difference to their future how well they do their present job.

Not to give adequate promotional opportunities to the supervis is a blow at the foundations of a free society, and a denial of the social responsibility of the business enterprise. For the strength and cohesion of a free society rest on the reality of its promise of equal opportunity. And in industrial society this means the chance to rise from worker into management according to ability, performance and effort. That in this country the job of supervisor has always been both the opportunity for the worker and the first rung on the management ladder explains in no small extent the absence of classes and class war.

For this reason, too, supervisors should be recruited from the rank-and-file. Denying the rank-and-file worker opportunities for promotion to supervisory jobs undermines his motivation. It is as incompatible with our social beliefs as is the denial of promotional opportunities to supervisors. Such a recruitment policy is also the only way to get good supervisors. There exists no acceptable substitute in the preparation of a supervisor for the actual experience of working as one of the team. The present trend toward staffing supervisory positions with boys out of college is basically irresponsible and anti-social. The same is true of the growing tendency to reserve higher management and specialist positions for college graduates recruited as "management trainees." I am old-fashioned enough to object to this on the grounds that education should confer duties rather than privileges. And I resent the theme of the propaganda campaign put on by some schools that education offers a bypath that leads around the need for performance and directly to position and income. Such a policy is contrary to the enterprise's social responsibility. It is contrary to its own needs for maximum utilization of its human resources. It is contrary to its needs for supervision capable of peak performance. It is the lazy man's way out of doing a job. And as always the lazy man's way causes more trouble and work in the end.

Manager development must therefore begin with the supervisors. And in the filling of middle-management and technical jobs the supervisors must be fully considered. The best preparation for most of the technical jobs in industrial engineering, in quality control, in production scheduling is successful performance as a first-line supervisor. Whatever specialized technical knowledge is needed can be acquired by the able supervisor in a training course. But the most important knowledge for these jobs—of the organization; of the needs of workers, supervisors and operating managers; of the place of technical activity in the work of the whole—one learns best in performing the job of a first-line supervisor.

Finally, the supervisor needs manager status. His own job must be meaningful enough in itself. It must be big enough to enable him to represent his men upward. He must hold such a position that management listens to him and takes him seriously. Indeed it could be considered *prima facie* evidence of poor organization of the supervisor's job if management has to make special efforts to give him a hearing—as so many do.

What the Job Should Be

The IBM example shows us what the supervisor's job should be. Indeed, there is probably no area in managing worker and work where business could learn as much from the experience of IBM as in the organization of the supervisor's job.

The first lesson is that the supervisor's job must be a genuine management job. The supervisor must carry a large measure of responsibility. At IBM, as manager of a project, he is responsible for getting a new design into production. He is in charge of working out individual output norms with his men. He is in charge of the scheduling of tools, materials and parts. That the supervisor should not be a "worker" himself is generally recognized; indeed, many union contracts forbid him to touch a machine except to repair it. But it is not sufficiently understood that he must be genuinely a manager, with significant planning and decision-making responsibility. Indeed, his job should be so big that it can have genuine objectives derived directly from the objectives of the business, and that its performance and results can be measured by their contribution to the performance and results of the business.

The second lesson is that the supervisor must have control over the activities needed to discharge his responsibility and must have adequate personnel to handle them. Even at its best a supervisor's day will always remain crowded. But if he is to do his job reasonably well, he simply has no time to fill out those printed forms on which most supervisors today spend up to one third of their time. For these he needs a clerk; IBM incidentally supplies him with one, known as "dispatcher."

He also has little time for the routine training of people in work with which senior workers are thoroughly familiar. He has enough to do in planning and scheduling, keeping materials flowing and equipment in good condition (which together account for well over half of the activities of the successful production supervisor, accord ing to the U.S. Army study quoted above). The rest of his time is fully occupied in personal contacts with his men on their problems, in work with the men on new techniques or processes, in keeping the men informed, in training new men and so on. He needs, in other words, one or more trainers—IBM's "job instructors."

But the supervisor also needs technical services. He may need help with industrial engineering, methods, cost accounting. He may need someone to keep track of the details of scheduling or of tool supply and machine repair. These are service functions to the supervisor. Like all service functions they should be discharged by someone on his own staff; for it is the supervisor who is responsible for performance.

Another lesson from IBM is that we have to reverse the trend toward narrowing the supervisor's authority. At IBM the supervisor hires, recommends, discharges, trains, promotes and schedules. And he alone handles all the relations of his department with the company, for instance, with the personnel department. Of course, all his decisions on people should first be reviewed by his superior—a rule that applies to all personnel decisions made by any manager. And the subordinate should always have a right of appeal. But the decisions themselves should be the supervisor's; otherwise he lacks the authority he needs to discharge his responsibility.

We have a great deal of additional evidence of the need for a larger scope for the supervisor and of the impact this has on his effectiveness.

A large automobile assembly plant recently switched from central hiring to hiring by the individual supervisor. The employment office still interviews, screens and tests applicants. But the supervisor makes the decision; and he is always sent several candidates for any job opening. The result has been a noticeable improvement in output. Supervisors explain it first by the improvement in placement. "I can pick the man who is just right for the job," is their typical comment. Secondly, they feel—and so do the men—that a worker knows much better what is expected of him when he is hired by the foreman. "The Employment Office," one union officer commented, "will always talk to a man about the marvelous opportunities, and about the good pension plan and the medical insurance. It won't tell him much about the job—it knows nothing about it. The supervisor, on the other hand, will tell a man realistically what he is expected to do and what's in it for him. As a result we have neither the wise guys who start out with a chip on their shoulder nor the disillusioned innocents who quit when they find out they aren't going to be plant managers in six weeks." And, finally, there has been a real improvement in union relations. For years the plant had been plagued by minor but painful union friction. Union relations at the top are still anything but good; but in the plant the supervisor can now operate without every step's becoming a union grievance, a precedent for the entire plant and cause for a slowdown.

Finally, the supervisor's unit should be much larger in numbers than it tends to be at present. The number itself will of course, vary with the circumstances of the job. But by and large we should aim at supervisory units at least twice and perhaps three times as large as those we now have. This will give the supervisor the status he needs to represent the worker in management. It will prevent his "supervising" people; instead, he will have to manage by setting objectives for his men, by placing them, training them and planning and scheduling their work. It will also allow us to pay a supervisor a decent management salary instead of the "10 per cent above the highest-rated rank-and-file job" that one finds today—a phrase which in itself reveals the gulf between reality and the fantasy of the supervisor's being management to the worker. (Yet, the larger salary for fewer supervisors will cost less money than today's low salaries for too many, even if the bill for the supervisor's new staff is included.)

If the supervisor has a genuine manager's job; if he is adequately supported by his own staff; if he has real authority; and if his unit is big enough—then his job will have become manageable again. Indeed, he will have much more time to work with his people than he has now. And he will know what work to do.

And the supervisor's job can again become the major gateway to opportunity it has traditionally been in this country. Being a "job instructor" trains a worker for a job as supervisor and tests him in actual performance. It is no accident that IBM is not much concerned with the problem of selecting candidates for supervisory positions—a problem that plagues practically every other manufacturing company. It is no accident that IBM management does not have to worry about the acceptance of a new supervisor by the men whose colleague he was only yesterday; accomplishment as "job instructor" is regarded by the work group as a fair and rational criterion for promotion. Finally, IBM only rarely has to demote a supervisor for failure to perform. Yet, in other companies in the same field it is not unusual to have two out of every four new supervisors fail—despite extensive training courses both before their promotion and on the job.

But perhaps even more important is the fact that proper organization of the supervisor's job alone can again make it possible to promote men as a matter of course from supervisory into managerial positions of greater responsibility. Today's supervisor may be an excellent manager in face-to-face relations with his men. But he is not being prepared to manage through setting objectives, through organizing work and jobs, through planning—in other words, through managing a component rather than through personal relationship. Yet, as soon as a man moves to a managerial position of greater responsibility he has to be able to manage a component, to set objectives, to organize, to plan. Even in the properly organized supervisory job the emphasis will be—and should be—on face-to-face relations. But there will be enough of conceptual, analytical, integrating management in the job to train the supervisor for larger responsibilities and to test him in actual performance.

If it be argued that, in the guise of making it manageable and meaningful, I propose to abolish the "supervisor's job," I would answer that this is indeed my intention. What the enterprise needs to obtain peak performance from the worker is a manager instead of a supervisor.

I do not like to quarrel with terms as such. But the term "supervisor" describes the opposite of what the job should be. I believe the term itself to be such an impediment that it would be better to change it to "manager" altogether (as IBM has done and as General Electric considers doing). Otherwise the old "gang leader" concept will continue to trip us up.

No matter what term we use, the job itself should make clear beyond doubt that its holder is the legitimate successor to the master craftsman of yesterday—a master craftsman who, instead of plying the trade of shoemaker or stonemason, practices management.

CHAPTER 26

THE PROFESSIONAL EMPLOYEE

Are professional employees part of management?—Professional employees the most rapidly growing group in the working population—Neither management nor labor—Professional employee and manager—Professional employee and worker—The needs of the professional employee—His objectives—His opportunities—His pay—Organizing his job and work—Giving him professional recognition.

SUPERVISORS are not alone in being described as part of management. The same assertion is made for—and usually by—the professional employee. And as in the case of the supervisor, the fact that this assertion has to be made bespeaks growing uneasiness over the organization of the work of the professional employee and the way he is being managed.

Professional employees constitute the most rapidly growing group in the business enterprise. At the end of World War II, for instance, seventy-five industrial companies in the U.S.A. had research laboratories employing more than a hundred professional people apiece. At that time this was considered by many a wartime phenomenon abetted by excess-profits tax largesse. But five years later, at the outbreak of the Korean War, the number of such large research laboratories in American industry had almost doubled. Counting large and small together, we now have well over three thousand industrial laboratories engaged in scientific research.

The scope of professional employment has also been widening steadily. To the layman—and to a great many businessmen—"professional employee" still means research engineer or chemist. But in addition to the physicists who have entered industry so spectacularly during these last ten years, business today is emplo ing thousands of geologists, biologists and other natural scientist and at least hundreds of economists, statisticians, certified publi accountants and psychologists—not to mention lawyers.

The new technology will greatly accelerate the trend and agai widen the scope of professional employment. In addition to creatin entirely new fields of research engineering, it will bring into th business enterprise in large numbers mathematical economists t study market and income patterns, experts in logical methods an mathematicians.

Wherever I go I find concern with the proper organization c these professional and technical experts.

The article I published on the subject ("Management and the Profe sional Employe," *Harvard Business Review,* May-June, 1952) has, fo instance, brought more demands for reprints than almost any other o my articles on management subjects. After every talk before a busines audience—whatever the subject—somebody asks: "How can we manag the professional specialist?" Almost every large company I know is work ing on the problem. And it seems to be as acute in nonbusiness organiza tions—for instance, in the Armed Services—as it is in business.

Yet so new is the phenomenon that we do not even really knov what to call the professional employee. Only General Electric ha coined a term; it calls these men "individual professional con tributors." Debatable as the term is (for these people usually do no work individually but in teams), it will have to do until a better on comes along.

Even the best term for the professional employee would not show us what the problem is nor how to tackle it; it would show us onl that a problem exists.

Neither Management nor Labor

Whenever it is asserted that the professional employee is " part of management," the purpose is to emphasize that the profes sional employee is not "labor." If a manager makes the assertion he usually means that professional employees must not be permittec to unionize. If a professional makes the assertion, he usually mean that the promotional opportunities, pay and status ought to be equal to that of a manager rather than of a highly skilled worker

It is, of course, one of the theses of this book that there is no suc

splendid professional job regardless of the performance of the company.

And what distinguishes the professional employee from the non-professional worker, whether skilled or unskilled? It is primarily that he is a professional, that is, that his work, its standards, its goals, its vision are set by the standards, the goals, the vision of a profession, that in other words, they are determined outside the enterprise. The professional must always determine himself what his work should be and what good work is. Neither what he should do nor what standards should be applied can be set for him. Moreover, the professional employee cannot be "supervised." He can be guided, taught, helped—just as a manager can be guided, taught, helped. But he cannot be directed or controlled.

These are, of course, blurred lines. Many professional employees will come close to being managers, and many will come close to being non-professional workers, that is, mere technicians. Many workers will work and behave like professionals; and under Automation the lines between the skilled worker, the technician and the professional may become hazy at times. Still, the differences between the groups are fundamental enough to indicate that the professional employee poses problems of his own. These problems cannot be solved by asserting that he is part of management. Indeed, this assertion may well make matters worse by creating unrealistic expectations in the minds of professional employee and management alike. The problems can, however, be solved even less by the traditional concepts of Personnel Administration. Indeed, their application to the professional employee underlies much of the discontent and unrest that are so marked among professional employees today.

The Needs of the Professional Employee

The professional employee has five specific needs that must be satisfied if he is to be an effective and productive member of the enterprise. (1) He must be a professional, yet must both make a contribution to the enterprise and know that he makes one and what it is. (2) He must have opportunities for promotion as a professional employee and individual contributor. (3) He must have financial incentives for improved performance and greater contribution as an individual contributor. (4) His job must be that of a professional. (5) He needs professional recognition both inside the enterprise and in the larger community.

1. The objectives of the professional's job have to remain professional objectives. Yet, they should at the same time always be set so as to include the maximum of business objectives. They should always provide both the maximum of managerial vision to the professional employee and a direct link between the work of the professional and its impact on the business.

One way to achieve this is to give the professional employee outside of, and separate from, his normal professional work a special assignment which will bring him into management. In one company, for instance, the senior chemist—a man concerned exclusively with long-range basic research in his own work—has been put on the budget committee of the company. That he knows nothing about finance—and cares less—was not considered an argument against his taking part in financial management. On the contrary, it was considered the strongest argument for it.

The same problem was solved in a different way by a major pharmaceutical company faced by the need to integrate its patent lawyers into the business without undermining their professional competence and integrity in the patent field.

Large patent departments present a particularly difficult problem of reconciling business objectives and professional standards. The high-grade patent lawyer is apparently apt to think in terms of "faultless patent work" rather than in terms of the company's needs. Yet, patents, particularly if taken out on a world-wide basis, are not only a major capital outlay. Patent strategy has decisive impact on the success of a pharmaceutical business.

In this particular company the problem has been solved by the formation of a Patent Committee, composed of the three senior men from the patent department, and the top marketing, research, financial and manufacturing people. Meeting once every two months for three whole days, the patent needs of the company and its patent strategy are worked out by the whole group. It is up to the patent lawyers after that to do their work according to their professional competence without any interference from management. "It took us ten years to think up this obvious solution," said the company's executive vice-president; "ten years during which there was constant friction between management and the patent people with each accusing the other of stubbornness and shortsightedness. Now we do an infinitely better patent job at half the cost."

To make the professional capable of seeing the objectives of the business therefore gets across to him what the business demands of him as an employee.

Bringing the individual contributor close to the business and its problems is also the only way to avoid "projectitis"—a common disease resulting from attempts by management to control professional work which they do not understand. Management understandably wants to see results; it gets "projects" going—usually focused on immediate urgencies rather than on long-range thinking. But the only way to get real benefit out of high-grade professional people is to hire good men and then let them do their own work. For that, however, they have to understand the business and its objectives and have to be able to figure out for themselves where they can make the greatest contribution and how.

2. It is in the area of promotional opportunities for professional employees that the plausible but false division of industrial society into managers and labor does particular harm. As a result, the typical enterprise knows only one kind of promotion: promotion to an administrative position that entails responsibility for managing the work of others.

But the best professional employee rarely makes a good administrator. It is not that he normally prefers to work alone, but that he is bored, if not annoyed, by administration. The good professional employee also has little respect for the administrator. He respects the man who is better professionally than he is himself. To promote the good professional employee into an administrative position will only too often destroy a good professional without producing a good manager. To promote only the good administrator—who more often than not will not be the outstanding professional in the group—will appear to the professional employee as irrational, as favoritism or as reward for mediocrity. Yet, so long as business has no promotional opportunities except into administrative positions it will be confined to choosing between these two evils.

What is needed is a promotion ladder for individual contributors that parallels the administrative one (General Electric is at present building such a ladder). Positions such as "senior metallurgist" or "chief consultant" are needed in addition to that of "manager of metallurgical research." And these new promotional opportunities should carry the same prestige, weight and position as the traditional opportunities for promotion to managerial positions.

3. They should also carry the same financial incentives. Again, largely because of the false either/or of manager or worker, pay incentives for the professional employee are largely tied today to promotion into administrative positions. But pay should always focus on a man's contribution to the business. And we must recognize that a man can make fully as great a contribution to the business in the role of professional contributor as he can make in the role of manager.

4. To make the professional employee's job truly that of a professional two things are needed. In the first place, he must not be "supervised." He needs rigorous performance standards and high goals. A great deal should be demanded of him, and poor or mediocre performance should not be accepted or condoned. But how he does his work should always be his responsibility and his decision. The professional employee's job should, in other words, be organized like the job of a manager; his relationship to his superior should be like that between the manager and his superior. The superior of professional people should therefore be chosen for his ability to assist them, to teach them, to guide them. And his relationship to them should be much closer to that between the senior in a university and the younger men on the faculty than that between boss and subordinate.

In the second place, we need special and continuous placement efforts for professional people. We must be able to place correctly the man who wants to devote his entire life to learning more and more about a small field, the man who wants nothing more than to become the world's greatest expert on, say, rheostats or depreciation allowances in the Revenue Code. We must also be able to place the man who wants to become master of a whole field, and who wants to move on from rheostats to other areas of electrical engineering, from tax law to general corporation law. Both kinds of men are needed in the enterprise. Yet they require different jobs, different challenges, different opportunities. That academic life allows both kinds of men to do what they are good at is one of its major attractions to the professional. And we need recognition, position and reward in the business enterprise for that rarest but most valuable of professionals, the inspiring teacher.

5. Finally, the professional needs recognition as a professional both inside and outside the enterprise. The distinguished older men need prestige positions inside the enterprise which clearly symbolize the value the company places on the contribution of the professional. The younger men need opportunities to participate in the work of the professional and learned societies, to teach part-time at a university or professional school, to continue to work both on their own education and on the advancement of their art. Such activities are usually permitted today to professional employees. They are of such value to the enterprise, however, that they ought to be encouraged if not rewarded by business, The professional employee who enjoys professional recognition has a real incentive to become more proficient in his field, to perfect himself or, at the least, to stay abreast of developments. And he is likely to attract the most promising of the next generation of professionals to his company—no small matter these days when professional employees are increasingly needed and when increasing demands on their competence are being made.

We hear a great deal today about the need for social responsibility on the part of the professional expert, a great deal about the need for his becoming a "broad humanist" rather than a "narrow specialist." Since more and more of the professionals in our society are working within a business enterprise and becoming effective in and through it, the professional will increasingly have to discharge his social responsibility through his contribution to the business enterprise, will have to acquire his broad humanism by understanding his place in the social structure of the business enterprise and his relationships to its objectives, its performance and its organization.

The proper management of professional employees is among the most difficult problems facing the business enterprise. It cannot be side-stepped by asserting that the professional employee is part of management. Nor would be it be solved, as traditional Socialist doctrine asserted, by considering the professional just a species of skilled worker and a "fellow-proletarian." Managing the professional employee requires recognition that he is distinct. He must have the managerial vision; but his primary function is not to manage. He is a worker; but he must determine his own work, set his own standards, have financial incentives and promotional opportunities equal to (though separate from) those of the manager. A great deal of inquiry and experimentation is still needed to teach us how to solve the problem. But in its main outlines the problem as well as the solutions are visible already. And in solving it the enterprise will not only solve one of its own most important problems; it will contribute to the solution of one of the central problems of modern society.

PART FIVE

WHAT IT MEANS TO BE A MANAGER

CHAPTER 27

THE MANAGER AND HIS WORK

"Long white beard" or "universal genius"?—How does the manager do his work?—The work of the manager—Information: the tool of the manager—Using his own time—The manager's resource: man—The one requirement: integrity—What makes a manager?—The manager as an educator—Vision and moral responsibility define the manager.

IT WAS Bismarck, I believe, who said: "It's easy enough to find a Minister of Education; all the job needs is a long white beard. But a good cook is different; that requires universal genius."

We have so far in this book discussed what management's job is—to the point where it should be evident that it takes more than a long white beard to discharge it. Clearly to be a manager it is not sufficient to have the title, a big office and other outward symbols of rank. It requires competence and performance of a high order. But is the job, then, one demanding universal genius? Is it done by intuition or by method? How does the manager do his work? And what in his job and work distinguishes the manager from the non-manager in the business enterprise?

A manager has two specific tasks. Nobody else in the business enterprise discharges these tasks. And everyone charged with them works as a manager.

The manager has the task of creating a true whole that is larger than the sum of its parts, a productive entity that turns out more than the sum of the resources put into it. One analogy is the conductor of a symphony orchestra, through whose effort, vision and leadership individual instrumental parts that are so much noise by themselves become the living whole of music. But the conductor has the composer's score; he is only interpreter. The manager is both composer and conductor.

This task requires the manager to bring out and make effective whatever strength there is in his resources—and above all in the human resources—and neutralize whatever there is of weakness. This is the only way in which a genuine whole can ever be created.

It requires the manager to balance and harmonize three major functions of the business enterprise: managing a business, managing managers and managing worker and work. A decision or action that satisfies a need in one of these functions by weakening performance in another weakens the whole enterprise. One and the same decision or action must always be sound in all three areas.

The task of creating a genuine whole also requires that the manager in every one of his acts consider simultaneously the performance and results of the enterprise as a whole and the diverse activities needed to achieve synchronized performance. It is here, perhaps, that the comparison with the orchestra conductor fits best. A conductor must always hear both the whole orchestra and the second oboe. Similarly, a manager must always consider both the over-all performance of the enterprise and, say, the market-research activity needed. By raising the performance of the whole, he creates scope and challenge for market research. By improving the performance of market research, he makes possible better over-all business results. The manager must continuously ask two double-barreled questions in one breath: What better business performance is needed and what does this require of what activities? And: What better performance are the activities capable of and what improvement in business results will it make possible?

The second specific task of the manager is to harmonize in every decision and action the requirements of immediate and long-range future. He cannot sacrifice either without endangering the enterprise. He must, so to speak, keep his nose to the grindstone while lifting his eyes to the hills—which is quite an acrobatic feat. Or, to vary the metaphor, he can neither afford to say: "We will cross this bridge when we come to it," nor "It's the next hundred years that count." He not only has to prepare for crossing distant bridges —he has to build them long before he gets there. And if he does not take care of the next hundred days, there will be no next hundred years; indeed, there may not even be a next five years. Whatever the manager does should be sound in expediency as well as in basic long-range objective and principle. And where he cannot harmonize the two time dimensions, he must at least balance them. He must carefully calculate the sacrifice he imposes on the long-range future of the enterprise to protect its immediate interests, or the sacrifice he makes today for the sake of tomorrow. He must limit either sacrifice as much as possible. And he must repair the damage it inflicts as soon as possible. He lives and acts in two time dimensions, and he is responsible for the performance of the whole enterprise and of his component.

The Work of the Manager

Every manager does many things that are not managing. He may spend most of his time on them. A sales manager makes a statistical analysis or placates an important customer. A foreman repairs a tool or fills in a production report. A manufacturing manager designs a new plant layout or tests new materials. A company president works through the details of a bank loan or negotiates a big contract—or spends dreary hours presiding at a dinner in honor of long-service employees. All these things pertain to a particular function. All are necessary, and have to be done well.

But they are apart from that work which every manager does whatever his function or activity, whatever his rank and position, work which is common to all managers and peculiar to them. The best proof is that we can apply to the job of the manager the systematic analysis of Scientific Management. We can isolate that which a man does because he is a manager. We can divide it into the basic constituent operations. And a man can improve his performance as a manager by improving his performance of these constituent motions.

There are five such basic operations in the work of the manager. Together they result in the integration of resources into a living and growing organism.

A manager, in the first place, *sets objectives.* He determines what the objectives should be. He determines what the goals in each area of objectives should be. He decides what has to be done to reach these objectives. He makes the objectives effective by communicating them to the people whose performance is needed to attain them.

Secondly, a manager *organizes*. He analyzes the activities, decisions and relations needed. He classifies the work. He divides it into manageable activities. He further divides the activities into manageable jobs. He groups these units and jobs into an organization structure. He selects people for the management of these units and for the jobs to be done.

Next a manager *motivates and communicates*. He makes a team out of the people that are responsible for various jobs. He does that through the practices with which he manages. He does it in his own relation to the men he manages. He does it through incentives and rewards for successful work. He does it through his promotion policy. And he does it through constant communication, both from the manager to his subordinate, and from the subordinate to the manager.

The fourth basic element in the work of the manager is *the job of measurement*. The manager establishes measuring yardsticks—and there are few factors as important to the performance of the organization and of every man in it. He sees to it that each man in the organization has measurements available to him which are focused on the performance of the whole organization and which at the same time focus on the work of the individual and help him do it. He analyzes performance, appraises it and interprets it. And again, as in every other area of his work, he communicates both the meaning of the measurements and their findings to his subordinates as well as to his superiors.

Finally, a manager *develops people*. Through the way he manages he makes it easy or difficult for them to develop themselves. He directs people or misdirects them. He brings out what is in them or he stifles them. He strengthens their integrity or he corrupts them. He trains them to stand upright and strong or he deforms them.

Every manager does these things when he manages—whether he knows it or not. He may do them well, or he may do them wretchedly. But he always does them.

Every one of these categories can be divided further into subcategories, and each of the sub-categories could be discussed in a book of its own. The work of the manager, in other words, is complex. And every one of its categories requires different qualities and qualifications.

Setting objectives, for instance, is a problem of balances: a balance between business results and the realization of the principles one believes in; a balance between the immediate needs of the business and those of the future; a balance between desirable ends and available means. Setting objectives therefore requires analytical and synthetizing ability.

Organizing, too, requires analytical ability. For it demands the most economical use of scarce resources. But it deals with human beings; and therefore it also stands under the principle of justice and requires integrity. Both analytical ability and integrity are similarly required for the development of people.

The skill needed for motivating and communicating, however, is primarily social. Instead of analysis, integration and synthesis are needed. Justice dominates as the principle, economy is secondary. And integrity is of much greater importance than analytical ability.

Measuring requires again first and foremost analytical ability. But it also requires that measurement be used to make self-control possible rather than be abused to control people from outside and above; that is, to dominate them. It is the common violation of this principle that largely explains why measurement is the weakest area in the work of the manager today. And as long as measurements are abused as a tool of "control" (as long, for instance, as measurements are used as a weapon of an internal secret policy that supplies audits and critical appraisals of a manager's performance to the boss without even sending a carbon copy to the manger himself) measuring will remain the weakest area in the manager's performance.

Setting objectives, organizing, motivating and communicating, measuring and developing people are formal, classifying categories. Only a manager's experience can bring them to life, concrete and meaningful. But because they are formal, they apply to every manager and to everything he does as a manager. They can therefore be used by every manager to appraise his own skill and performance, and to work systematically on improving himself and his performance as a manager.

Being able to set objectives does not make a man a manager, just as ability to tie a small knot in confined space does not make a man a surgeon. But without ability to set objectives a man cannot be an adequate manager, just as a man cannot do good surgery who cannot tie small knots. And as a surgeon becomes a better surgeon by improving his knot-tying skill, a manager becomes a better manager by improving his skill and performance in all five categories of his work.

Information: The Tool of the Manager

The manager has a specific tool: information. He does not "handle" people; he motivates, guides, organizes people to do their own work. His tool—his only tool—to do all this is the spoken or written word or the language of numbers. No matter whether the manager's job is engineering, accounting or selling, his effectiveness depends on his ability to listen and to read, on his ability to speak and to write. He needs skill in getting his thinking across to other people as well as skill in finding out what other people are after.

Of all the skills he needs, today's manager possesses least those of reading, writing, speaking and figuring. One look at what is known as "policy language" in large companies will show how illiterate we are. Improvement is not a matter of learning faster reading or public speaking. Managers have to learn to know language, to understand what words are and what they mean. Perhaps most important, they have to acquire respect for language as man's most precious gift and heritage. The manager must understand the meaning of the old definition of rhetoric as "the art which draws men's heart to the love of true knowledge." Without ability to motivate by means of the written and spoken word or the telling number, a manager cannot be successful.

Using His Own Time

Everybody has the problem of time; for of all resources it is the scarcest, the most perishable and the most elusive. But the manager must solve what is a common problem in very specific ways.

Managers are forever pursuing some glittering panacea for their time problem: a course in faster reading, a restriction of reports to one page, a mechanical limitation of interviews to fifteen minutes. All such panaceas are pure quackery and, in the end, a waste of time. It is, however, possible to guide a manager toward an intelligent allocation of his time.

Managers who know how to use time well achieve results by planning. They are willing to think before they act. They spend a great deal of time on thinking through the areas in which objectives should be set, a great deal more on thinking through systematically what to do with recurrent problems.

Most managers spend a large amount of time—in small driblets—on attempts to appraise the performance and quality of the men who work under them. Good time users do not. Instead, they systematically appraise their men once a year. As the result of a few hours' work, they then have the answers for all the decisions—concerning a man's salary, for instance, or his promotion or work assignment—on which judgment is required.

Good time users do not spend a great deal of time on the modification engineering of their products. They sit down once a year—for a few days perhaps—and work out with their sales and manufacturing departments the basic policy, the objectives and the rules for the necessary modifications, determining then how much of it there should be—and assign engineering manpower in advance to the job. In their eyes it is no praise to say: "This year we managed to get through this inventory crisis, thanks to the experience we had acquired last year." If they have a recurrent crisis, they spend the time to find out what causes it so as to prevent its repetition. This may take time, but in the long run it saves more.

The good time users among managers spend many more hours on their communications up than on their communications down. They tend to have good communications down, but they seem to obtain these as an effortless by-product. They do not talk to their men about their own problems, but they know how to make the subordinates talk about theirs. They are, for instance, willing to spend a great deal of their time on the half-yearly Manager Letter, in which each subordinate sets down the objectives of his job, his plans, and what his superior does to help and to hamper him. They may spend a whole day every six months with each of their ten or twelve men going carefully over the Manager Letter—and as a result they do not have to worry much in between about their communications down.

The manager who utilizes his time well also spends a great deal of time on considering his boss's problems, and on thinking what he can do to contribute to the success of his boss, of the whole activity and of the business. He takes responsibility, in other words, for his boss's job—considering this a part of his own job as a manager. As a result, he seems to need no extra time for clearing up the messes that result from a confusion of objectives and viewpoints.

The Manager's Resource: Man

The manager works with a specific resource: man. And the human being is a unique resource requiring peculiar qualities in whoever attempts to work with it.

For man, and man alone, cannot be "worked." There is always a two-way relationship between two men rather than a relationship between man and a resource. It is in the nature of this interrelationship that it changes both parties—whether they are man and wife, father and child, or manager and the man he manages.

"Working" the human being always means developing him. And the direction this development takes decides whether the human being—both as a man and as a resource—will become more productive or cease, ultimately, to be productive at all. This applies, as cannot be emphasized too strongly, not alone to the man who is being managed, but also to the manager. Whether he develops his subordinates in the right direction, helps them to grow and become bigger and richer persons, will directly determine whether he himself will develop, will grow or wither, become richer or become impoverished, improve or deteriorate.

One can learn certain skills in managing people, for instance, the skill to lead a conference or to conduct an interview. One can set down practices that are conducive to development—in the structure of the relationship between manager and subordinate, in a promotion system, in the rewards and incentives of an organization. But when all is said and done, developing men still requires a basic quality in the manager which cannot be created by supplying skills or by emphasizing the importance of the task. It requires integrity of character.

There is tremendous stress these days on liking people, helping people, getting along with people, as qualifications for a manager.

These alone are never enough. In every successful organization there is one boss who does not like people, does not help them, does not get along with them. Cold, unpleasant, demanding, he often teaches and develops more men than anyone else. He commands more respect than the most likeable man ever could. He demands exacting workmanship of himself as well as of his men. He sets high standards and expects that they will be lived up to. He considers only what is right and never who is right. And though usually himself a man of brilliance, he never rates intellectual brilliance above integrity in others. The manager who lacks these qualities of character—no matter how likeable, helpful, or amiable, no matter even how competent or brilliant—is a menace and should be adjudged "unfit to be a Manager and a Gentleman."

It may be argued that every occupation—the doctor, the lawyer, the grocer—requires integrity. But there is a difference. The manager lives with the people he manages, he decides what their work is to be, he directs it, he trains them for it, he appraises it and, often, he decides their future. The relationship of merchant and customer, professional man and client requires honorable dealings. Being a manager, though, is more like being a parent, or a teacher. And in these relationships honorable dealings are not enough; personal integrity is of the essence.

We can now answer the question: Does it require genius, or at least a special talent, to be a manager? Is being a manager an art or an intuition? The answer is: "No." What a manager does can be analyzed systematically. What a manager has to be able to do can be learned (though perhaps not always taught). Yet there is one quality that cannot be learned, one qualification that the manager cannot acquire but must bring with him. It is not genius; it is character.

What Makes a Manager?

The standard definition is that a man is a manager if he is in charge of other people and their work. This is too narrow. The first responsibility of a manager is upward: to the enterprise whose organ he is. And his relations with his superior and with his fellow-managers are as essential to his performance as are his relations and responsibilities to the people under him.

Another definition—though one that is usually implied rather than spelled out—is that importance defines the manager. But in the modern enterprise no one group is more essential than another. The worker at the machine, and the professional employee in the laboratory or the drafting room, are as necessary for the enterprise to function as is the manager. This is the reason why all members of the enterprise have to have the managerial vision. It is not importance but function that differentiates the various groups within the enterprise.

The most common concept of what defines the manager is rank and pay. This is not only wrong, but it is destructive. Even today we find incidentally, so-called rank-and-file workers who have higher incomes than the majority of managers; there are model makers in the automobile industry, for instance, whose annual income exceeds $15,000 and who are yet considered workers and are indeed members of the union's bargaining unit. And unless we can pay professional contributors adequately, can give them promotional opportunities as individual contributors, and can provide for them the status, dignity and self-respect of the true professional, we will simply not be able to manage their ever-increasing numbers.

Altogether the idea that rank and pay define the manager is not much more than a fallacious conclusion from the individual proprietor of yesterday to the manager of today's business enterprise.

Who is a manager can be defined only by a man's function and by the contribution he is expected to make. And the function which distinguishes the manager above all others is his *educational* one. The one contribution he is uniquely expected to make is to give others vision and ability to perform. It is vision and moral responsibility that, in the last analysis, define the manager.

CHAPTER 28

MAKING DECISIONS

"Tactical" and "strategic" decision—The fallacy of "problem-solving"—The two most important tasks: finding the right questions, and making the solution effective—Defining the problem—What is the "critical factor"?—What are the objectives?—What are the rules?—Analyzing the problem—Clarifying the problem—Finding the facts—Defining the unknown—Developing alternative solutions—Doing nothing as an alternative—Finding the best solution—People as a factor in the decision—Making the decision effective—"Selling" the decision—The two elements of effectiveness: understanding and acceptance—Participation in decision-making—The new tools of decision-making—What is "Operations Research"?—Its dangers and limitations—Its contribution—Training the imagination—Decision-making and the manager of tomorrow.

WHATEVER a manager does he does through making decisions. Those decisions may be made as a matter of routine. Indeed, he may not even realize that he is making them. Or they may affect the future existence of the enterprise and require years of systematic analysis. But management is always a decision-making process.

The importance of decision-making in management is generally recognized. But a good deal of the discussion tends to center on problem-solving, that is, on giving answers. And that is the wrong focus. Indeed, the most common source of mistakes in management decisions is the emphasis on finding the right answer rather than the right question.

The only kind of decision that really centers in problem-solving is the unimportant, the routine, the tactical decision. If both the conditions of the situation and the requirements that the answer has to satisfy, are known and simple, problem-solving is indeed the only thing necessary. In this case the job is merely to choose between a few obvious alternatives. And the criterion is usually one of economy: the decision shall accomplish the desired end with the minimum of effort and disturbance.

In deciding which of two secretaries should go downstairs every morning to get coffee for the office—to take the simplest example—the one question would be: What is the prevailing social or cultural etiquette? In deciding the considerably more complex question: Shall there be a "coffee break" in the morning, there would be two questions: Does the "break" result in a gain or in a loss in work accomplished, that is, does the gain in working energy outweigh the lost time? And (if the loss outweighs the gain): Is it worth while to upset an established custom for the sake of the few minutes?

Of course, most tactical decisions are both more complicated and more important. But they are always one-dimensional, so to speak: The situation is given and the requirements are evident. The only problem is to find the most economical adaptation of known resources.

But the important decisions, the decisions that really matter, are strategic. They involve either finding out what the situation is, or changing it, either finding out what the resources are or what they should be. These are the specifically managerial decisions. Anyone who is a manager has to make such strategic decisions, and the higher his level in the management hierachy, the more of them he must make.

Among these are all decisions on business objectives and on the means to reach them. All decisions affecting productivity belong here: they always aim at changing the total situation. Here also belong all organization decisions and all major capital-expenditures decisions. But most of the decisions that are considered operating decisions are also strategic in character: arrangement of sales districts or training of salesmen; plant layout or raw-materials inventory; preventive maintenance or the flow of payroll vouchers through an office.

Strategic decisions—whatever their magnitude, complexity or importance—should never be taken through problem-solving. Indeed, in these specifically managerial decisions, the important and difficult job is never to find the right answer, it is to find the right question. For there are few things as useless—if not as dangerous—as the right answer to the wrong question.

Nor is it enough to *find* the right answer. More important and more difficult is to make effective the course of action decided upon. Management is not concerned with knowledge for its own sake; it is concerned with performance. Nothing is as useless therefore as the right answer that disappears in the filing cabinet or the right solution that is quietly sabotaged by the people who have to make it effective. And one of the most crucial jobs in the entire decision-making process is to assure that decisions reached in various parts of the business and on various levels of management are compatible with each other, and consonant with the goals of the whole business.

Decision-making has five distinct phases: Defining the problem; analyzing the problem; developing alternate solutions; deciding upon the best solution; converting the decision into effective action. Each phase has several steps.

Making decisions can either be time-wasting or it can be the manager's best means for solving the problem of time utilization. Time should be spent on defining the problem. Time is well spent on analyzing the problem and developing alternate solutions. Time is necessary to make the solution effective. But much less time should be spent on finding the right solution. And any time spent on selling a solution after it has been reached is sheer waste and evidence of poor time utilization in the earlier phases.

Defining the Problem

Practically no problem in life—whether in business or elsewhere—ever presents itself as a case on which a decision can be taken. What appear at first sight to be the elements of the problem rarely are the really important or relevant things. They are at best symptoms. And often the most visible symptoms are the least revealing ones.

Management may see a clash of personalities; the real problem may well be poor organization structure. Management may see a problem of manufacturing costs and start a cost-reduction drive; the real problem may well be poor engineering design or poor sales planning. Management may see an organization problem; the real problem may well be lack of clear objectives.

The first job in decision-making is therefore to find the real problem and to define it. And too much time cannot be spent on this phase. The books and articles on leadership are full of advice on how to make fast, forceful and incisive decisions. But there is no more foolish—and no more time-wasting—advice than to decide quickly what a problem really is.

Symptomatic diagnosis—the method used by most managers—is no solution. It is based upon experience rather than upon analysis, which alone rules it out for the business manager who cannot systematically acquire this experience. We cannot put sick businesses into a clinic and exhibit them to students as we do with sick people. We cannot test whether the manager has acquired enough experience to diagnose correctly before letting him loose on actual problems. We can—and do—use cases to prepare men to make business decisions. But the best of cases is still a dead specimen preserved, so to speak, in alcohol. It is no more a substitute for the real business problem than the specimens in the anatomical museum are a substitute for the live patient in the clinical ward.

Moreover, symptomatic diagnosis is only permissible where the symptoms are dependable so that it can be assumed that certain visible surface phenomena pertain to certain definite diseases. The doctor using symptomatic diagnosis can assume that certain symptoms do not, on the whole, lie (though even the physician today tries to substitute strict, analytical methods for symptomatic diagnosis). The manager, however, must assume that symptoms do lie. Knowing that very different business problems produce the same set of symptoms, and that the same problem manifests itself in an infinite variety of ways, the manager must analyze the problem rather than diagnose it.

To arrive at the definition of the problem he must begin by finding the "critical factor." This is the element (or elements) in the situation that has to be changed before anything else can be changed, moved, acted upon.

A fairly large kitchenware manufacturer bent all management energies for ten years toward cutting production costs. Costs actually did go down; but profitability did not improve. Critical-factor analysis showed that the real problem was the product mix sold. The company's sales force pushed the products that could be sold the easiest. And it put all its emphasis on the most obvious sales appeal: lower price. As a result the company sold more and more of the less profitable lines where its competitors made the least efforts. And as fast as it reduced manufacturing costs it cut its price. It gained greater sales volume—but the gain was pure fat rather than growth. In fact, the company became progressively more vulnerable to market fluctuations. Only by defining the problem as one of product mix could it be solved at all. And only when the question was asked: What is the critical factor in this situation? could the right definition of the problem be given.

To find the critical factor by straight analysis of the problem is not always easy. Often two subsidiary approaches have to be used. Both are applications of a principle developed by the classical physicists of the eighteenth century to isolate the critical factor: the principle of "virtual motion." One approach assumes that nothing whatever will change or move, and asks: What will then happen in time? The other approach projects backward and asks: What that could have been done or left undone at the time this problem first appeared, would have materially affected the present situation?

One example of the use of these two approaches is the case of a chemical company that faced the need to replace the executive vice-president who had died suddenly. Everybody agreed that the dead man had made the company; but everybody agreed also that he had been a bully and a tyrant and had driven out of the company all independent people. Consequently the problem, as management saw it, seemed to be that of deciding between not filling the job at all or filling it with another strong man. But if the first were done who would run the company? If the second, would there not be another tyrant?

The question of what would happen if nothing were done revealed both that the problem was to give the company a top management, and that action had to be taken. Without action the company would be left without top management. And sooner or later—probably sooner—it would decline and disintegrate.

The question of what could have been done ten years ago then brought out that the executive vice-president, his function and his personality were not the problem at all. The problem was that the company had a president in name but not in fact. While the executive vice-president had had to make all the decisions and take full responsibility, final authority and its symbols were still vested in a president who guarded his rights jealously, though he had abdicated in effect. Everything that could have been done ten years earlier to secure to the company the benefit of the dead man's strength and safeguard it against his weaknesses would have required clear establishment of the man's authority and responsibility as the top man. Then constitutional safeguards—team organization of the top job; assignment of the objective-formulating part of the job to the vice-presidents operating as a planning committee, or federal decentralization of product businesses—could have been provided. This analysis thus revealed that removal of the president was the first thing that had to be done—and once that was done the problem could be solved.

The second step in the definition of the problem is to determine the conditions for its solution.

The objectives for the solution must be thought through.

In replacing the deceased executive vice-president the objectives for the solution of the problem were fairly obvious. It had to give the company an effective top management. It had to prevent a recurrence of one-man tyranny. And it had to prevent the recurrence of a leaderless interregnum; it had to provide tomorrow's top managers.

The first objective ruled out the solution most favored by some of the vice-presidents: an informal committee of functional vice-presidents working loosely with the nominal president. The second ruled out the solution favored by the Board chairman: recruitment of a successor to the executive vice-president. The third objective demanded that, whatever the organization of top management, federally decentralized product businesses had to be created to train and test future top managers.

The objectives should always reflect the objectives of the business, should always be focused ultimately on business performance and business results. They should always balance and harmonize the immediate and the long-range future. They should always take into account both the business as a whole and the activities needed to run it.

At the same time the rules that limit the solution must be thought through. What are the principles, policies and rules of conduct that have to be followed? It may be a rule of the company never to borrow more than half its capital needs. It may be a principle never to hire a man from the outside without first considering all inside managers carefully. It may be considered a requirement of good manager development not to create crown princes in the organization. It may be established policy that design changes must be submitted to manufacturing and marketing before being put into effect by the engineering department.

To spell out the rules is necessary because in many cases the right decision will require changing accepted policies or practices. Unless the manager thinks through clearly what he wants to change and why, he is in danger of trying at one and the same time both to alter and to preserve established practice.

The rule is actually the value-system within which the decision has to be made. These values may be moral; they may be cultural; they may be company goals or accepted principles of company structure. In their entirety they constitute an ethical system. Such a system does not decide what the course of action should be; it only decides what it should not be. Management people often imagine that the Golden Rule of doing unto others as you would have them do unto you, is a rule of action. They are wrong; the Golden Rule only decides what action should not be taken. Elimination of the unacceptable courses of action is in itself an essential prerequisite to decision. Without it there will be so many courses to choose from as to paralyze the capacity to act.

Analyzing the Problem

Finding the right question, setting the objectives and determining the rules together constitute the first phase in decision-making. They define the problem. The next phase is analyzing the problem: classifying it and finding the facts.

It is necessary to classify the problem in order to know who must make the decision, who must be consulted in making it and who must be informed. Without prior classification, the effectiveness of the ultimate decision is seriously endangered; for classification alone can show who has to do what in order to convert the decision into effective action.

The principles of classification have been discussed earlier (see Chapter 16). There are four: the futurity of the decision (the time-span for which it commits the business to a course of action and the speed with which the decision can be reversed); the impact of the decision on other areas and functions; the number of qualitative considerations that enter into it; and the uniqueness or periodicity of the decision. This classification alone can insure that a decision really contributes to the whole business rather than solves an immediate or local problem at the expense of the whole. For the classification proposed sorts out problems according to their correlation both with over-all business goals and with the goals of the component that the individual manager runs. It forces the manager to see his own problem from the point of view of the enterprise.

"Get the facts" is the first commandment in most texts on decision-making. But this cannot be done until the problem has first been defined and classified. Until then, no one can know the facts; one can only know data. Definition and classification determine which data are relevant, that is, the facts. They enable the manager to dismiss the merely interesting but irrelevant. They enable him to say what of the information is valid and what is misleading.

In getting the facts the manager has to ask: What information do I need for this particular decision? He has to decide how relevant and how valid are the data in his possession. He has to determine what additional information he needs and do whatever is necessary to get it.

These are not mechanical jobs. The information itself needs skillful and imaginative analysis. It must be scrutinized for underlying patterns which might indicate that the problem has been wrongly defined or wrongly classified. In other words, "getting the facts" is only part of the job. Using the information as a means to test the validity of the whole approach is at least as important.

A monthly trade magazine found itself in financial difficulties. The problem was defined as one of advertising rates. But analysis of the facts and figures showed something no one at the magazine had ever suspected: whatever success the magazine had had was as a source of news for its subscribers. The subscribers were oversupplied with weighty monthlies; they lacked a smaller news publication and valued the particular magazine the more the closer it came to a news magazine in format and editorial content. As a result of this analysis of readership figures the whole problem was redefined: How can we become a news magazine? And the solution was: by becoming a weekly. It was the right solution, too, as the magazine's subsequent success showed.

The manager will never be able to get all the facts he should have. Most decisions have to be based on incomplete knowledge—either because the information is not available or because it would cost too much in time and money to get it. To make a sound decision, it is not necessary to have all the facts; but it is necessary to know what information is lacking in order to judge how much of a risk the decision involves, as well as the degree of precision and rigidity that the proposed course of action can afford. For there is nothing more treacherous—or, alas, more common—than the attempt to make precise decisions on the basis of coarse and incomplete information. When information is unobtainable, guesses have to be made. And only subsequent events can show whether these guesses were justified or not. To the decision-making manager applies the old saying of doctors: "The best diagnostician is not the man who makes the largest number of correct diagnoses, but the man who can spot early, and correct right away, his own mistaken diagnosis." To do this, however, the manager must know where lack of information has forced him to guess. He must define the unknown.

Developing Alternative Solutions

It should be an invariable rule to develop several alternative solutions for every problem. Otherwise there is the danger of falling into the trap of the false "either-or." Most people would protest were one to say to them: "All things in the world are either green or red." But most of us every day accept statements—and act on them—that are no whit less preposterous. Nothing is more common than the confusion between a true contradiction—green and non-green, for instance—which embraces all possibilities, and a contrast—green and red, for instance—which lists only two out of numerous possibilities. The danger is heightened by the common human tendency to focus on the extremes. All color possibilities are indeed expressed in "black or white," but they are not contained in it. Yet, when we say "black or white," we tend to believe that we have stated the full range simply because we have stated its extremes.

The old plant of a small plumbing equipment manufacturer had become obsolete and threatened the company with the total loss of market position in a highly competitive and price-conscious industry. Management rightly concluded that it had to move out of the plant. But because it did not force itself to develop alternate solutions, it decided that it had to build a new plant. And this decision bankrupted the company. Actually nothing followed from the finding that the old plant had become obsolete but the decision to stop manufacturing there. There were plenty of alternative courses of action: to sub-contract production, for instance, or to become a distributor for another manufacturer not yet represented in the territory. Either one would have been preferable, would indeed have been welcomed by a management that recognized the dangers involved in building a new plant. Yet, management did not think of these alternates until it was too late.

Another example is that of a big railroad which, in the postwar years, experienced a sharp increase in traffic volume. It was clear that facilities had to be expanded. The bottleneck seemed to be the company's biggest classification yard. Situated halfway between the main terminal points the yard handled all freight trains, breaking them up and rearranging them. And the jam in the yard had become so bad that trains were sometimes backed up for miles outside either end and had to wait twenty-four hours before they could even get in. The obvious remedy was to enlarge the yard. And this was accordingly done at a cost running into many millions. But the company has never been able to use the enlarged facilities. For the two subsidiary yards that lie between the main yard and the two terminals, north and south respectively, simply could not handle such additional loads as would be imposed on them were the new facilities put to use. Indeed it speedily became clear that the real problem all along had been the limited capacity of the subsidiary yards. The original main yard would have been able to handle a good deal more traffic if only the subsidiary yards had been larger and faster. And the enlargement of these two yards would have cost less than a fifth of the sum that was wastefully invested in enlarging the main yard.

These cases reveal how limited most of us are in our imagination. We tend to see one pattern and to consider it the right if not the only pattern. Because the company has always manufactured its own goods, it must keep on manufacturing. Because profit has always been considered the margin between sales price and manufacturing costs, the only way to raise profitability is cutting production costs. We do not even think of subcontracting the manufacturing job or of changing the product mix.

Alternative solutions are the only means of bringing our basic assumptions up to the conscious level, forcing ourselves to examine them and testing their validity. Alternative solutions are no guarantee of wisdom or of the right decision. But at least they prevent our making what we would have known to be the wrong decision had we but thought the problem through.

Alternative solutions are in effect our only tool to mobilize and to train the imagination. They are the heart of what is meant by the "scientific method." It is the characteristic of the really first-class scientist that he always considers alternative explanations, no matter how familiar and commonplace the observed phenomena.

Of course, searching for and considering alternatives does not provide a man with an imagination he lacks. But most of us have infinitely more imagination than we ever use. A blind man, to be sure, cannot learn to see. But it is amazing how much a person with normal eyesight does not see, and how much he can perceive through systematic training of the vision. Similarly, the mind's vision can be trained, disciplined and developed. And the method for this is the systematic search for, and development of, the alternative solutions to a problem.

What the alternatives are will vary with the problem. But one possible solution should always be considered: taking no action at all.

To take no action is a decision fully as much as to take specific action. Yet, few people realize this. They believe that they can avoid an unpleasant decision by not doing anything. The only way to prevent them from deceiving themselves in this way is to spell out the consequences that will result from a decision against action.

Action in the enterprise is always of the nature of a surgical interference with the living organism. It means that people have to change their habits, their ways of doing things, their relationship to each other, their objectives or their tools. Even if the change is slight there is always some danger of shock. A healthy organism will withstand such shock more easily than a diseased one; indeed, "healthy" with respect to the organization of an enterprise means the ability to accept change easily and without trauma. Still it is the mark of a good surgeon that he does not cut unless necessary.

The belief that action on a problem has to be taken may in itself be pure supersition.

For twenty years a large shipping company had difficulty filling one of its top jobs. It never had anyone really qualified for the position. And whoever filled it soon found himself in trouble and conflict. But for twenty years the job was filled whenever it became vacant. In the twenty-first year a new president asked: What would happen if we did not fill it? The answer was: Nothing. It then turned out that the position had been created to perform a job that had long since become unnecessary.

It is particularly important in all organization problems that one consider the alternative of doing nothing. For it is here that traditional ways of doing things and positions reflecting past rather than present needs have their strongest hold on management's vision and imagination. There is also the danger of the almost automatic growth of layers and levels of management which will be continued unless the decision not to fill a vacant job is always considered as part of the decision how to fill it.

Finding the Best Solution

Only now should the manager try to determine the best solution. If he has done an adequate job, he will either have several alternatives to choose from each of which would solve the problem, or he will have half a dozen or so solutions that all fall short of perfection but differ among themselves as to the area of shortcoming. It is a rare situation indeed in which there is one solution, and one alone, In fact, wherever analysis of the problem leads to this comforting conclusion, one may reasonably suspect the solution of being nothing but a plausible argument for a preconceived idea.

There are four criteria for picking the best from among the possible solutions.

1. The risk. The manager has to weigh the risks of each course of action against the expected gains. There is no riskless action nor even riskless non-action. But what matters most is neither the expected gain nor the anticipated risk but the ratio between them. Every alternative should therefore contain an appraisal of the odds it carries.

2. Economy of effort. Which of the possible lines of action will give the greatest results with the least effort, will obtain the needed hange with the least necessary disturbance of the organization?

Far too many managers pick an elephant gun to chase sparrows. Too many others use slingshots against forty-ton tanks.

3. Timing. If the situation has great urgency, the preferable course of action is one that dramatizes the decision and serves notice on the organization that something important is happening. If, on the other hand, long, consistent effort is needed, a slow start that gathers momentum may be preferable. In some situations the solution must be final and must immediately lift the vision of the organization to a new goal. In others what matters most is to get the first step taken. The final goal can be shrouded in obscurity for the time being.

Decisions concerning timing are extremely difficult to systematize. They elude analysis and depend on perception. But there is one guide. Wherever managers must change their vision to accomplish something new, it is best to be ambitious, to present to them the big view, the completed program, the ultimate aim. Wherever they have to change their habits it may be best to take one step at a time, to start slowly and modestly, to do no more at first than is absolutely necessary.

4. Limitations of resources. The most important resource whose limitations have to be considered, are the human beings who will carry out the decision. No decision can be better than the people who have to carry it out. Their vision, competence, skill and understanding determine what they can and cannot do. A course of action may well require more of these qualities than they possess today and yet be the only right program. Then efforts must be made—and provided for in the decision—to raise the ability and standard of the people. Or new people may have to be found who have what it takes. This may sound obvious; but managements every day make decisions, develop procedures, or enact policies without asking the question: Do we have the means of carrying these things out? and do we have the people?

The wrong decision must never be adopted because people and the competence to do what is right are lacking. The decision should always lie between genuine alternates, that is, between courses of action every one of which will adequately solve the problem. And if the problem can be solved only by demanding more of people than they are capable of giving, they must either learn to do more or be replaced by people who can. It is not solving a problem to find a solution that works on paper but fails in practice because the human resources to carry it out are not available or are not in the place where they are needed.

Making the Decision Effective

Finally, any solution has to be made effective in action.

A great deal of time is spent today on "selling" solutions. It is wasted time. To attempt to sell a solution is both too little and too much. It implies that all is well if only people will "buy." However, it is of the essence of a manager's decision that other people must apply it to make it effective. A manager's decision is always a decision concerning what other people should do. And for this it is not enough that they buy it. They must make it their own.

To speak of "selling" also implies that what is the right decision be subordinated to what the "customer" wants; but this is poisonous and dishonest doctrine. What is right is decided by the nature of the problem; the wishes, desires and receptivity of the "customers" are quite irrelevant. If it is the right decision, they must be led to accept it whether at first they like it or not.

If time has to be spent on selling a decision, it has not been made properly and is unlikely to become effective. Presentation of the final results should never be a great concern, though, in line with the oldest and most basic rule of rhetoric, a decision should always be presented to people in language they use and understand.

Though it is a questionable term the emphasis on "selling" the decision points up an important fact: it is the nature of the managerial decision to be made effective though the action of other people. The manager who "makes" the decision actually does no such thing. He defines the problem. He sets the objectives and spells out the rules. He classifies the decision and assembles the information. He finds the alternative solutions, exercises judgment and picks the best. But for the solution to become a decision, action is needed And that the decision-making manager cannot supply. He can only communicate to others what they ought to be doing and motivate them to do it. And only as they take the right action is the decision actually made.

To convert a solution into action requires that people understand what change in behavior is expected of them, and what change to expect in the behavior of others with whom they work. What they have to learn is the minimum necessary to make them able to act the new way. It is poor decision-making to present a decision as if it required people to learn all over again or to make themselves over into a new image. The principle of effective communication is to convey only the significant deviation or exception—and that in clear, precise and unambiguous form. It is a problem in economy and precision.

But motivation is a problem in psychology and therefore stands under different rules. It requires that any decision become "our decision" to the people who have to convert it into action. This in turn means that they have to participate responsibly in making it.

They should not, to be sure, participate in the definition of the problem. In the first place, the manager does not know who should participate until the definition and classification are done; only then does he know what impact the decision will have and on whom. Participation is unnecessary—and usually undesirable—in the information-gathering phase. But the people who have to carry out the decision should always participate in the work of developing alternatives. Incidentally, this is also likely to improve the quality of the final decision, by revealing points that the manager may have missed, spotting hidden difficulties and uncovering available but unused resources.

Precisely because the decision affects the work of other people, it must help these people achieve their objectives, assist them in their work, contribute to their performing better, more effectively and with a greater sense of achievement. It cannot be a decision designed merely to help the manager perform better, do his job more easily or obtain greater satisfaction from it.

The New Tools of Decision-Making

Nothing I have said so far about decision-making is new; on the contrary, it only repeats what has been known for thousands of years. But while many managers use the decision-making method well, few understand clearly what they are doing.

Two new developments, however, make it important that every manager understand the process. In the first place, a whole new battery of tools to help in decision-making has become available. These are powerful and valuable tools; but they cannot be used unless the manager understands their purpose.

Secondly, the new technology is rapidly shifting the balance between tactical and strategic decisions. Many decisions that have always been tactical, if not routine, are rapidly becoming strategic decisions containing a high degree of futurity, a great impact and a large number of qualitative considerations; they are becoming decisions of a high order, in other words. And they can only be taken successfully and effectively if the manager knows what he is doing and does it systematically.

The new tools have been introduced under the rather confusing name of "Operations Research." They are neither "operations" nor "research." They are the tools of systematic, logical and mathematical analysis and synthesis. Actually it is not even correct to say that the tools are new; they differ very little from the tools used by the medieval symbolical logician, such as St. Bonaventure. The only new things are a few mathematical and logical techniques.

It is not sufficient therefore to train people in using the new tools and then turn management decisions over to them. Management decisions still have to be made by the manager. And they are still decisions based on judgment. But the new tools can help greatly in some phases of decision-making.

In any new tool it is important to say first what it cannot do. Operations Research and all its techniques—mathematical analysis, modern symbolical logic, mathematical information theory, the "Theory of Games," mathematical probability and so on—cannot help in defining what the problem is. They cannot determine what is the right question. They cannot set objectives for the solution. Nor can they set rules. Similarly, the new tools cannot make the decision concerning the best solution; they cannot by themselves make a decision effective. Yet these are the most important phases in decision-making.

But the new tools can be of great help in the two middle stages: analyzing the problem and developing alternatives. They can find and bring out the underlying patterns in the behavior of the business and in its environment, including those that have hitherto lain beyond the manager's field of vision or range of imagination. They can thus bring out alternative courses of action. They can show which factors are relevant (that is, facts) and which are irrelevant (that is, mere data). They can show the degree of reliability of the available data and what additional data are required to arrive at sound judgment. They can show what resources will be needed in any of the alternative courses of action, and what contribution from each component or function would be required. They can be used to show the limitations of each available course of action, its risks and its probabilities. They can show what impact a given action would have on other areas, components and functions, the relationship between input and output and the location and nature of bottlenecks. They can tie together the work and contribution of each function or component with those of all others and show this total impact on the behavior and results of the entire business.

The new tools are also not without danger. In fact, unless properly used they can become potent means for making the wrong decisions. Precisely because they make possible concrete and specific analysis of problems which hitherto could only be roughly defined or sensed, the new tools can be abused to "solve" the problems of one small area or of one function at the expense of other areas or functions or of the entire business. They can be abused, as the technician calls it, to "sub-optimize." And it is important to stress that practically all the problems which are given in the literature so far as illustrations of Operations Research are problems which should never be solved by themselves as such a solution inevitably results in serious "sub-optimization." In fact proper use of these tools is possible only if they are first applied to the analysis and definition of the characteristics of the whole business. Only then can they be profitably used for the analysis of individual problems and for the improvement of individual decisions.

Finally, the new tools promise help in making others understand what action is required of them and what to expect from associates. Mathematical information theory is still in its infancy. But it is likely to produce tools capable of identifying the relevant and new deviation in an action pattern and defining it in precise symbols.

All these things have been done for generations by imaginative people. What the new tools do is to bring this accomplishment within everybody's reach. They arm the imagination, develop it, guide it.

In essence these are tools of information, and of information-processing, not of decision-making. As tools of information, they are the best. In fact, it is not too fanciful to expect that within ten or twenty years these new tools of logical and mathematical analysis will have superseded the traditional financial accounting methods with which we are so familiar today.

For the new tools raise the question of what underlies the phenomena, rather than merely describing them. They focus on action, showing what alternative courses of action there are and what each implies. They therefore make possible decisions with a high degree of rationality in respect to futurity, risk and probability. This is the kind of information each manager needs to set his objectives so as to contribute the most to the business, and to control himself. Accounting will still be needed for financial reporting to stockholders, tax work and custodial work. Management information, however, will increasingly be mathematical and logical.

The manager may not have to be able to work these tools personally (even though their use for a great many applications does not require greater mathematical skill than is required for the reading of sales charts today). But it is essential that he understand them, know when to call in a specialist in their use, and know what to demand of the specialist.

But, above all, he must understand the basic method involved in making decisions. Without such understanding he will either be unable to use the new tools at all, or he will overemphasize their contribution and see in them the key to problem-solving which can only result in the substitution of gadgets for thinking, and of mechanics for judgment. Instead of being helped by the new tools, the manager who does not understand decision-making as a process in which he has to define, to analyze, to judge, to take risks, and to lead to effective action, will, like the Sorcerer's Apprentice, become the victim of his own bag of tricks.

The Greater Importance of Decision-Making

At the same time the manager—whatever his function or level—will have to make more and more strategic decisions. Less and less will he be able to rely on his ability to make intuitively the right tactical decision.

Tactical adjustments will, of course, always be needed. But they will have to be made within a framework of basic strategic decisions. No amount of skill in making tactical decisions will free tomorrow's manager from the necessity of making strategic decisions. Even the manager who today gets by without any knowledge of, or insight into, the decision-making method will tomorrow have to understand it, to know it and to use it.

CHAPTER 29

THE MANAGER OF TOMORROW

The new demands—The new tasks—But no new man—Exit the "intuitive" manager—The preparation of tomorrow's manager—General education for the young—Manager education for the experienced—But central will always be integrity.

THE demands on the skill, knowledge, performance, responsibility and integrity of the manager have doubled in every generation during the past half century. Things which in the twenties only a few pioneers in top management were aware of we now expect young men straight out of school to be able to do. Daring innovations of yesterday—market research, product planning, human relations, or trend analysis, for instance—have become commonplace. Operations Research is fast becoming so. Can we expect this almost explosive increase in the demands on the manager to continue? And what can we expect to be demanded of the manager of tomorrow?

Throughout this book we have repeatedly referred to the new pressures, the new demands on the manager. Let me refer again briefly to the most important ones:

The new technology will demand the understanding of the principles of production and their consistent application by all managers. It will require that the entire business be seen, understood and managed as an integrated process. Even if distribution of the product is carried on in physical separation from production and by a legally distinct and independent distributor, it will have to be considered an integral part of the process. And the same applies to raw-materials procurement or to customer service.

This process requires a maximum of stability and of ability to anticipate future events. Hence it must be based on careful objectives and on long-range decisions in all key areas. But it also requires great internal flexibility and self-guidance. Hence managers on all levels must be able to make decisions which adapt the whole process to new circumstances, changes in the environment and disturbances and yet maintain it as a going process.

In particular the new technology demands that management create markets. Management can no longer be satisfied with the market as it exists, it can no longer see in selling an attempt to find a purchaser for whatever it is that the business produces. It must create customers and markets by conscious and systematic work. Above all, it must focus continuously on creating mass purchasing power and mass purchasing habits.

Marketing itself is affected by the basic concepts of the new technology. We have, on the whole, discussed Automation as if it were exclusively a principle of production. It is, however, a principle of work in general. Indeed, the new methods of mass marketing may require greater application of the principles of Automation than the automatic factory, even though not one single automatic machine or electronic relay may be used. Marketing itself is becoming an increasingly integrated process. And increasingly it requires close integration with all other phases of the business. Instead of putting the emphasis on selling the individual customer, marketing centers more and more in product and market planning, product design and styling, product development and customer service. Instead of the individual sale, the creation of mass demand will be the pay-off. Television advertising is as much Automation, in other words, as is a mechanized machine feed. And the technological changes in distribution and marketing have as much impact as the technological changes in production.

This will demand that tomorrow's managers, regardless of their level and function, understand the marketing objectives and policies of their company, and know what they have to contribute to them. Business management will have to be able to think through long-range market objectives and to plan and build a long-range marketing organization.

The new technology will make new demands for innovation. Not only must the chemist, designer or engineer work closely with production and marketing men, but there will have to be the kind of systematic approach to innovation that Sears, Roebuck, for instance, applies to its merchandise planning and its development of suppliers. Innovation will have to be managed by objectives that reflect long-term market goals. It will also have to attempt much more systematically to foresee the inherent possibilities of technological and scientific development and to shape manufacturing and marketing policies accordingly.

The new technology will result in greater competition. True, it will broaden the market and raise the level of production and consumption, but these new opportunities will also demand consistent efforts to do better on the part of the enterprise and its managers.

Both because the new technology requires it and because social pressures demand it, the manager of tomorrow will have to make it possible to anticipate employment and to maintain it as close to stability as possible. At the same time, as today's semi-skilled machine operator becomes tomorrow's highly trained maintenance man, and today's skilled worker tomorrow's individual professional contributor, labor will become a more expensive resource—a capital investment of the business rather than a current cost. And its performance will have a much greater impact on the performance of the whole business.

the manager will have to acquire a whole new set of tools which he will have to develop himself. He needs to acquire adequate yardsticks for performance and results in the key areas of business objectives. He needs to acquire economic tools to make meaningful decisions today for a long-range tomorrow. He will have to acquire the new tools of the decision-making process.

The New Tasks

We can summarize by saying that the new demands require that the manager of tomorrow acquit himself of *seven new tasks*:

1. He must manage by objectives.
2. He must take more risks and for a longer period ahead. And

risk-taking decisions will have to be made at lower levels in the organization. The manager must therefore be able to calculate each risk, to choose the most advantageous risk-alternative, to establish in advance what he expects to happen and to "control" his subsequent course of action as events bear out or deny his expectations.

3. He must be able to make strategic decisions.

4. He must be able to build an integrated team each member of which is capable of managing and of measuring his own performance and results in relation to the common objectives. And there is a big task ahead in developing managers equal to the demands of tomorrow.

5. He will have to be able to communicate information fast and clearly. He will have to be able to motivate people. He must, in other words, be able to obtain the responsible participation of other managers, of the professional specialists and of all other workers.

6. Traditionally a manager has been expected to know one or more functions. This will no longer be enough. The manager of tomorrow must be able to see the business as a whole and to integrate his function with it.

7. Traditionally a manager has been expected to know a few products or one industry. This, too, will no longer be enough. The manager of tomorrow will have to be able to relate his product and industry to the total environment, to find what is significant in it and to take it into account in his decisions and actions. And increasingly the field of vision of tomorrow's manager will have to take in developments outside his own market and his own country. Increasingly he will have to learn to see economic, political and social developments on a world-wide scale and to integrate worldwide trends into his own decisions.

But No New Man

But there will be no new men to do these staggering tasks. The manager of tomorrow will not be a bigger man than his father was before him. He will be possessed of the same endowments, beset by the same frailties and hedged in by the same limitations. There is no evidence that the human being has altered much in the course of recorded history, certainly none that he has grown in intellectual stature or emotional maturity. The Bible is still the fullest measure of man's nature, Aeschylus and Shakespeare still the best textbooks of psychology and sociology, Socrates and St. Thomas Aquinas still the high-water marks of human intellect.

How then can we accomplish these new tasks with the same men?

There is only one answer: the tasks must be simplified. And there is only one tool for this job: to convert into system and method what has been done before by hunch or intuition, to reduce to principles and concepts what has been left to experience and "rule of thumb," to substitute a logical and cohesive pattern for the chance recognition of elements. Whatever progress the human race has made, whatever ability it has gained to tackle new tasks has been achieved by making things simple through system.

The manager of tomorrow will not be able to remain an intuitive manager. He will have to master system and method, will have to conceive patterns and synthesize elements into wholes, will have to formulate general concepts and to apply general principles. Otherwise he will fail. In small business and in large, in general management and in functional management, a manager will have to be equipped for the Practice of Management.

To find the necessary general concepts, to develop the right principles, to formulate the appropriate system and method and to show basic patterns has, of course, been the main purpose of this book. It has been based on the premise that in our management of today we have the experience out of which we can distill valid methods and general conclusions for the management task of tomorrow.

The Preparation of Tomorrow's Manager

If a man is to manage by concepts, patterns and principles, if he is to apply system and methods he can, however, also prepare himself for the job. For concepts and principles can be taught as can system, method and the formulation of patterns. Indeed, perhaps the only way to acquire them is by systematic learning. At least I have never heard of anyone acquiring those basic patterns, the alphabet and the multiplication table, by experience.

Tomorrow's manager will actually need two preparations rather than one. Some things a man can learn before he becomes a manager;

he can acquire them as a youth or as he goes along. Others he can learn only after he has been a manager for some time; they are adult education.

One does not have to have been a manager to learn reading and writing. Indeed, these skills are best acquired in one's youth.

It can be said with little exaggeration that of the common college courses being taught today the ones most nearly "vocational" as preparation for management are the writing of poetry and of short stories. For these two courses teach a man how to express himself, teach him words and their meaning and, above all, give him practice in writing. It can also be said that nothing would help so much to prepare young men for management as a revival of the honorable practice of the oral defense of one's "thesis"—only it should be made a frequent, normal, continuing part of college work rather than something that happens once, at the end of formal schooling.

In one's youth one can also most easily acquire knowledge and understanding of logic and of its analytical and mathematical tools. A young man can also learn the basic understanding of science and scientific method which the manager of tomorrow will need. He can acquire the ability to see the environment and to understand it through history and the political sciences. He can learn economics and acquire the analytical tools of the economist.

To prepare himself to be a manager, a young man can, in other words, acquire a general education. He may acquire it through formal schooling. Or, as so many of the best have always done, he may educate himself. But all these things together constitute what has always been considered the general knowledge and discipline of the educated man.

I do not mean to imply that what the young man needs to prepare himself for management is incompatible with specific business or engineering training. On the contrary, there is no reason why the required general education should not be an integral part of the business-school or engineering-school curriculum (as is indeed being recognized increasingly by our engineering schools). I also do not mean that there is no value to specific business or engineering subjects. On the contrary; they give a man ability to perform functional work with some degree of workmanship. And it is not only still important that everyone in an enterprise possess the ability to do functional work—at least on the journeyman's level—but it is crucial that every manager acquire the respect for workmanship which only a technical or craft skill can give. The young man who only acquires functional skills, however, and only learns specific business or engineering subjects, is not being prepared to be a manager. All he is being prepared for is to get his first job.

Indeed, the demands that tomorrow will make on the manager may well force us to create anew what we have all but lost: the liberal education for use. It will be very different (at least in outward appearance) from what our grandfathers knew by that name. But it will again have strict method and real standards, especially of self-discipline and of ethics, instead of the abandonment of method and standards that characterizes so much of today's so-called "progressive education." It will again have a unified focus rather than be fragmented departmentally. And, like every living liberal education in the past, it will be preparation for work as an adult and citizen rather than merely "general culture."

One needs experience in management as well as maturity, however, to learn to manage by objectives, to analyze the company's business, to learn to set objectives and to balance them, to learn to harmonize the needs of immediate and long-range future. Without experience as a manager—or at least as an adult—one can learn to recite these things; but one cannot learn to do them.

One needs experience as a manager to learn how to assess and to take risks. One needs experience to learn how to exercise judgment and make decisions. One needs experience to see the business in society, to assess the impact of the environment on the business and to decide what management's public responsibilities are.

One cannot, as a young man, learn what managing managers means, nor managing worker and work. Nothing is as futile or as pathetic as the young man who has learned "personnel management" in a business school and then believes himself qualified to manage people. And no one can do quite as much harm—or as little good.

The specific work of the manager makes sense only to men who have set objectives, organized, communicated and motivated, measured performance and developed people. Otherwise it is formal, abstract and lifeless. But to a manager who can put the flesh of his own experience on these bones, the terms can become extremely meaningful. Their classification can become a tool by means of which he can organize his own work, examine his own performance and improve his own results. For young people who have no management experience this classification appears the way French irregular verbs appear to a schoolboy in rural Idaho: an assignment to be learned mechanically. All they can do is to parrot: "The sixteen principles of control are . . ."; this may get them a good mark in an examination but it is of little meaning to them in their work. The experienced manager, however, can be brought to see and to use these classifications the way a mature French poet would use the study of the same irregular verbs: as a tool to gain greater insight into his language, greater skill as a writer and greater depth as a thinker.

To discharge tomorrow's management tasks we therefore will need advanced education for people already in management. We have already made the first steps in this direction, as witness the countless "advanced management programs" that have come into being in this country in the last ten years. And it is a fairly safe bet that the focus in education for management will increasingly shift to advanced work for the adult, experienced manager.

The business manager's need for a systematic attempt at his own advanced education is a new development; but it is not unprecedented. All armies have what is called in this country the "Command and General Staff School," for professional training in the specific work of a senior officer. All armies have learned that this training cannot be given to young men learning to be officers but only to mature men with considerable experience in actual command and performance of military duties. Similarly, the oldest elite corps, the Jesuit Order, does not subject its men to training in advanced theology and philosophy until they have had many years of practical experience in the study of such lay subjects as medicine, sociology or meteorology, in teaching and in administrative work. It has found that the most advanced, the really professional training for being a Jesuit, does not "take" until a man has acquired the actual experience in the work that his advanced studies organize, make meaningful, appraise and focus.

In fact, that management has a need for advanced education—as well as for systematic manager development—means only that management today has become an institution of our society.

But Central Will Always Be: Integrity

Yet intellectual and conceptual education alone will not enable the manager to accomplish the tasks of tomorrow.

The more successfully tomorrow's manager does his work, the greater will be the integrity required of him. For under the new technology the impact on the business of his decisions, their time-span and their risks, will be so serious as to require that he put the common good of the enterprise above his own self-interest. Their impact on the people in the enterprise will be so decisive as to demand that the manager put genuine principles above expediency. And their impact on the economy will be so far-reaching that society itself will hold the manager accountable. Indeed, the new tasks demand that the manager of tomorrow root every action and decision in the bedrock of principles, that he lead not only through knowledge, competence and skill but through vision, courage, responsibility and integrity.

No matter what a man's general education or his adult education for management, what will be decisive above all, in the future even more than in the past, is neither education nor skill; it is integrity of character.

CONCLUSION

THE RESPONSIBILITIES OF MANAGEMENT

THE RESPONSIBILITIES OF MANAGEMENT

Enterprise and society—The threefold public responsibility of management—The social developments that affect the enterprise—The social impact of business decisions—Making a profit the first social responsibility—Keep opportunities open—Management as a leading group—Asserting responsibility always implies authority—What is management's legitimate authority?—Management and fiscal policy—The ultimate responsibility: to make what is for the public good the enterprises' own self-interest.

OUR discussion has so far treated the business enterprise as primarily existing by and for itself. True, we have stressed the relationship to the outside—to customers and market, to the labor union, to the social, economic and technological forces at work in our society. But these relations have been viewed somewhat like the relationship between a ship and the sea which engirds it and carries it, which threatens it with storm and shipwreck, which has to be crossed, but which is yet alien and distinct, the environment rather than the home of the ship.

But society is not just the environment of the enterprise. Even the most private of private enterprises is an organ of society and serves a social function.

Indeed the very nature of the modern business enterprise imposes responsibilities on the manager which are different in kind and scope from those of yesterday's businessman.

Modern industry requires an organization of basic resources

which is radically different from anything we have known before. In the first place, the time span of modern production and of business decisions is so long that it goes way beyond the life span of one man as an active factor in the economic process. Secondly, the resources have to be brought together into an organization —both of material objects and of human beings—which has to have a high degree of permanence to be productive at all. Next, resources, human and material, have to be concentrated in large aggregations—though there is of course a question how large they have to be for best economic performance and how large they should be for best social performance. This in turn implies that the people who are entrusted with the direction of this permanent concentration of resources—the managers—have power over people, that their decisions have great impact upon society, and that they have to make decisions that shape the economy, the society and the lives of individuals within it for a long time to come. In other words, modern industry requires the business enterprise, which is something quite different and quite new.

Historically, society has always refused to allow such permanent concentrations of power, at least in private hands, and certainly for economic purposes. However, without this concentration of power which is the modern enterprise, an industrial society cannot possibly exist. Hence society has been forced to grant to the enterprise what it has always been most reluctant to grant, that is, first a charter of perpetuity, if not of theoretical immortality to the "legal person," and second a degree of authority to the managers which corresponds to the needs of the enterprise.

This, however, imposes upon the business and its managers a responsibility which not only goes far beyond any traditional responsibility of private property but is altogether different. It can no longer be based on the assumption that the self-interest of the owner of property will lead to the public good, or that self-interest and public good can be kept apart and considered to have nothing to do with each other. On the contrary, it requires of the manager that he assume responsibility for the public good, that he subordinate his actions to an ethical standard of conduct, and that he restrain his self-interest and his authority wherever their exercise would infringe upon the commonweal and upon the freedom of the individual.

And then there is the fact that the modern business enterprise for its survival needs to be able to recruit the ablest, best educated and most dedicated of young men into its service. To attract and to hold such men a promise of a career, of a living, or of economic success is not enough. The enterprise must be able to give such men a vision and a sense of mission. It must be able to satisfy their desire for a meaningful contribution to their community and society. It must in other words embrace public responsibility of a high order to live up to the demands the manager of tomorrow must make on himself.

No discussion of the practice of management could therefore leave out those functions and responsibilities of management that arise out of the social character and the public existence of even the most private of enterprises. In addition the enterprise itself must demand that management think through its public responsibilities. For public policy and public law set the range for the actions and activities of the enterprise. They decide what forms of organization are open to it. They prescribe marketing, pricing, patent and labor policies. They control the ability of the enterprise to obtain capital and its price. They decide altogether whether private enterprise is to remain private and autonomous and to be governed by managements of its own choosing.

The responsibility of management in our society is decisive not only for the enterprise itself but for management's public standing, its success and status, for the very future of our economic and social system and the survival of the enterprise as an autonomous institution. The public responsibility of management must therefore underlie all its behavior. Basically it furnishes the ethics of management.

The discussion of management's public responsibility tends today, at least in this country, to begin with the consideration of management as a leading group in society. But properly it should begin with management's responsibility to the enterprise of which it is an organ. This responsibility cannot be compromised or side-stepped.

For the enterprise is management's specific trust; everything else arises out of this trust.

The first responsibility which management owes to the enterprise in respect to public opinion, policy and law is to consider such demands made by society on the enterprise (or likely to be made within the near future) as may affect attainment of its business objectives. It is management's job to find a way to convert these demands from threats to, or restrictions on, the enterprise's freedom of action into opportunities for sound growth, or at least to satisfy them with the least damage to the enterprise.

Even the staunchest friend of management would not claim that the job done so far could not be improved upon.

One illustration should suffice. It should have been clear ten years ago that the changing age structure of the American population, coupled with the steady drop in the purchasing power of the dollar, would produce an irresistible demand on business to do something for old employees. Some managements faced the problem years ago; we have good pension plans going back to 1900. But many more refused to see the inevitable. As a result they were forced to accept demands for employee pensions which tend to impose the greatest rather than the least burden on the enterprise though they do not actually meet the issue. For it is becoming increasingly obvious that pensions will not solve the problem of the old employee. If one fifth of the work force is of pensionable age, as it soon will be in our society, compulsory pensioning of the older people puts an all but unbearable burden on the production of the younger men. At the same time the great bulk of the people who reach what used to be considered old age are both able physically to continue work and eager to do so. What management should have done was to work out plans for keeping employed those older people who want to work and are able to do so, with pensions as something to fall back on for those who are unable or unwilling to keep on working. At the same time these plans would have to make sure that the older employees who are retained do not bottle up the promotional opportunities for younger men or endanger their employment security. Having failed to think through the problem, managements will almost certainly find themselves faced with compulsory employment programs for older people—imposed by unions or by government—which will mean additional cost and new restrictions.

American managements are on the verge of making the same mistake in respect to the stability of income and employment. That this demand will have to be met can hardly be disputed any more. It expresses not only the need of the worker for income security, but the need of our society to symbolize the worker's middle-class status. Also the demand has behind it the force of the deep "depression psychosis" that we inherited from the thirties.

I have tried to show earlier that this demand could be satisfied in such a way as to improve and strengthen the enterprise, increase its productivity and raises its over-all profits. If managements, however, refuse to face the responsibility to make the inevitable productive for the enterprise, they will only saddle their businesses with the guaranteed annual wage—both the most expensive and the least effective way to take care of a real social need.

Management is also responsible for making sure that the present actions and decisions of the business enterprise will not create future public opinion, demands and policies that threaten the enterprise, its freedom and its economic success.

During the last years many companies have dispersed their plants geographically. In doing so many of them have simply built, in a new location, a replica of the original plant, turning out the same product for the same market. In many cases both the old and the duplicate plants are the main source of employment in their respective communities. Examples are a rubber company with old plants in Akron and a new plant in a small southern town; a ball-bearing company with an old plant in a small New England town and a new plant in a small town in Ohio; a shirt maker with old plants in upstate New York and a new plant in rural Tennessee.

In a depression this can only lead to serious public reaction. For management will then be forced to decide which of these plants to close down and which to keep open—the new plants which represent a high capital investment, have by and large a high break-even point and thus require capacity operations to be profitable, or the old plants around which a whole community may have grown up. But will any community, no matter how eager it was to obtain the new industry, take quietly a decision to deprive it of its main source of income so as to keep up employment in some other place? If the market and the forces of the business cycle bring about unemployment, that is one thing. But if management, by unilateral action, does so, it is quite another. It may therefore be a vital management responsibility to organize new plants so that they have their own market and their own product rather than only be separated geographically. Otherwise expansion will lead to a clash between management and the community, between the requirements of the business and of public policy.

Other practices which may tend to breed public opinion and policies hostile to the enterprise, are the exclusive hiring of college graduates for management positions, thus cutting off chances for men inside the company; the narrowing of promotional opportunities for foremen, thus cutting off the most important rungs on the traditional American ladder of success; or the policy of not hiring older workers or disabled people. To discharge its responsibility to the enterprise management must carefully think through these practices and their impact upon the public welfare.

In brief, management, in every one of its policies and decisions, should ask: What would be the public reaction if everyone in industry did the same? What would be the public impact if this behavior were general business behavior? And this is not just a question for the large corporations. In their totality, small businesses and their managements have fully as much of an impact on public opinion and policy. And all, large and small, should remember that if they take the easy way out and leave these problems to "the other fellow," they only assure that their solution will eventually be imposed by government.

The Social Impact of Business Decisions

This discussion should have made it clear that the impact of management's decisions on society is not just "public" responsibility but is inextricably interwoven with management's responsibility to the enterprise. Still, there is a responsibility of management to the public interest as such. This is based on the fact that the enterprise is an organ of society, and that its actions have a decisive impact on the social scene.

The first responsibility to society is to operate at a profit, and only slightly less important is the necessity for growth. The business is the wealth-creating and wealth-producing organ of our society. Management must maintain its wealth-producing resources intact by making adequate profits to offset the risk of economic activity. And it must besides increase the wealth-creating and wealth-producing capacity of these resources and with them the wealth of society

It may seem paradoxical that this responsibility of management is most clearly recognized in the Soviet Union. Profitability is the first and absolute law for Soviet management and the essence of what the Russians proudly proclaim to be their great economic discovery: "management by the ruble." But a source which the Kremlin would hardly admit as authority has said as much; I refer, of course, to Our Lord's Parable of the Talents.

This responsibility is absolute and cannot be abdicated. No management can be relieved of it. Managements are in the habit of saying that they have a responsibility to the shareholder for profits. But the shareholder, at least in a publicly owned company, can always sell his stock. Society, however, is stuck with the enterprise. It has to take the loss if the enterprise does not produce adequate profits, has to take the impoverishment if the enterprise does not succeed in innovation and growth.

For the same reason management has a public responsibility to make sure of tomorrow's management without which the resources would be mismanaged, would lose their wealth-producing capacity and would finally be destroyed.

Management is responsible for conducting the enterprise so as not to undermine our social beliefs and cohesion. This implies a negative responsibility: not to usurp illegitimate authority over citizens by demanding their absolute and total allegiance.

In a free society the citizen is a loyal member of many institutions; and none can claim him entirely or alone. In this pluralism lies its strength and freedom. If the enterprise ever forgets this, society will retaliate by making its own supreme institution, the state, omnipotent.

The tendency today of so many, especially of our larger, enterprises to assume paternal authority over their management people and to demand of them a special allegiance, is socially irresponsible usurpation, indefensible on the grounds alike of public policy and the enterprise's self-interest. The company is not and must never claim to be home, family, religion, life or fate for the individual. It must never interfere in his private life or his citizenship. He is tied to the company through a voluntary and cancellable employment contract, not through some mystical and indissoluble bond.

But responsibility for our social beliefs and cohesion also has a positive component. At least in this country it imposes on management the duty to keep open the opportunity to rise from the bottom according to ability and performance. If this responsibility is not disch rged, the production of wealth will, in the long run, weaken rather than strengthen our society by creating social classes, class hatred and class warfare.

There are other areas in which responsibilities can be asserted. I would, for instance, consider it a responsibility of the management of the large company to develop a capital-expenditure policy which tends to counteract the extremes of the business cycle (with Automation such a policy becomes a business necessity). I believe that management has a responsibility to develop policies that will overcome the deep-seated hostility to profits, for the simple reason that this is a threat to our economic and social system. I finally believe that any business, in the present world situation, has the responsibility to make its best contribution to the defensive strength of its country.

But what is most important is that management realize that it must consider the impact of every business policy and business action upon society. It has to consider whether the action is likely to promote the public good, to advance the basic beliefs of our society, to contribute to its stability, strength and harmony.

Management as a Leading Group

Only now can we raise the question of the responsibility that management should assume by virtue of being one of the leading groups in society—responsibilities over and above those grounded in the business itself.

Hardly a day goes by when a spokesman of management does not assert a new public responsibility of this kind. We have been told that management should hold itself responsible for the survival of the liberal arts colleges, for the economic education of workers, for religious tolerance or for a free press, for strengthening the United Nations or for abolishing it, for "culture" in its broadest form and for every one of the arts in particular.

There is no doubt that being a leading group entails heavy responsibility; and there is nothing more destructive than to shirk these responsibilities. There is also, however, nothing more destructive than to assert responsibilities for a group which it does not have, nothing more dangerous than to usurp responsibilities. The present management approach tends to do both: it shirks responsibilities that exist and usurps others that do not and must not exist.

For whoever says "responsibility" also implies "authority." One does not exist without the other. To assert management's responsibility in any area is therefore to assign it authority in the area in question. Is there any reason to believe that management in a free society should have any authority over the colleges, over culture and the arts, over the freedom of the press or over our foreign policy? To raise the question is to answer it: such authority would be intolerable. Even the impassioned twaddle permitted, by hoary custom, to the commencement speaker or the boss at the annual employees' picnic should avoid such a claim.

Managament's public responsibility as one of the leading groups should therefore be restricted to areas in which management can legitimately claim authority.

As a "rule of thumb" I recommend that management religiously avoid asserting or assuming responsibility for any activities it does not want to see controlled either by the union leader or by government. These are the activities which should be free, that is, organized by spontaneous, local, pluralist action of the citizens, not by any one group or any governing organ. If management does not want the union leader to control an activity, it is a fair assumption that the union leader (and his sizable following) would not want management to control the activity either. And it would be reasonable to assume that society would find sole control of such an activity by either management or union leader intolerable. It would demand the obvious and easy substitute for non-control of these areas: control by the organized-government as the representative of the entire people.

And if the business enterprise becomes a source of financial support for important causes and institutions—as our tax laws force it increasingly to be—management must take scrupulous care not to let financial support become "responsibility," not to let itself be misled into usurping authority where it has and should have none.

But from the fact that responsibility and authority go together, it follows also that management owes to society responsibility wherever its special competence gives it authority.

One major area here is that of fiscal policy. Because we have not modernized our tax structure even though it was built when the maximum income tax was 4 per cent (and that rate applied to millionaires only), we have today an illogical, unmanageable, indeed an immoral system of taxation that encourages and rewards irresponsible actions and decisions of businesses and private individuals alike. Here management can make a major contribution—and it has therefore a major responsibility. But it has responsibility for positive action.

It is not enough to scream that taxes are too high as some people in management have been doing. What we need is a policy that reconciles the necessity of continuing high government expenditures, in the world we live in, with the requirements of society and economy. As long as management confines itself to shouting "down with taxes" it will not have discharged its responsibility for fiscal policy. In fact, it will have been totally ineffectual and will only have made itself look irresponsible.

Wherever management's competence gives it authority, wherever therefore management has a responsibility, this responsibility must be discharged on the basis of the public interest. It is not good enough to start out with the premise that "what is good for the business is good for the country," even though the assertion may be substantially correct for the very large company which is in effect a cross section of the American economy. For while its competence is the basis for management's authority, the only basis on which this authority can be used is the public interest. What is good for the business—or even for all businesses—is irrelevant.

But the final conclusion from the consideration of management's public responsibility as one of the leading groups is the most important one: It is management's public responsibility to *make* whatever is genuinely in the public good *become* the enterprise's own self-interest.

To be disinterested is not enough for a leading group in society. It is not even enough that the group subordinate its own interests to the common good. It must succeed in harmonizing public and private interest by making what is the common good coincide with its own self-interest. "This company must be so managed as to make everything likely to strengthen our country, or to advance its prosperity, add strength to the company and advance its prosperity"; thus the management of one of our most successful companies, Sears, Roebuck. In economic fact, "what is good for the country must be made to be good for Sears" may not be so different from "what is good for the business is good for the country." In spirit, in essence, in assertion of responsibility, however, it is completely different.

The Sears statement does not imply pre-established harmony between the private self-interests of a group and the commonweal. On the contrary; to make what is good for the country good for the enterprise requires hard work, great management skill, high standards of responsibility and broad vision. It is a counsel of perfection. To carry it out completely would require the philosopher's stone that can transmute the basest element into pure gold. But if management is to remain a leading group—indeed, if it is to remain autonomous management running free enterprises—it must make this rule the lodestar of its conduct, must consciously strive to live up to it, and must actually do so with a fair degree of success.

Two hundred and fifty years ago an English pamphleteer, de Mandeville, summed up the spirit of the new commercial age in the famous epigram: "private vices become public benefits"—selfishness unwittingly and automatically turns into the common good. He may have been right; economists since Adam Smith have been arguing the point without reaching agreement.

But whether he was right or wrong is irrelevant; no society can lastingly be built on such belief. For in a good, a moral, a lasting society the public good must always rest on private virtue. No leading group can be accepted on de Mandeville's foundation. Every leading group must, on the contrary, be able to claim that the public good determines its own interest. This assertion is the only legitimate basis for leadership; to make it reality is the first duty of the leaders.

That "capitalism," as the nineteenth century understood the term (and as Europe still too prevalently understands it), was based on de Mandeville's principle may explain its material success. It certainly explains the revulsion against capitalism and capitalists that has swept the Western world during the last hundred years. The economic doctrines of the enemies of capitalism have been untenable and often childish. Their political doctrines have carried the threat of tyranny. But these answers have not been sufficient to quiet the critics of capitalism. Indeed they have usually appeared quite irrelevant to the critics, as well as to the people at large. For the hostility to capitalism and capitalists is moral and ethical. Capitalism is being attacked not because it is inefficient or misgoverned but because it is cynical. And indeed a society based on the assertion that private vices become public benefits cannot endure, no matter how impeccable its logic, no matter how great its benefits.

Fifty years ago de Mandeville's principle was as fully accepted here as it still is in Europe. But today it has become possible if not commonplace in this country to assert the opposite principle that the business enterprise must be so managed as to make the public good become the private good of the enterprise. In this lies the real meaning of the "American Revolution" of the twentieth century. That more and more of our managements claim it to be their responsibility to realize this new principle in their daily actions is our best hope for the future of our country and society, and perhaps for the future of Western society altogether.

To make certain that this assertion does not remain lip service but becomes hard fact is the most important, the ultimate responsibility of management: to itself, to the enterprise, to our heritage, to our society and to our way of life.

SELECTED BIBLIOGRAPHY

INTRODUCTION: THE NATURE OF MANAGEMENT

PETER F. DRUCKER. *The New Society; the Anatomy of the Industrial Order* (New York: Harper & Brothers, 1950).

OSWALD KNAUTH. *Managerial Enterprise, its growth and methods of operations* (New York: Norton, 1948).

JOSEPH A. SCHUMPETER. *Capitalism, Socialism and Democracy.* 3rd edition (New York: Harper & Brothers, 1950).

JOHN DIEBOLD. *Automation* (New York: Van Nostrand, 1953).

M. L. HURNI. "Increasing Opportunities for Automaticity," *Mechanical Engineering,* April, 1954.

KENDRICK PORTER and EDWARD A. MAHONEY. "Cybernetics and Product Design," *The Consulting Engineer,* February, 1954.

PART ONE: MANAGING A BUSINESS

J. M. CLARK. *Guideposts in a Time of Change* (New York: Harper & Brothers, 1949).

JOEL DEAN. *Managerial Economics* (New York: Prentice-Hall, 1951).

———"Measuring the Productivity of Capital, *Harvard Business Review,* January-February, 1954.

GEORGE KATONA. *Psychological Analysis of Business Behavior* (New York: McGraw-Hill, 1951).

PART TWO: MANAGING MANAGERS

PETER F. DRUCKER. *Concept of the Corporation* (New York: John Day, 1946).

R. E. GILLMOR. *A Practical Manual of Organization* (New York: Funk & Wagnalls, 1948).

HENRI FAYOL. *Industrial and General Administration* (English Translation, London: Pitman, 1930).

JAMES D. MOONEY and ALAN C. REILEY. *The Principles of Organization* (New York: Harper & Brothers, 1939).

ORDWAY TEAD. *The Art of Administration* (New York: McGraw-Hill, 1951).

LYNDALE URWICK. *Notes on the Theory of Organization* (New York: American Management Association, 1952).

JAMES C. WORTHY. "Democratic Principles in Business Management," *Advanced Management,* March, 1949.

———"Organizational Structure and Employe Morale," *American Sociological Review,* April 1950.

PART THREE: THE STRUCTURE OF MANAGEMENT

HOLDEN, FISH and SMITH. *Top Management Organization and Control* (Stanford: Stanford University Press, 1948).

ERNEST DALE. *Planning and Designing the Company Organization Structure* (New York: American Management Association, 1952).

PART FOUR: THE MANAGEMENT OF WORKER AND WORK

E. W. BAKKE. *Bonds of Organization* (New York: Harper & Brothers, 1950).

ALEXANDER R. HERON. *Why Men Work* (Stanford: Stanford University Press, 1948).

———*No Sale, No Job* (New York: Harper & Brothers, 1954).

ELTON MAYO. *Human Problems of an Industrial Civilization* (New York: Macmillan, 1933).

———*Social Problems of an Industrial Civilization* (Cambridge, Mass.: Harvard University Press, 1945).

DOUGLAS MCGREGOR. *Line Management's Responsibility for Human Relations* (New York: American Management Association, Manufacturing Series No. 213, 1953).

PAUL PIGORS and CHARLES A. MYERS. *Personnel Administration* (New York: McGraw-Hill, 1947).

FREDERICK W. TAYLOR. *Scientific Management* (New York: Harper & Brothers last reprinted in 1947).

CHARLES R. WALKER and F. L. W. RICHARDSON. *Human Relations in an Expanding Company* (New Haven: Yale University Press, 1948).

CHARLES R. WALKER and ROBERT H. GUEST. *The Man on the Assembly Line* (Cambridge, Mass.: Harvard University Press, 1952).

PART FIVE: WHAT IT MEANS TO BE A MANAGER

CHESTER I. BARNARD. *The Functions of the Executive* (Cambridge, Mass.: Harvard University Press, 1938).

PETER F. DRUCKER. "Management Sciences and the Manager," *Management Sciences,* Vol 1, No. 1, 1954.

M. L. Hurni. "Observations on Operations Research," *Operations Research Journal,* July 1954.
W. A. R. Leys. *Ethics for Policy Decisions* (New York: Prentice-Hall, 1952).
Mary Follett Parker. *Dynamic Administration* (New York: Harper & Brothers, 1941).

CONCLUSION: THE RESPONSIBILITIES OF MANAGEMENT

Howard R. Bowen. *Social Responsibilities of the Businessman* (New York: Harper & Brothers, 1953).
H. F. Merrill, editor. *Responsibilities of Business Leadership* (Cambridge, Mass.: Harvard University Press, 1948).
Clarence Randall. *A Creed for Free Enterprise* (Boston: Little Brown, 1952).

INDEX